THE SYSTEMS LIBRARIAN

The role of the library systems manager

THE SYSTEMS LIBRARIAN

The role of the library systems manager

Edited by

Graeme Muirhead
Bibliographic Database Manager, Solihull Libraries and Arts

Library Association Publishing

London

© Library Association Publishing Ltd 1994

Published by
Library Association Publishing Ltd
7 Ridgmount Street
London WC1E 7AE

First published 1994

British Library Cataloguing in Publication Data

A catalogue record for this book is available from the British Library

ISBN 1-85604-116-6

Typeset in 10/13pt Palermo from author's disk by Library Association Publishing Ltd
Printed and made in Great Britain by Bookcraft (Bath) Ltd

❖

For my parents

❖

❖ Contents

❖ Acknowledgements

The research reported in Chapters 1 and 13 was funded by a grant from the British Library Research & Development Department. I am grateful to Bob McKee, Director of Libraries & Arts, Solihull MBC, for providing the necessary institutional backing and for his personal encouragement.

In the course of the research many groups and individuals gave of their time and contributed ideas, advice, and, not least, moral support. Special thanks are due to members of the BLCMP System Managers User Group and the Dynix User Group, and to the many systems librarians who completed questionnaires or supplied other information about their posts.

Staff at Library Association Publishing Ltd gave much helpful guidance while the book was in preparation, and of course it would not have been possible at all without the expertise and cooperation of the contributors.

❖ Contributors

David Bovey

David Bovey held a number of posts in the British Library of Political and Economic Science (London School of Economics) before taking up his present appointment as Deputy Librarian, University College London. He has been a lecturer on Aslib courses on external information sources and sat on the Executive Committee of the Aslib Social Sciences Group. He has also been a member of the British Library's Social Sciences Steering Group.

Arthur Brady

Arthur Brady has worked for Dynix since 1984 and is currently its European General Manager, based at Dynix UK. Before this he was Vice-President for Sales and Marketing for Dynix North America. This appointment followed three years in Canada where he set up the Dynix Canada office, increasing the staff there from 1 to 35, and expanding the client base to 55 in less than three years. Arthur has a degree in Japanese and Asian Studies as well as a Master of Library and Information Sciences.

Janet Broome

Janet Broome graduated in Library and Information Studies from Brighton University in 1987. In 1989 she joined CLSI (Computer Library Services International) as support librarian with responsibility for the day-to-day support, implementation, training, and software installation of Unix-based library systems. From April 1993 to August 1994 she was Systems Librarian at Middlesex University, and she is now a senior consultant with McDonnell Information Systems.

Christine Dobbs

Christine Dobbs has over 12 years' experience as a professional training consultant in the field of computer software. Having worked previously for Digital Equipment Corporation, she joined BLCMP in 1993 to create a comprehensive training programme for the new TALIS system.

Gordon Dunsire

Gordon Dunsire is Information Systems Librarian of Napier University in Edinburgh. He is currently Vice-Chair of the Cataloguing and Indexing

Group in Scotland, and is their representative on the Scottish Library Association Council. He is also Development Officer of the Dynix Users Group, and advises Dynix Library Systems (UK) Ltd on the development of its Marquis system.

Shelagh Fisher

Shelagh Fisher is a Senior Lecturer in the Department of Library and Information Studies at Manchester Metropolitan University. Her teaching and research responsibilities are concerned with access to electronic information. She managed the introduction of the use of 'real' library systems into the teaching curriculum, which forms the basis of her chapter. Shelagh has previously worked as a library consultant with the Specialist Computer Group and established an IT-based library service at Bradford Grammar School. Her career began in the Reader Services department at the University of Lancaster. Recent publications include *BookshelF: a guide for librarians and system managers* (with J.E. Rowley). She has also published several articles on the use of library systems in teaching, on the selection of library systems, and on management information from library systems.

F. J. Friend

Frederick Friend is Librarian of University College London. His earlier career was in other UK university libraries at Manchester, Leeds, Nottingham, and Essex. In 1993 he coordinated an electronic document delivery trial using the SuperJANET network. He has published several papers, mainly on future developments in libraries, and is a member of a number of professional committees.

A. J. Meadows

Professor A.J. Meadows trained in Russian at Cambridge University and Physics at Oxford University before obtaining postgraduate qualifications in Astronomy and in History and Philosophy of Science from the Universities of Oxford and London. In the 1960s he worked at the British Museum Department of Printed Books and Manuscripts and subsequently went to Leicester University and became Head of the Departments of Astronomy and History of Science, and Project Head of the Primary Communications Research Centre and the Office for Humanities Communication. From 1986 to 1990 he was Head of Library and Information Studies at Loughborough University, where he is now Professor of Library and Information Studies and Dean of the School of Education and the Humanities.

Lindsay Mitchell

Lindsay Mitchell is Manager of Library Services at the University of Limerick. She has an MA from the University of Aberdeen and postgraduate qualifications in librarianship and computing. Her work experience has included a variety of posts in the University of Limerick Library and also with a library system supplier. Her professional interests include the impact of information technology and systems on work, staff development, and the management of change.

Graeme Muirhead

Graeme Muirhead is currently Bibliographic Database Manager with Solihull Libraries and Arts Department, and Editor of *Catalogue & index*, the periodical of the Library Association Cataloguing and Indexing Group.

Frances Richardson

A graduate in Chemistry from the University of Durham, Frances Richardson is a member of the Chartered Institute of Marketing, and has held a number of posts in marketing and information management. Her work as Marketing Consultant at BLCMP includes facilitating the exchange of experience between customers through seminars, technology days, user groups, and the BUG (BLCMP User Group) customer conference, as well as coordinating the company's publicity.

Sally Ryan

Before joining Dynix, Sally Ryan worked in public libraries and the Tavistock Joint Library, and for the cancer information charity BACUP, where she was responsible for setting up their library and information systems. Sally joined Dynix in 1988 as Support Librarian, became Customer Support Manager in 1989, and is currently Operations Manager.

Michael R. Schuyler

Michael R. Schuyler is Chief of Support Services with Kitsap Regional Library, Bremerton, Washington, and owner of Skysoft Enterprises, a company which specializes in software publishing and marketing, training, and consultancy work in automated systems for libraries and small businesses. He has published extensively on the subject of library automation and is an Associate Editor with Meckler Corporation where he has responsibility for articles and information on integrated library systems for *Computers in libraries*. His most recent books include *Dial-in 1991-1992: an annual guide to library online public access catalogs in North America, The systems librarian guide to computers, PC management*, and *Now what?: how to get your computer up and keep it running*.

Angela Warlow

Angela Warlow is Systems Librarian/Database Manager at Manchester Metropolitan University Library and currently convener of the BLCMP Systems Managers Group and BLCMP Systems Development Group. She is interested in 'all areas of library automation but preferably those that make life simpler!'.

Duncan Westlake

Duncan Westlake has spent all his working life with Hillingdon Borough

Libraries, beginning as a junior professional in the Bibliographic Services Department ('an excellent apprenticeship for anyone, but one that is sadly uncommon now') and progressing to systems management by way of branch librarianship and reference work. Along the way he has collected an MA in Librarianship and Art Administration from the City University, but apart from the IT modules on this course he has no formal training in computing. He is the author of *Geac: a guide for librarians and systems managers* (with John E. Clarke and others).

Hazel Woodward

Hazel Woodward is Information Services Librarian at Loughborough University. Her current areas of professional interest and research include the scholarly communications process, electronic information, and electronic journals. She has contributed many articles and book chapters to the professional literature, presented papers at national and international conferences, and is a member of various UK Serials Group, SCONUL, and IFLA committees.

Introduction

❖ *Graeme Muirhead*

The past 30 years have seen some astonishing changes in libraries and information centres. Computerized library management systems are widely used across all sectors of the library and information world and in organizations of all sizes. Information retrieval has come to embrace a variety of computer-based products and services including online retrieval from external databases, CD-ROM, TIMS (text information management systems), and printed indexes and current awareness services. Networking has enabled libraries to share their resources more efficiently and, in the face of increasing financial constraints, to move away from custodial policies and adopt policies in which access to information is given greater emphasis than collection development within the local library. The sights and sounds that greet today's library users convey vividly how far we have come along the road of automation. Light pens bleep, keyboards click, screens flicker, disk drives whirr. OPACs (Online Public Access Catalogues) have replaced oak cabinets and five-by-three cards, and the Oxford English Dictionary is stored on a couple of shiny, saucer-sized disks. Behind the scenes, a single keystroke can send screens of information to a library supplier or retrieve a MARC (Machine Readable Cataloguing) record from a bibliographic utility. As a profession we not only navigate cyberspace and surf the Internet, we are also involved in a more active capacity, building databases, designing software, engineering intelligent systems, helping to construct this brave new virtual library world. In short, computers, developments in communications technology, and the appearance of new multimedia formats for the storage of information have revolutionized the services we provide, the skills we require, the staffing structures we have adopted, and the physical environment in which we work.

These changes have been copiously documented. There are many books covering all aspects of library automation, some of which have already gone through a number of editions. In addition to coverage in generalist library and information services (LIS) periodicals, there are many well-established journals devoted entirely to library automation broadly or to specific formats and applications. A useful introduction to this vast and growing literature is given by Tedd in her standard textbook on computer-based systems.[1] Technical matters and management issues naturally feature prominently in this literature, and within the latter category there is a substantial amount of material dealing with the staffing implications and personnel aspects of automation.[2,3] Much of this has tended to concentrate on issues such as the management of change, organizational/departmental restructuring, changes in job content, training, job satisfaction, and 'technostress'. But the agents of this change have been given much less attention. Since the early days when researchers, practising librarians, and computer personnel collaborated to develop and implement the first experimental systems, an entirely new breed of library professional, the library systems specialist or 'systems librarian', has appeared largely unnoticed. This book is an attempt to make good this omission.

The book began life as a research project funded by the British Library Research & Development Department (BLR & DD) which aimed to investigate the roles and activities of systems librarians in UK libraries. The research is described in detail in Chapters 1 and 13, but it is worth stating here its original objectives, as these remain valid for this book. These objectives were:

- to raise awareness of the role of the systems librarian in an increasingly automated environment;
- to identify the skills and qualifications necessary to pursue a career as a systems librarian, and the prospects for anyone who applies for such a post;
- to indicate to employers and potential employers the qualities and experience needed by systems librarians, as well as the training and opportunities that should be provided;
- to investigate further the apparent lack of uniformity across this field of employment;
- to throw new light on how IT is being implemented and managed in the library and information world;
- to point out areas of overlap between LIS and other employment sectors.

The research generated considerable interest among those who were involved. There was an overwhelmingly high response rate to the questionnaire which was used to collect the data, and a great deal of warmth and enthusiasm was expressed in marginal comments and covering letters. It was evident that the survey had tapped into an area of high interest. It was clear, too, that the original list of objectives and many of the issues raised in the course of the study would make it of interest to a much wider audience than just systems librarians. The IT revolution has changed the distribution of employment, undermining the position and importance of manufacturing industries, creating a new class of information professional, and giving rise (in theory at least) to new patterns of work. Many organizations have undergone major structural upheaval, leading to new staffing configurations, new posts, and the transformation of traditional ones beyond recognition. New skills have had to be learned, and learned again and again as part of a lifelong process of continuous development, or even, some might say, survival. Interacting with these movements have been other powerful forces in the wider external environment which have compelled libraries to become more efficient, more competitive, and more customer-orientated. As the chapters which follow amply show, the systems librarian represents in miniature the profession as a whole in the face of these changes, a kind of Everyman figure with whom a cross-section of library and information professionals will be able to identify, whatever their background. And so while the book is aimed primarily at systems librarians and library systems managers, the convergence of these broader issues on the systems function make it relevant to a much wider readership, including:

- senior library managers responsible for the implementation and management of IT systems within their own organizations, and possibly considering the future development of their own systems unit;
- the growing number of library and information professionals and students interested in pursuing a career as a systems librarian (in the past, librarians have drifted into systems posts with little forethought); also, those existing and prospective systems librarians interested in using their IT skills to move up the career structure within library and information work or move into the 'emerging market';
- the increasing number of practising librarians whose duties involve an element of systems work;
- those involved in the education and training of information professionals in an automated environment;
- all library and information workers concerned about their professional status, the dangers of a transfer of control and professional knowledge to other sectors (such as systems suppliers), and the future role of libraries in society;
- members of other professions whose work has been similarly transformed by automation.

Furthermore, because the questions raised in the course of the original research were broad it became clear that there was potential input from a number of different fields and areas of practice to counterbalance the perspective of the automation specialists who had been the focus of the BLR & DD survey. So as the concept of the book grew, it was always intended to be more than simply another book-of-the-research-project. Before proceeding to outline the remainder of the book, there are some preliminary questions which need to be addressed.

WHAT IS A SYSTEMS LIBRARIAN?

The short answer to this question is that 'systems librarians are the people responsible for managing computerized library systems'.[4] Again, systems librarians are 'the people who identify the needs of the library for automated systems, cause these systems to be implemented, and analyze the operations of the library'.[5] As often happens, the short answer raises further questions and so needs to be qualified and extended. This is one of the tasks which will occupy us on and off throughout the rest of the book as we look in some detail at what the job entails. Here at the very outset, though, it will be helpful to clarify some of the points arising from the above definitions.

To answer the question 'What is a systems librarian?', perhaps we need to take a step further back and ask the question 'What do we mean by "the system"?' The word is enshrouded in a 'penumbra of uncertainty' and this gives it certain awe-inspiring qualities. Its ubiquity in marketing and advertising is an indication of this power to impress. Products and services as diverse as vacuum cleaners and video recorders, car washes and waste disposal use it to imply that their combination of methods, materials, and techniques have been devised logically and scientifically to create a new and more effective synergy, or that what they offer is more holistic, dealing not simply with isolated phenomena but embracing a range of approaches to deliver a comprehensive solution. It could be argued that there is an element of incongruity about the term 'systems librarian', juxtaposing as it does these rather nebulous but impressive associations with the mundane and often negative connotations evoked by libraries and librarians. However, the appropriation of the word by information workers is much more than jumping on the bandwagon. Libraries and information centres have a long and outstanding track record in the use of automation. Computerized systems for the basic library housekeeping functions of cataloguing and circulation control can be traced back as far as the mid-1960s. Many of the systems which were developed during this experimental phase were failures, and it was not until the 1970s that real growth occurred, facilitated by progress on a number of fronts: the development and widespread use of the MARC format; the adoption by the publishing industry, libraries, and cataloguing agencies of the ISBN (International Standard Book Number) as a unique identifier for each bibliographic item; the publication of bibliographic standards such as ISBD (International Standard Bibliographic Description) and AACR (Anglo-American Cataloguing Rules); and the rise of the major library cooperatives and bibliographic utilities, BLCMP (originally Birmingham Libraries Cooperative Mechanization Project) and SWALCAP (South West

Academic Libraries Cooperative Automation Project, now SLS) in the UK, and in the USA and Canada OCLC (originally Ohio College Library Center, now Online Computer Library Center), WLN (formerly Washington but now Western Library Network), UTLAS (University of Toronto Library Automation System), RLIN (Research Libraries Information Network) and others.

During this first phase of automation, computer-based acquisitions and cataloguing systems were usually quite independent from circulation systems, and libraries generally made use of an institutional mainframe, though by the late 1970s some libraries had begun to install their own minicomputers. This trend continued into the 1980s, and so the market rapidly grew for the turnkey systems which are now the choice of most large and medium-sized libraries, in which hardware and software are sold together as a package, and the various housekeeping functions are integrated into a single system. The systems available from most of the main vendors now offer a much extended range of functions, including OPAC, interlibrary loans, serials control, community information, and thesaurus modules in addition to the basic housekeeping processes of ordering and acquisitions, cataloguing, and circulation control, and most of these can be parameterized to local requirements. Developments in microcomputers have meant that these sophisticated systems are now within the grasp of even the smallest of information services. In the 1990s, in an increasingly competitive market, a number of system suppliers are developing and marketing 'third generation' library management systems with more user-friendly interfaces based on an open systems approach. The effect of these advances in computers and communications technology extend far beyond the routine library housekeeping tasks. The spread of the personal computer has given library managers access to a range of microcomputer-based business applications software, management information systems, and decision support systems to assist them in the processes of planning and control. New services such as online information retrieval and CD-ROM databases are now available to library users, while the delivery of traditional databases such as the library catalogue has been radically transformed. Developments in networking locally, nationally, and internationally have increased the potential for machines and systems to communicate with each other. Systems, and indeed libraries, are no longer discrete. In consequence physical access to the library is becoming less important and there is a growing trend towards end-user access to remote databases of bibliographic, statistical, graphic, and full-text information. Again, Tedd provides an excellent and manageably concise introduction to these trends with pointers to further more detailed readings.[6]

This potted summary of the development of computerized library systems reveals two important points about the systems librarian's job which our preliminary definitions glossed over. First, by looking more carefully at what we mean when we talk about 'the system' we have seen that it is seldom possible to equate the responsibility of the systems librarian with the library management system alone. The scope of the job has progressively widened as new technologies have been embraced by libraries and information centres. In Chapter 3 Dunsire takes this discussion further by bringing in the human components of the system and non-automated library procedures, and by considering the library system within the context of the organization and the wider network of information systems. Second, because there is now such a range of constituent parts within any one library system, and because the take-up of this new technology in libraries has been uneven, determined by a range of factors such as local and institutional politics, human and financial resources, and the needs of the user community, heterogeneity is a salient feature of the systems librarian position. Other groups in LIS have found their work radically altered by the implementation of new technology, but the diversity is more marked among systems librarians, where there is no established and time-honoured blueprint for the post, and where changes in technology impact more directly on duties and responsibilities.

Given this diversity it is perhaps not surprising that there is some inconsistency in the terminology of systems posts. 'Systems librarian' has probably gained the widest currency, but a glance at some of the job titles of the contributors to this volume is revealing. Titles such as Automated Systems Librarian, IT Librarian, Automation Librarian, Computer Officer, Assistant Librarian (Automation), and many others abound in job advertisements, each carrying its own nuances and overtones. A useful distinction, one which serves as a touchstone in this debris of terms but which is not always easy to apply in practice, is between systems librarians, where there is more or less a one-to-one correspondence between the post and the tasks of systems management, and systems administrators or systems managers, for whom the task of administering the system is merely one of several duties and whose main responsibilities lie elsewhere. By giving this book the title *The systems librarian* the intention was to draw attention to the unique role of the dedicated or full-time systems specialist where the whole range of systems duties are to be found in their 'purest' form. This does not mean that systems managers or administrators are excluded. Thus, in Chapter 6, Brady and Ryan adopt a wider definition of 'systems librarian' than that given above and include in the term part-timers as well as specialists; similarly, the hybrid post of Systems Librarian/Database Manager described by Warlow in Chapter 7 is not uncommon as an alternative to the dedicated systems librarian; Woodward and Meadows like Ryan and Brady use the term inclusively to refer to systems administrators more generally; and finally, in other chapters where the term is used in its narrower sense, much of the discussion is equally valid and relevant to the growing number of library and information workers who find themselves performing systems work in whatever capacity.

ARE SYSTEMS LIBRARIANS SPECIAL?

Although systems-related duties are becoming more and more common on the job descriptions of many non-systems posts, the systems librarian as defined in the last section is unique. Other library and information professionals perform their duties in ways they could not have imagined 20–30 years ago. What distinguishes the systems librarian is that the job itself was inconceivable until the widespread use of computers, and many of the duties involved do not fall within the traditional confines of library and information work.

Despite their singularity and despite the importance of the systems function, systems librarians have certainly not (until recently) been the focus of special attention in the professional literature. All of the standard texts on library automation deal with the requirements of the post in so far as they describe the procedures involved in planning for, implementing, and managing IT-based systems. Many also draw attention to the need for a library systems manager or systems unit as one of the staffing implications of automation. However, the treatment is usually incidental and seldom recognizes the post as a distinct specialism in its own right.

Historically, the emergence of the post is not easy to trace in the literature. A glance at some of the issues of *Vine* and *Program* dating back to the late 1960s and early 1970s shows how much of the initiative during the early phases of IT in libraries came from the fruitful collaboration between far-sighted library staff and their colleagues in computer departments. Systems posts only became common after the early trail-blazing had been done, and their rise can be traced in two surveys which were the forerunners of Chris Batt's surveys of IT in public libraries.[7] In the first survey, concerned specifically with the effects of computerization on staffing, no library authority mentioned the existence of such a post, though the need clearly existed. One respondent notes the 'disproportionate amount of professional time spent on non-professional work within the computer systems'. In another case, a full-time copy-typist is given clerical and liaison duties on the computer system. A third respondent comments that there is

> much less routine clerical work than with manual system, but there is a distinct increase in the workload of senior staff (e.g., dumping the store every evening). Much of this is borne by the 2 senior non-professional assistants . . . . Another point that has been stressed . . . is the need to designate one or more senior officers to oversee all computer matters and to liaise with the computer staff. Two are preferable: a senior professional for planning and

policy, and administrative officer for dealing with the necessary forms, maintenance, etc. Unless the size of the library and the degree of computerisation justify it, it is not essential for these officers to be full-time on computer work: it might, in fact, be considered better if they have other interests to give a broader outlook.[8]

Some years later, in the 1982 survey into computerization in public libraries carried out by the Technical Panel of the Association of London Chief Librarians, libraries were asked who managed the day-to-day running of their system. The report concludes:

There is a clear trend for authorities to have developed better organisation in the control of both routine procedures and future developments. Since the 1979 report more logical and consistent staffing hierarchies of responsibility seem to have evolved or been implemented by changes in management structure. This increase in control is one of the most significant changes to have taken place since the last survey.

There are now more posts defined as technical, development or liaison than was previously the case. Overall responsibility for computer systems now lies generally at second or third level whilst day to day running is the responsibility of a less senior officer often within a bibliographical services section. Only two authorities, Bexley and Westminster, reported that this function lay with the staff of the data processing section.[9]

Published case studies of library automation projects can also provide useful and informative instances of the formation and development of systems units within particular organizations. Typical of the parenthetical treatment which the systems librarian usually receives in such studies is Gratton's account of the implementation of the first automated system in Derbyshire County Libraries in 1978.[10] Gratton reproduces the job description for the new post of Computer Liaison Officer and justifies the need for it in an exchange of letters between himself and the Senior Depute Librarian with Renfrew District Libraries. Systems posts are featured more prominently in Craghill, Neale and Wilson's study of the impact of IT on staff deployment in public libraries in the UK, which included case studies of six public libraries.[11] The creation of systems-related posts is singled out as one of the few direct organizational effects which can be attributed to IT alone; other organizational changes related to IT usually had other additional causes in the internal or external environment. In their conclusions about the impact of automation on individuals and on the nature of library work, the authors describe in some detail the characteristics of systems work and the qualities and qualifications it requires. A further example, this time an academic library in the United States, is found in Begg's case study of automation in Boston College Library.[12] Begg begins with the first in-house acquisition system in 1978/9 and goes on to describe the implementation of a Geac system in 1983 and the subsequent migration to NOTIS (Northwestern Online Total Integrated System) in 1990. Over this 12-year period the systems staff grow from a single systems librarian in 1982 to a team of three: the Automation Librarian, 'who coordinates all library automation implementation and ongoing operations', 'the more technically focused Library Systems Manager', and a temporary Technical Assistant. The systems staff report to the Assistant University Librarian for Automation and Technical Services, 'who has overall planning and management responsibility for library technology and its applications'.

An even more elusive source than the published literature is the grey literature of internal reports, job advertisements, and the career histories of individual librarians. The chapters in this collection can be seen as an attempt to bring some of this material to light by charting the career progression of individual systems librarians and the varying fortunes of the systems function in particular organizations from their earliest days of automation.

Despite this dearth of material documenting the rise of the systems librarian in the historical context of progressive library automation, a small but growing number of articles dealing specifically with the systems librarian's post have been added to the literature over the years.[13–19] These have tended to be essentially descriptive in their approach, and in them two themes are often repeated, both of which have already been mentioned above: the range of duties and skills involved in system management, and the widening of the systems librarian's responsibilities beyond merely administering an integrated library system. The literature also includes three surveys of systems posts, all of them of geographically or otherwise restricted and therefore of limited value,[20–22] and a series of articles which focused on single issues such as the training of automation specialists,[23] relations with computer personnel,[24–27] and salaries.[28]

This rapid survey of the literature serves to illustrate that the systems librarian has, until fairly recently, been treated very much as a footnote in the history of library automation. The reasons for this neglect are not hard to find. In part, it can be explained by the excitement that accompanied the IT revolution. Any diversion of attention away from the novelty of the technology itself or its impact on traditional services would have been a narcissistic distraction. But there are other reasons too. Paradoxically, some of the very qualities which make the post so distinctive also account for its low profile. The emergence of the position is still a relatively recent phenomenon. It has occurred gradually, and, like the take-up of IT itself, it has been an uneven process. Overall, the number of systems librarians is comparatively small: not all libraries choose to (or are able to) create a dedicated full-time systems post when they automate, and its specialist nature has tended to restrict it to a single post, generally in large and medium-sized libraries. Where the position does exist, the duties it encompasses seem to vary a great deal. Some systems librarians are responsible purely for the major library housekeeping operations. This in itself entails a not inconsiderable range of duties and skills and allows scope for much variation from post to post. As Chu comments, to expect a single individual to be equally well-versed in all the areas associated with the maintenance and development of a large system is akin 'to having one person build a house, and do an equally good job in installing the electrical system, the plumbing, and the heating system'.[29] In addition to these responsibilities, many systems librarians find themselves participating to varying degrees in a range of other IT initiatives in their organizations. This may be input at a strategic level, technical support and hardware maintenance, or merely providing advice and support to colleagues.

The aforementioned absence of uniformity in the terminology of system-related posts has merely added to the nebulousness and uncertainty which surrounds these posts, and may, along with the other factors mentioned above, have contributed to the fragmented impact which systems librarians have had on the profession. And any sense of cohesion and group identity is virtually non-existent: there are no professional groups consisting purely of systems librarians (though user groups of particular library systems may be made up largely of systems managers), and no journals or newsletters produced by and for systems librarians alone. (An electronic mailing-list for systems librarians, LIS-SYS, is being set up on Mailbase at the time of writing.)

In contrast with this low profile within the library and information community as a whole, systems librarians seem often to be highly influential within their own organizations. Existing on the margins in the sense that they do not use their information skills directly, their activities are nonetheless central to service provision since all library operations depend on them alone. This influence is further enhanced by a 'here be dragons' attitude to computers which is still found among some library staff and which endues the systems librarian with a heroic glamour and the mystique associated with being the guardian of arcane and esoteric knowledge. The very title 'systems librarian' seems to encapsulate something of this mystery by juxtaposing the familiar connotations of libraries with the mist of uncertainty that surrounds the word 'systems'.

From this brief discussion, it should be apparent that systems librarians are indeed special. The post is a unique one and an intriguing one, not least because of its ability to hold together so many apparent contradictions and irreconcilables: the world of humans and the world of machines; a low group profile externally and nationally and yet much influence internally; on the periphery of library work, yet indispensible for the day-to-day operation of the most basic services; a specialism with no real homogeneity or uniformity in terms of the job content, and in which the postholder can expect to find him/herself cast in a variety of roles – librarian, technician, computer professional, manager, educator; the glamour, the high drama, and the stress of crisis situations, and the tedium of system error reports or ongoing minor hardware faults.

ARE SYSTEMS LIBRARIANS IMPORTANT?

Some of the milestones and landmarks along the road of ever-increasing dependence on automated systems have already been indicated: the development of experimental in-house systems running on institutional mainframes; the birth of MARC and the rise of the major bibliographic utilities and cooperatives; the growth in the 1980s of the market for integrated standalone systems; dramatic progress in the computer industry, including falling hardware costs, increasing storage capacity and processing power, the proliferation of the microcomputer, the emergence of standard, high-performance relational database management systems, and the development of more user-friendly interfaces; and the development of communications technologies which permit the high-speed transfer of enormous quantities of data resulting in the increasing use of networks. There can be few library services which are not largely dependent on technology for service delivery as well as for the numerous support operations and background activities. This represents a huge financial investment, and although new technology is sometimes introduced for questionable motives or with unrealistic expectations, a carefully managed automation project can bring many benefits. These benefits could include greater efficiency and the ability to handle heavier workloads, more cooperation and centralization, and the introduction of new services such as OPAC or self-service reservation or issue facilities. These three factors – the almost universal dependence on IT for the provision of a full range of services, the financial cost of computer-based systems, and the benefits and raised expectations that automation brings – place a very heavy burden of responsibility on those whose job it is to manage these systems. It is a job that requires a person of the highest calibre, one who possesses exceptional and wide-ranging abilities. Something of the variety of skills involved will emerge in the chapters written by systems librarians themselves. It is worth noting, though, that hard technological skills are only one aspect of the job and are often less important than communication and management skills.

Whether systems librarians will continue to be important is an issue that is dealt with by several of the contributors to this volume. Libraries of all kinds face an uncertain future as a result of changes in government policy, economic performance, trends in education and leisure, demographic shifts, and, not least, new technologies. In the long term, network access to remote databases of full-text and other information is seen by some as a threat to the very existence of libraries as we know them. In this scenario systems will replace the physical structures. Thus the question of the future of the systems librarian is bound up with the question of the future of libraries, and for this reason, too, systems librarians are important.

WHERE ARE SYSTEMS LIBRARIANS FOUND?

We noted above the role of organization-specific variables in determining the nature of the systems librarian's duties. In the same way, a large number of local factors, acting singly or in combination, will influence the particular staffing configuration adopted to execute the systems function. In the two case studies of the University of Limerick Library and the Library of University College London featured in Part 2 the decision to adopt a team approach to system management was the outcome of a definite policy decision. By contrast, an Association of Research Libraries' survey of systems office organization in academic libraries in the USA mentions the importance of historical and sometimes arbitrary factors such as 'the subsystem that was implemented first, the location of interested staff, and the physical location of major computing equipment'.[30] Other relevant considerations include staffing levels, the pool of IT expertise among staff, the level of support available from the system supplier or computer department, the availability of funding, and the need for training and in-house documentation.

The research reported in Chapter 1 selected a small number of what were felt to be significant and measurable influencing factors in an attempt to obtain a profile of libraries in which there was a systems librarian.[31] The results of the survey largely confirmed the initial expectations. Systems librarians were found to be more common in public libraries and the libraries of large and medium-sized academic institutions. The most obvious explanation for this is that such libraries are more likely to have the financial resources and staffing levels to permit the appointment of a dedicated systems specialist. For many smaller libraries this would be an unthinkable luxury, which explains why the incidence of systems administrators was found to be higher in these libraries. The nature of the systems also had a bearing in that libraries with large sophisticated library management systems (measured in terms of the size of machine, the number of terminals, and the number of modules which had been implemented) were more likely to have a systems librarian. The established vendor names were common in this category: BLCMP, Dynix, Geac, and the others. Smaller systems – usually low-cost, single application software packages running on PCs, or systems designed in the first instance for information retrieval but which also offer some housekeeping facilities (for example Cardbox Plus,

CAIRS LMS, Inmagic, etc.) usually required less attention, and were looked after by a systems manager on a part-time basis. One unforeseen result of this analysis was that a majority of libraries with a system that had been designed in-house had no systems librarian (56.7%). One reason for this might be that where the high level of knowledge required to develop a system from scratch already exists in an organization there is no need for the library to duplicate that skill by employing its own specialist. However the sample is so small (30 responses) that it would be unwise to read too much into this.

The organizations which responded to the survey showed much less variation when analysed in terms of other aspects of automation. For example, the implementation of other IT applications additional to the library management system was equally high irrespective of the presence or otherwise of a full-time systems librarian. Similarly, there were no significant differences between libraries with a full-time systems librarian and libraries where the post did not exist regarding the location of the computer. However, where there is no systems librarian, the availability of expert computer advice and support from the parent organization, over and above vendor support, is important: of 136 libraries with no systems librarian which replied to a question on this subject in the survey, 75.7% received support from a central computer section.

SUMMARY OF CONTENTS
The book is divided into four parts.

Part 1   The role of the systems librarian
The chapters in this section attempt to give an insight into some aspects of the work of the systems librarian and discuss some of the issues arising from this.

Chapter 1 reports the findings of a postal survey of systems librarians carried out at the end of 1991 in libraries throughout the UK. A wide range of data concerning many aspects of the post was collected and analysed. This included objective information about the duties performed, wider professional activities beyond the workplace, and the educational qualifications and previous work experience of the sample, as well as 'softer', more subjective data regarding levels of stress and the rewards of being a systems librarian as indicated by status and job satisfaction.

The purpose in presenting this material here is to provide a general framework for the remaining chapters in this part of the book, which exemplify and expand on many of the survey findings as these are found in real settings. These remaining chapters have all been written by authors with long experience of managing IT systems in libraries (as have those in the second part) and they are thus able to look back at some of the changes that have occurred as systems have developed, and also glance ahead at where these changes seem to be taking us.

In Chapter 2 Westlake describes the history of automation in Hillingdon Borough Libraries focusing on the decision (in the early 1980s) to create the new post of Library Systems Manager with the initial task of specifying a planned new system. The varying fortunes of this post in all its manifestations are chronicled through several organizational restructurings, and there is a detailed description, with journal entries for a typical week, of the kind of work currently performed. In developing this, Westlake expounds the belief that a systems librarian should be dedicated to these tasks rather than diverted by also having to work in other areas of the library's activities. He also argues strongly that this kind of job is so strategically important that the systems librarian should be included on the organization's key decision-making body. In conclusion Westlake looks at how the job may develop as a result of technological and organizational changes. Hillingdon, like many other local authorities, is going through major changes of philosophy regarding the organization of service delivery, and these, together with the prospect of competitive tendering, are likely to have a significant impact on the work of the Information Technology Team.

If, as a former British prime minister has observed, a week is a long time in politics, it can be equally long for the systems librarian. In Chapter 3, 'A life in the week . . .', Dunsire examines some of the general issues concerning the systems librarian in an informal and at times provocative manner. Among some of the questions raised are:

- What constitutes the system? Are staff and non-automated procedures included? Is the systems librarian's system a component of the larger library system or is it coextensive? Does the system extend beyond the library?
- What are the problems of keeping up with developments? What are the relative merits of seminars, meetings, publications, and e-mail? Can the net be cast wide or will overload result?
- How do you communicate the system to its users? Is it better to 'train' the system or train the user?
- Is the role of the systems librarian reactive or proactive? Should the systems librarian have a mission beyond that of keeping it up and running? What drives system changes, the 'goal' of the system (its environment) or its internal potential (the technology)?
- Will the systems librarian eventually replace the chief librarian? Should the systems librarian be in a position to take strategic decisions, and is the formal authority to do so available? Does the systems/chief librarian have a wider role to play within the organization?

- What lies in the future? Will the systems librarian outlive the library? Can the systems librarian role be automated?

The relationship between the library systems vendor and its customers is in some ways akin to a marriage: there is often a honeymoon period followed by a time of disillusionment when all the golden promises fail to materialize, which in turn gives way to the normal ups and downs of a realistic working partnership. However, there is nothing in the contract which binds the two sides 'till death do us part'. Many of the library systems which were implemented in the early to mid-1980s are now in the final stages of their life cycle. Systems managers in these libraries are discovering that the range of choices brought about by new technological developments has made the task of finding a replacement more difficult, since simple off-the-shelf solutions may no longer offer the most attractive deal.

In Chapter 4 Broome surveys some recent developments in the library systems market-place and how these will influence the skills required during the process of migrating to a new system. With first and second generation systems technical constraints prevented system suppliers from providing librarians with the level of functionality they and their clients required. The development and widespread adoption of industry standards has removed this constraint, and the way is now clear for librarians to assert their requirements and to take the lead in shaping the future development of library management systems. Broome argues that in order to do this, and in order to ensure that their employers' investment is well spent, systems librarians will need to increase their technical knowledge of hardware and software, operating systems, and database management tools, and also develop a new market awareness. In the first section of her chapter Broome examines these technical developments in detail and questions whether library systems suppliers are doing all they can to make the benefits of open systems – portability, flexibility and freedom of choice – available to their customers. The chapter then presents a framework for procuring an 'open systems'-based library system from the very earliest stages of costing the new system and preparing a system specification through to the problems involved in data conversion and the various migration options available.

Schuyler, in Chapter 5, describes Kitsap Regional Library's search for a new system, and demonstrates well the value of having a well-informed systems librarian with business acumen and market awareness in addition to solid technical know-how. As frame relay technology is developed and becomes more widely available commercially, Schuyler's account of the implementation of a frame relay network will be of interest to librarians from all sectors of the information world. Of special interest to those working in the public library sector will be his experience of the technical and political barriers which preserve the information divide between the 'information rich' who have access to the global network of electronic information and the 'information poor', mostly public library clients, who do not. The success of public libraries in confronting such challenges and in meeting the competition head-on will be a key factor in determining their future role in society. As Schuyler points out, systems librarians have a central role in achieving this:

> A push to the centre of the information revolution is central to libraries' survival. For better or worse, the systems librarian is thrown into the middle of this fray. We are often faced with pulling a reluctant institution into the twenty-first century in spite of ourselves, attempting to explain a vision of the future that isn't quite here yet, justifying a budget request before the Board of Trustees for what appears to be another project, and pulling yet another wire, all in the same day.[32]

In Chapter 6, 'The system vendor's perspective', Brady and Ryan of Dynix Library Systems adopt a wide definition of the systems librarian to include part-time systems managers as well as full-time specialists. The chapter discusses the relationship between the vendor and the systems librarian with particular reference to the skills and qualities required by the 'ideal' systems librarian before, during, and after the installation of a new system. Among the many points the authors make is the belief that a systems librarian appointed at the very beginning of an automation project, and thus able to drive the pre-purchase, pre-installation procedures, brings clear benefits in term of continuity, an early agreement of the project's basic aims and objectives, and an improvement in 'the tone and personality of the entire experience', including the minimization of many of the traditional '"people" challenges' which often arise in such projects. They also express a strong preference for a '"one point of contact" systems librarian who has a recognized position within the library's management structure and is empowered to give final decisions on all aspects of the installation'.

The second part of Chapter 6 throws new light on the system supplier–library relationship by examining the extent to which the skills acquired in the two environments are transferable, using as a basis for the discussion a survey of former systems librarians currently employed by Dynix.

Part 2 Alternatives to the systems librarian
As we saw earlier, the 'pure' systems librarian is generally found in large and medium-sized libraries, and so it is, and will remain, comparatively rare. The alternative arrangements for administering the systems function vary from institution to institution. The purpose of Part 2 is to present two alternative

staffing structures drawn from three libraries, each large enough to have considered appointing a full-time systems specialist, but each of which decided that this did not suit their best interests.

In Chapter 7 Warlow tracks the course of library automation in the library of the Manchester Metropolitan University (formerly Manchester Polytechnic), where a dual-function post has evolved combining database management and systems administration. Warlow presents the case for combining both roles in a single post by demonstrating the continuity of skills required. Underpinning this continuity is a 'systems approach' similar to that proposed by Dunsire in Chapter 3, in which the library system is seen as a series of subsystems – hardware and software, library staff, clients, and the database:

> In order to achieve both efficiency and effectiveness a sound knowledge and understanding of the creation and content of the databases is required. This in turn leads to a sensitivity to the needs of all the users of the system, both library staff and library patrons. An integrated system requires an 'integrated manager' and therefore if this is to be believed, separation of the responsibilities for system management and database management would not seem to be an advantage for the Manchester Metropolitan University Library.[33]

Using this model one could equally justify combining the systems function with a user services post. As the above quotation implies, there is no universal solution, and the one described in Chapter 7 is the one that works best for the Manchester Metropolitan University Library.

Chapters 8 and 9 are case studies of two academic libraries which differ from each other considerably in terms of size, traditions, automation history, and user community, but alike in that they have both adopted a team approach to system management. The University of Limerick is a relatively new university which has expanded rapidly over the past 20 years. Mitchell recounts the development of automated systems in the Library during this time, and the philosophy and policy decisions which have driven them, focusing specifically on how a 'customer first' ethos, a democratic culture in which change is encouraged from the bottom up, and a belief that communication is more effective when library staff have direct contact with system support staff rather than through library systems staff, have developed into an approach to system management in which systems knowledge, skills, and responsibilities are diffused throughout the organization. The Library of University College London, with twice as many students as the University of Limerick and a history many times longer, lays equal stress on a customer-orientated approach, which is embodied in its subject specialist tradition. In this case, however, the driving force behind the team approach to systems administration has been the benefits to the organization of flexibility, spreading workloads more evenly, and improving communication and fostering a sense of involvement among staff. It is hoped that the case studies presented in this section will, amongst other things, assist library managers and systems administrators by providing them with models with which to compare their own structures and distribution of systems tasks.

Part 3   Education and training

There is growing recognition throughout the profession of the importance of education and training. In Chapter 10 Woodward and Meadows examine how far educational institutions in the UK and the USA are able to meet the special requirements of systems posts, and identify some solutions to the problems mentioned. The chapter goes on to argue that access to further education and training may be more important for systems librarians than for any other group within the library and information field, and looks at ways in which this training can be delivered.

Following on from this wider examination of the education and training of systems staff, Fisher in Chapter 11 describes what is currently being done in one particular institution. On the BA (Hons) Information and Library Management course at the Manchester Metropolitan University, four working library systems are available to students and serve as a vehicle for a variety of teaching methods and learning approaches including practical exercises and project-based work. From the detailed descriptions given by Fisher, and from the student profiles and experiences which follow, it is evident that the library system can be used not only to provide a solid grounding for future systems specialists, but can also work as a powerful teaching aid, integrating diverse course components, and introducing and reinforcing principles which have relevance for all library and information workers, specifically the theory and practice of information retrieval, basic library operations, and the principles of library management. Furthermore, students develop a range of information, problem-solving, and evaluative skills which are transferable and highly marketable in related employment sectors.

Part 3 concludes with a chapter which looks at the system supplier's contribution to the training of systems staff. Dobbs and Richardson describe the formal training available for system managers from BLCMP Library Services Ltd. In addition, they review the broader collection of events, activities, and services which, though not strictly training, facilitate the exchange of information or form the basis for collaborative problem-solving and thus contribute to the process of learning and development. Chapter 12 also deals with the support a system vendor can provide to the systems librarian in his/her role as trainer of other staff. The benefits of supplier input to staff training programmes will be felt by both parties, the training provider as well as the library itself. Well-trained library staff will place fewer demands on the resources of the help desk and customer support services. More importantly, at a time when the move to open systems promises libraries greater freedom in their choice of hardware, thus undermining the library systems suppliers' main source of revenue, vendors who can offer customers the added value of high quality training programmes will have a competitive edge in the market-place as well as an additional source of income.

Part 4 The future

This book is the first to deal specifically with the systems librarian. Will it be the last? Several contributions elsewhere in the book speculate about what lies ahead for libraries and for systems librarians. This theme is taken up and developed at length in Chapter 13, which presents further analyses of data obtained in the survey reported in Chapter 1. The chapter begins by assessing the job market and career prospects for individuals intent on a career in library systems management and concludes with a more general discussion of how technological advances and wider social, political, and economic trends could impact on the position of systems librarians collectively.

REFERENCES

1 Tedd, L. A., *An introduction to computer-based library systems*, 3rd edn, Chichester, Wiley, 1993.

2 Dyer, H., Fossey, D., and McKee, K., 'The impact of automated library systems on job design and staffing structures', *Program*, **27** (1), 1993, 1–16.

3 Myers, M., 'Library automation and personnel issues: a selected bibliography', *Journal of library administration*, **13** (1/2), 1990, 205–14.

4 Chan, G. K. L., 'The systems librarian', in Revill, D. H. (ed.), *Personnel management in polytechnic libraries*, Aldershot, Gower in association with COPOL, 1987, 175–99.

5 Martin, S.K., 'The role of the systems librarian', *Journal of library administration*, **9** (4), 1988, 57–68.

6 Tedd, op. cit.

7 Batt, C., *Information technology in public libraries*, 4th edn, London, Library Association Publishing, 1992.

8 LAMSAC, *Staffing of public libraries: a report of the research undertaken by the Local Authorities Management Services and Computer Committee for the Department of Education and Science. Vol. 1: General report*, London, HMSO, 1976.

9 Association of London Chief Librarians, *Computerisation in public libraries: a report of the survey carried out by the Technical Panel of the Association of London Chief Librarians during 1982*, London, The Association of London Chief Librarians, 1983.

10 Gratton, P. D., *Automation in Derbyshire County Libraries*, London, The Library Association, 1983.

11   Craghill, D., Neale, C. and Wilson, T. D., *The impact of IT on staff deployment in UK public libraries* (British Library research paper, 69), London, The British Library Research and Development Department, 1989.

12   Begg, K., 'Changing systems: putting it all together and making it work – or, How we did it good at Boston College', in Pitkin, G. M. (ed.), *Library systems migration: changing automated systems in libraries and information centers*, Westport, Meckler, 1991, 102–23.

13   Chan, op. cit..

14   Martin, op. cit..

15   Sherwood, M., 'The systems librarian or library systems analyst', *Australian library journal*, **29** (4), 1980, 176–9.

16   Holbrook, L. L., 'The information systems analyst: an emerging profession', in Williams, M. E. and Hogan, T. (eds.), *Proceedings of the 5th National Online Meeting, New York, April 10–12, 1984*, Medford, NJ, Learned Information, 1984, 107–13.

17   Manchovec, G. S., 'The broadening role of the systems librarian', *Online libraries and microcomputers*, **7** (10), 1989, 1–4.

18   Chu, F. T., 'Evaluating the skills of the systems librarian', *Journal of library administration*, **12** (1), 1990, 91–102.

19   Epstein, S. B., 'Administrators of automated systems: a job description', *Library journal*, 15 March, 1991, 66–7.

20   Jenkins, D. L., 'Do you want to be a systems or planning librarian? Or management analyst in an academic library?', in Lunin, L.F., Henderson, M. and Wooster, H. (eds.), *The information community: an alliance for progress: proceedings of the 44th ASIS Annual Meeting 1981, Vol.18, Washington, D.C.*, White Plains, NJ, Knowledge Industry Publications, 1981, 150–3.

21   Association of Research Libraries, Office of Management Studies, *Systems office organization* (SPEC kit 128), Washington, DC, ARL, 1986.

22   Dynix Inc., *Dynix dataline*, **8** (2) March 1991, 4-6. Also reported in *Dynix global update*, **5** (3) April 1991, 1-3.

23   McLain, J. P., Wallace, D. P. and Heim, K. M., 'Educating for automation: can the library schools do the job?', *Journal of library administration*, **13** (1/2), 1990, 7–20.

24   McWilliams, J., 'Preparing for the programmer/information specialist interchange', in Lunin, L.F., Henderson, M. and Wooster, H., (eds.), *The information community: an alliance for progress: proceedings of the 44th ASIS Annual Meeting 1981, Vol. 18, Washington, D.C.*, White Plains, NJ, Knowledge Industry Publications, 1981, 160–2.

25   Allen, L., 'From librarian to systems analyst', in Thuraisingham, A. (ed.), *The new professionals: proceedings of the Singapore-Malaysia Congress of Librarian [sic] and Information Scientists, Singapore 4–6 September 1986*, Aldershot, Gower, 1987, 158–67.

26   Scanlon, J. L., 'How to mix oil and water: or, getting librarians to work with programmers', *College and research libraries news*, **5** (4), 1990, 320–2.

27   Waters, D. J., '"We have a computer": administrative issues in the relations between libraries and campus computing organizations', *Journal of library administration*, **13** (1/2), 1990, 117–38.

28 Budd, J. M., 'Salaries of automation librarians: positions and requirements', *Journal of library administration*, **13** (1/2), 1990, 21–9.

29 Chu, op. cit..

30 Association of Research Libraries, op. cit..

31 For a fuller account of this aspect of the research see Muirhead, G. A., 'System management in UK libraries: some preliminary findings of a survey', *Information services & use*, **12**, 1992, 177–93.

32 Schuyler, Michael R., Ch.3, p.110 (this volume).

33 Warlow, Angela, Ch.7, p.137 (this volume).

❖ Acronyms and abbreviations

AACR	Anglo-American Cataloguing Rules
ANSI	American National Standards Institute
ASCII	American Standard Code for Information Interchange
AT & T	American Telephone and Telegraph Company
BCS	British Computer Society
BIDS	Bath Information and Data Services
BLCMP	Birmingham Libraries Cooperative Mechanization Project
BLR & DD	British Library Research and Development Department
BT	British Telecom
BUBL	Bulletin Board for Libraries
CALIM	Consortium of Academic Libraries in Manchester
CCT	compulsory competitive tendering
CCTA	Central Computer and Telecommunications Agency
CD-ROM	compact disc-read only memory
CIG	Cataloguing and Indexing Group of the Library Association
CLSI	Computer Library Services International
COM	computer output on microfiche
CPD	continuing professional development
CPU	central processor unit
DOS	disk operating system
EC	European Community
EDI	electronic data interchange
E-mail	electronic mail
FCC	Federal Communications Commission
FTE	full-time equivalent
IIS	Institute of Information Scientists

ILL	interlibrary loans
IR	information retrieval
IRDAC	Industrial Research and Development Advisory Committee of the Commission of the European Community
ISBN	International Standard Book Number
ISO	International Standards Organization
IT	information technology
JANET	Joint Academic Network
JUGL	JANET User Group for Libraries
LA	Library Association
LAITG	Library Association Information Technology Group
LAN	local area network
LAVA	Local Authority Viewdata Association
LIS	library and information services
MARC	machine readable cataloguing
MDIS	McDonnell Information Systems
NISS	National Information on Software Services
NOTIS	Northwestern Online Total Integrated System
OCLC	Online Computer Library Center
OPAC	online public access catalogue
OR	operational requirements
OSI	Open Systems Interconnection
PAC	public access catalogue
PC	personal computer
RAM	random access memory
RDBMS	relational database management system
RFP	request for proposal
RLIN	Research Libraries Information Network
SCOLCAP	Scottish Library Cooperative Automation Project
SLA	service level agreement
SLS	SWALCAP Library Services
SWALCAP	South Western Academic Libraries Cooperative Automation Project

TCP/IP	Transmission Control Protocol/Internet Protocol
TIMS	text information management system
UKOLUG	UK Online User Group
UTLAS	University of Toronto Library Automation System
VDU	video display unit
VGA	video graphics adaptor
WAIS	Wide Area Information Service
WAN	wide area network
WLN	Western Library Network
WWW	World Wide Web

❖ Part 1
The role of the systems librarian

1   Systems librarians in the UK: the results of a survey*

❖   Graeme Muirhead

INTRODUCTION

This chapter and Chapter 13 describe a survey to investigate the roles and activities of systems librarians in UK libraries and information centres. The specific objectives of the research are given in the introduction to this volume (see p. xv). The questionnaire which was used for the survey was designed to collect data concerning the most important issues which emerged from a reading of the literature, and its content was extremely wide-ranging. (The text of the questionnaire and the guidance notes which accompanied it are reproduced as the appendix to this chapter.) Consequently this chapter, too, covers much ground and so gives a context for subsequent chapters, which take up specific topics and themes and develop them with reference to a specific organization or a particular career, or discuss them in the light of the authors' specialist skills and experience.

After a brief analysis of the response to the questionnaire the chapter looks at what systems librarians actually do, beginning with the job itself, then moving on to look between the lines of the job description at how systems librarians communicate and at the area of work-related professional activities. It next examines the qualifications and experience which systems librarians require, before ending with a discussion of some of the 'softer' survey data concerning how systems librarians feel about what they do: Are they adequately compensated in terms of salary and status? Are they more prone to stress and burnout than colleagues in less high-profile positions? And what is it about systems work that keeps them going in spite of the pressures? What are its rewards?

---

* Aspects of Chapters 1 and 13 of this book are based on articles written by the author and published by Bowker-Saur in *Journal of librarianship and information science*, **25** (3), September 1993, and by Learned Information Ltd in *The electronic library*, **11** (2), April 1994.

1   RESPONSE RATE AND PROFILE OF THE SAMPLE

Data was collected by means of a postal survey of libraries in the UK which was conducted between October and December 1991. The libraries contacted were those in which it was thought a systems librarian post might conceivably exist, namely all public library authorities, libraries in the main academic institutions, and a selection of government, special, and larger college libraries. At the time of the survey the 'new universities' had not yet been established, and the following account preserves the now obsolete distinction between polytechnics and the older universities for the differences it exposes between these two groups.

From a total of 503 questionnaires sent out 416 replies were received, giving an overall response rate of 82.7%. The slightly lower response rate from university libraries was disappointing only by comparison with the exceptional response from polytechnics, colleges, and public libraries (see Table 1.1). Fewer responses from the remainder of the libraries in the sample (75.3%) was not unexpected. This category probably contains a higher proportion of small to medium-sized organizations, mainly government and special libraries, where, as was suggested in the Introduction (see p. xxvi), there is less likely to be staff assigned solely to the systems function, and for whom the questionnaire may therefore have seemed less relevant.

Table 1.1   Response rate

	Univ	Poly/Coll.	Public	Other	Total
No. questionnaires sent	97	70	170	166	503
No. responses received	72	67	152	125	416
% response	74.2	95.7	89.4	75.3	82.7

Figure 1.1 analyses in more detail the response rate from each sector, expressed as a percentage of the 416 respondents. Of the libraries which responded, 55% said they had a systems librarian as defined in the guidance notes. However, 49 of the remaining libraries did not have a systems post because they were still using manual systems. So by excluding this group we can say that of those libraries in the the sample which had an automated housekeeping system, 62.9% also had a systems librarian.

Figure 1.2 shows the distribution of systems librarian posts across the various sectors. In comparison with Figure 1.1, special libraries are underrepresented here. Again, the likely explanation for this is the higher proportion of small to medium-sized libraries in this category, where either the system size does not require, or else staffing constraints do not permit, the 'luxury' of a full-time systems person.

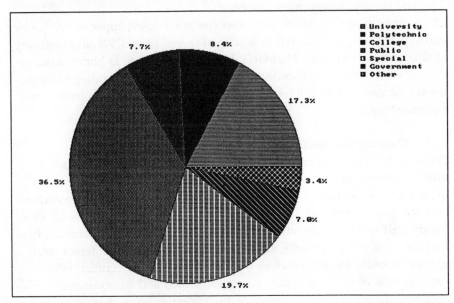

Fig. 1.1   Respondents by LIS sector

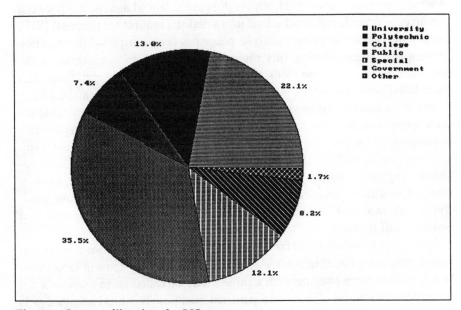

Fig. 1.2   Systems librarians by LIS sector

2   JOB DUTIES

2.1   The library management system

Library management systems, like other computer-based applications, can be said to pass through a life cycle consisting of several phases. A convenient way of discussing the systems librarian's duties as they relate to library management systems is to group them into three broad areas corresponding to the successive phases of a simplified automation cycle: planning, implementation, and maintenance.

2.1.1   *Planning and implementation*

Planning for a new automated library system or for a major upgrade to an existing system usually consists of a number of discrete stages. The first of these is a systems analysis involving detailed research into current procedures and the requirements of the replacement system. Consultation with other library staff will be an essential part of this process, and the systems librarian may be required to provide advice or arbitrate between different interest groups in order to resolve areas of non-cooperation or conflict. When the requirements of the new system have been costed and authorization to proceed with the project has been given by the governing body, the systems librarian can then begin the task of preparing a detailed technical specification or operational requirement (OR) in which the initial research and an awareness of what is currently available from vendors are balanced against the financial resources allocated, and synthesized into a realistic request for proposal (RFP) document. When the systems analysis phase has been completed the selection process can begin. During this phase there will be an evaluation of the responses to the RFP, site visits and demonstrations, and negotiations with short-listed system vendors, leading finally to the signing of a formal contract.

The main tasks of the second phase, implementation, include arranging for data conversion (in liaison with the system supplier) and stock preparation; organizing all the practicalities of the installation project – ordering new furniture, organizing and scheduling site preparation by contractors (telecommunications engineers, carpenters, electricians, etc.), and ensuring that work is clearly specified in advance and completed as agreed; testing hardware; modifying software and parameters; and finally, documenting the system and training staff to use it.

From even these brief and far from comprehensive descriptions it is evident that during these two stages of the automation process a systems librarian who is responsible for managing such a project may be called on to exercise a not inconsiderable range of skills and personal qualities. Technical knowledge is required to prepare the OR document, and also during the installation. At all stages of an automation project it is essential to have an overview of library operations and service requirements, and to possess the array of management skills necessary to plan and coordinate a large-scale project involving considerable resources and many staff. Not the least of these skills will be the ability to communicate effectively with a range of individuals and groups of all levels and in a variety of contexts – academics/elected members, library staff, sales representatives, computer professionals, telephone engineers, electricians, etc.

In the questionnaire, systems librarians were asked if they had been involved in either of these stages of library automation and whether they had taken the leading role as project manager. The results are shown in Table 1.2.

Table 1.2   Participation in planning/implementation

	n (100%)	Yes %	No %
Planning for new system	228	70.6	29.4
Planning for major upgrade	228	80.7	19.3
Project manager during installation	198	69.2	30.8

Not all systems librarians will be required to participate in all the stages of planning for and installing the system or participate to the same degree. Thus respondents were able to describe a range of levels of involvement in the planning process, for example. Some were leaders and coordinators, others were merely members of a team. Some specified that their input had been that of a technical expert, often as author or co-author of the capital bid/business case or the technical specification/OR document, but that they were excluded from the financial and policy decisions. Others said they were involved in the evaluation process – site visits, negotiations, etc. In the past, it has not been uncommon for the planning process to be carried out by existing staff, and for a systems librarian to be appointed at a later date to manage the post-selection coordination at the library end, train staff, document the system, and generally promote its use (though one can expect this arrangement to become rarer now that many organizations have a systems librarian who can see any future automation development through from beginning to end).

It is also worth bearing in mind that the term system 'upgrade' used in this question (Q19B) is open to some variation in interpretation, from the routine installation of a new memory board or loading of a new software revision to the wholesale replacement of the system centre.

But despite these qualifications, the fact that so many respondents had had some input during both the planning and implementation phases, in addition to the ongoing duties of maintaining and operating the system which are discussed below, gives some idea of the range of skills which this post requires. Quite often one person is carrying out what are effectively three jobs single-handed.

2.1.2   *System maintenance*

The tasks involved in the ongoing maintenance of a library housekeeping system are many and varied, and cannot always be clearly separated from the planning and implementation processes described above. For example, once the system has gone live, implementation fades imperceptibly into system maintenance. Some responsibilities, such as user education, staff training, and documention writing, are equally a part of the preparation for implementation and also a continuous requirement to ensure that the system's potential is realized. Likewise, monitoring and evaluating system performance is a continuous task, but feeds into the process of planning for the next system.

The questionnaire listed seven of the areas which are associated with keeping the system running, and asked respondents which of these fell within their remit. The responses are presented in Figure 1.3. The additional system-related duties specified in the 'other' category were wide-ranging, and included

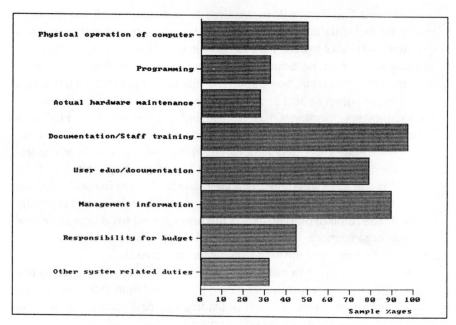

Fig. 1.3   System maintenance duties

staffing a help desk, troubleshooting hardware and software malfunctions, system development (for example loading new software, index building, etc.), ensuring compliance with health and safety requirements, organizing demonstrations for visitors, negotiating maintenance contracts, developing IT strategy, and responsibility for staff rotas and appointments.

In interpreting these responses it is important to remember that they do not indicate the time spent on each task. And as was also the case with the planning stage, some allowance must be made for variations in how individual respondents understood the terms used. For example, 'programming' for some systems librarians may mean writing a set of instructions for a particular application using a specific programming language, while for others (the majority, probably) it is merely adjusting the parameters of a turnkey system to meet local requirements. And there are widely varying arrangements for the maintenance and repair of equipment. In many cases the systems librarian's responsibility will extend only as far as elementary and routine repairs, testing hardware, and arranging for any internal repairs to be carried out by trained engineers as part of a maintenance contract. It is likely, therefore, that the 32.5% of systems librarians who said their duties included programming, and the 27.6% who mentioned hardware maintenance are overestimates of the numbers who actually perform these tasks in the stricter senses intended. So, if anything the clear contrast in Figure 1.3 between the low scores of those areas where technical skills are required, and the higher results achieved in the areas where the role is that of a mediator or human interface between technology and its users – user education, staff training, system documentation, and providing management reports – understates the importance of these mediating skills.

The importance of the intermediary role rather than technical skills is further underlined by the systems librarians' responsibility for liaising with various external bodies (see Figure 1.4).

2.2   Other IT duties

Systems librarians have traditionally been appointed to look after large-scale library management systems. It was suggested in the Introduction that as IT has penetrated further into library and information services many of the other computer-based systems have fallen within the systems librarian's purview. This is confirmed by the results of the survey. Out of 227 respondents, 165 (72.7%) said they were involved in IT developments additional to managing their library management system. Standard office automation, CD-ROM, PC-based applications, and network management were among the most frequently mentioned areas, but the range extended as far as theatre automation and security systems.

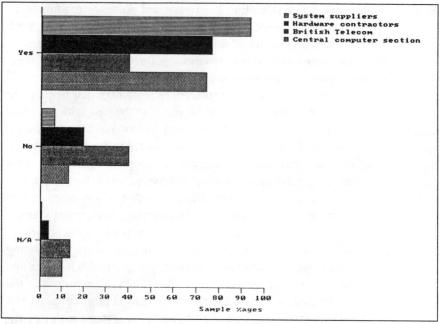

Fig. 1.4   External contacts

Participation in these developments again showed a great deal of variation. The three areas identified above in relation to automating library housekeeping operations and their associated skills apply equally to automation in the wider sense, and the extent to which a systems librarian is called on to develop these will depend on local conditions. There was also considerable variation in the type involvement, from a strategic and policy-making level through an advisory and consultative role to the practicalities of installation, hardware support, and staff training.

2.3 Non-IT duties

In addition to the duties discussed above, 70.5% of systems librarians said they also had duties which were completely unrelated to IT. These spanned the whole range of library and information work, from a few hours on an information desk or shelving, through stock selection, cataloguing, subject responsibility, and departmental liaison, to section head responsibility for varying numbers of staff.

The amount of time which systems librarians spent on their non-IT duties varied a great deal and is shown in Table 1.3.

Table 1.3   Time spent on non-IT duties

Hours per week	<5	6-10	11-15	16-20	21-30	>31
% of systems librarians	31.2	33.3	7.2	14.5	11.6	2.2

Total responses: 138

It is interesting to compare the figures in Table 1.3 with the amount of time spent on systems work in libraries with no dedicated systems staff. In 23 of these libraries systems-related work occupied more than 10 hours per week (though in some of these the work would be shared between two or more staff). It is quite possible that some of this group were spending more time on system management than some of the 39 systems librarians who said they spent more than 15 hours per week on non-IT duties. This illustrates the difficulty of arriving at a precise definition of what a systems librarian is. Systems management in libraries is best conceived of as a continuum rather than as an enclave with clear lines of demarcation. At one extreme there is the 'pure' systems librarian with responsibility only for the library management system, and at the other, the systems administrator who turns his/her hand to library automation as one job among many. Where one begins and the other ends is not clear, and staff can find themselves at any point on this line.

In some cases the systems librarians' additional non-IT tasks were assigned to the systems post for operational reasons. In others they were a legacy from a pre-automation era. As the case studies which follow this chapter illustrate, a not uncommon scenario is for an interested member of staff, or a section head who is highly involved in the automation project, to be seconded to work as project manager, or more frequently simply to take on automation duties as an extra while continuing to carry out his/her normal duties at a reduced level, and for this arrangement to become permanent.

2.4   Job duties – conclusions
To summarize so far, the survey shows that the systems librarian's post is not simply a matter of administering an automated library system (in itself no mean feat). The scope of the job often extends to other computer applications as well as duties completely unrelated to IT. A point which emerged from a considerable number of replies was that as technologies merge, making the distinction between the library system and the range of other internal and external IT systems less distinct, and as open systems make physical access to the library collection less important, so the role of the systems librarian is not only widening but also evolving from an essentially supporting role into a more high-profile post providing a direct service to a range of customers.

3   PROFESSIONAL ORGANIZATIONS AND ACTIVITIES

The duties delineated in the previous section and the kind of pressures they exert suggest that the flow of information and the benefits of peer group support that can be obtained by participation in professional activities could be especially important for systems librarians. Paradoxically, systems librarians are potentially restricted in their professional involvement by the very factors that make it so valuable for them: heavy workloads, the 'isolation factor', the 24-hour demands of the system, and lack of time.

Figure 1.5 shows membership of professional bodies. Among the most frequently mentioned groups in the 'other' category were JUGL (JANET User Group for Libraries), UKOLUG (UK Online User Group), LAVA (Local Authority Viewdata Association), LIRG (Library and Information Research Group), Scottish Electronic Information Group, and the Circle of State Librarians.

The 59.9% of respondents who belonged to a special interest group includes 49.1% who specified the LAITG (Library Association Information Technology Group). Neither this nor the high membership of system supplier user groups is surprising. What is more interesting, particularly in the light of the discussion of education and employment background (see section 5 below), is the overwhelming predominance of the Library Association, not only over the British Computer Society, but also over other information service groups such

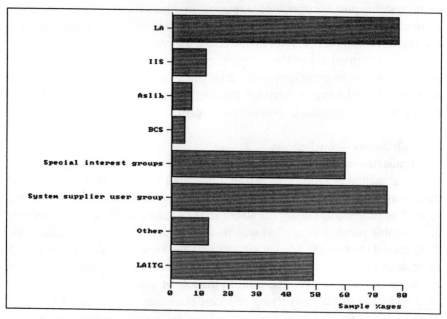

Fig. 1.5   Membership of professional organizations

as Aslib and the Institute of Information Scientists.

It is also worth noting that 29.2% said they were actively involved in a professional organization (for example, through committee membership). Comparative data is not readily available, but this figure of almost 30% would seem to indicate a fairly high level of professional commitment.

Only 56 respondents mentioned other professional activities (see Figure 1.6), but the fact that almost 25% of the sample participate in such a variety of other professional activities indicates not only commitment but also a high degree of expertise and experience.

4 USE OF JOURNALS AND E-MAIL

The questionnaire asked respondents to state the three journals which they found most useful to them in carrying out their duties as systems librarians. In the replies, five journal titles and the publications emanating from one professional association were mentioned with sufficient frequency to merit a category of their own. The journal titles were *Computers in libraries, The Electronic library, Library micromation news, Vine,* and *Program.* The professional association was Aslib, which publishes *Aslib proceedings, Aslib information, Aslib online notes, Aslib current awareness bulletin,* and *Journal of documentation* (*Program* is also produced by Aslib but its frequency in reply sheets merited a category of its own). The remainder of the responses were sorted into the following broad

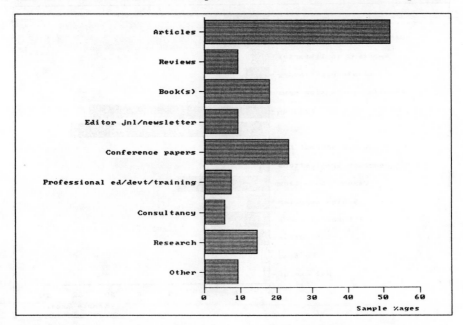

Fig. 1.6 Other professional activities

categories: general library and information services (for example, *British journal of academic librarianship, Library Association record, Information world review, Journal of librarianship and information science,* etc.), general computing (for example, *What's new in computing, Byte, Which computer?, Personal computer, What micro?,* etc.), library automation (for example, *CD-ROM librarian, IT in libraries, Libraries in automation,* etc.), other computer applications (for example, *Information technology in local government, Computers in teaching, Government computing,* etc.), other journals (for example, *The Bookseller,* the *Guardian, New scientist, Education review,* etc.), system supplier documentation and newsletters, and the publications of special interest groups such as LAITG, UKOLUG, and LACIG (Library Association Cataloguing and Indexing Group). As Figure 1.7 shows, *Vine* and *Program* emerged as the clear front runners, with mentions in 61.6% and 55% of the reply sheets respectively. Otherwise the results are a reflection of the professional interests of the sample, with a heavy bias towards library automation. It is worth observing that general computing magazines and journals score considerably higher than general LIS publications, which suggests that systems librarians have as much (perhaps more) in common with computer professionals as with their colleagues in libraries. Four respondents said they had no time to read journals, and three said they found them of no

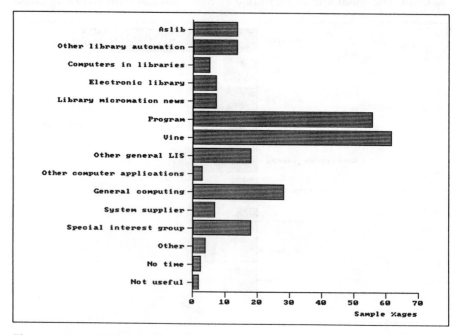

Fig. 1.7   Journal titles mentioned

value, though the comparatively low response rate to this question (185 replies) may in itself indicate that these views are held more generally.

There was a surprisingly low use of e-mail by systems librarians, and some possible reasons for this are suggested in the concluding paragraphs of this section. Of a total of 225 responses, 40% said they were regular users of e-mail, 21.3% said they used it occasionally, and 38.7% said they never used it. As Table 1.4 shows, there was variation between sectors, with the heaviest use in the university and polytechnic libraries.

Table 1.4 Use of e-mail

	n (100%)	Regularly (%)	Occasionally (%)	Never (%)
University	49	83.6	16.4	0.0
Polytechnic	30	56.7	30.0	13.3
College	17	17.6	29.4	52.9
Public	80	21.2	18.8	60.0
Special	28	17.9	21.4	60.7
Government	17	29.4	17.6	52.9
Other	4	50.0	50.0	0.0
Total	225	40.0	21.3	38.7

Less surprising than the low use of e-mail was the lack of interest in the electronic mailing-lists and discussion groups which many librarians now have access to via JANET: only 23.2% said they used these services, and several commented that they found it difficult to distinguish between them or took no notice of where the messages originated. Predictably, the use of these services was almost exclusively among the academic community, with university and polytechnic libraries representing 63.5% and 28.8% of users respectively.

Finally, respondents were asked to state the source of information and support to which they attached most importance. The responses are represented in Figure 1.8 (many were unable to limit themselves to a single answer, and so this question should be regarded as a multi-answer question).

In the absence of readily available data of a similar nature for other library and information specialists or for the profession as a whole it is impossible to say to what extent these preferences distinguish systems librarians. However, on the basis of these findings three cautious observations can be made:

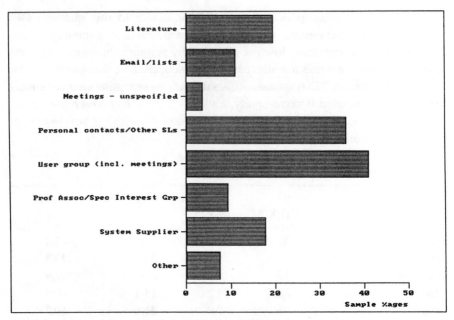

Fig. 1.8   Main sources of information and support

1   The high scores for user groups and personal contacts (Figure 1.8) seem to suggest that systems librarians depend more on external contacts for information and support than on colleagues within their own organizations.

2   The relatively low score for e-mail can be interpreted in several ways. It may be the case that some systems librarians did not regard their own internal library system-based communications as 'true' e-mail and so disregarded it in their responses. The problem is therefore one of semantics. Another consideration is the lack of hardware connections from the library machine to a wide area network, especially in public libraries. If, as has been suggested above, external contacts are more important to systems librarians than contacts within their own organizations, and if most e-mail systems are library or institutional LANs, then the value of these local systems to systems librarians will be genuinely diminished, as they do not provide contact with the people who matter.

3   Systems librarians seem to value face-to-face interaction with other professionals with shared interests and common problems more highly than other less personal methods of communicating, and their active participation in professional affairs shows that they will make time for this despite the many factors which militate against their doing so. Again, with no comparative data it is impossible to say if their needs in this respect are stronger than for other subgroups in the library and information world. But there are certainly reasons inherent in the nature of their work why this might be the case: they often

work long hours, at times under conditions of great stress, and are frequently isolated in their specialist function by inadequate staffing levels; and although communication and interpersonal skills are important in executing their duties, the kind of communication they habitually engage in is carried out on the basis of their outsider status and non-membership of the various groups between which they mediate.

5 QUALIFICATIONS AND EXPERIENCE

The questionnaire asked respondents to give their formal education qualifications. Their answers are presented in Figures 1.9 and 1.10.

These results show unequivocally that systems librarians are on the whole computer-trained librarians rather than library-trained computer experts. Those possessing a BLib or equivalent accounted for 17.3% of respondents and 52.4% had a postgraduate diploma in library and information studies. Library and information studies also accounted for 19.4% of the subjects studied for other qualifications. The range of subjects otherwise reflects the strong humanities bias of the sample. Only 17 respondents specified computer studies as a subject in which they had a formal qualification, and only 15 had any previous work experience in the computer industry. This last figure contrasts strikingly with the positive wealth of previous library experience represented in Figure 1.11.

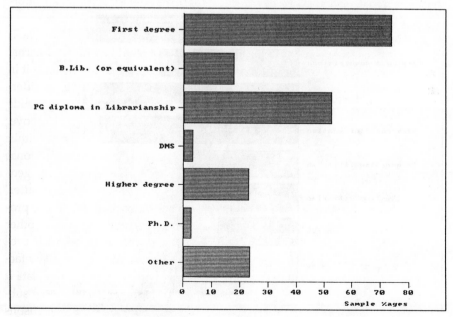

Fig. 1.9   Formal educational qualifications

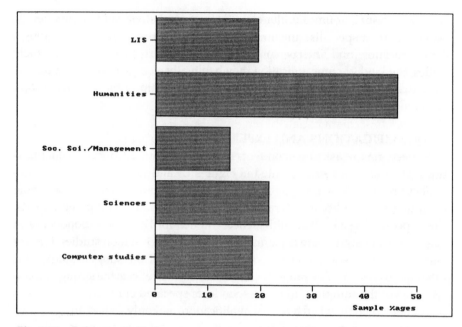

Fig. 1.10   Subjects studied

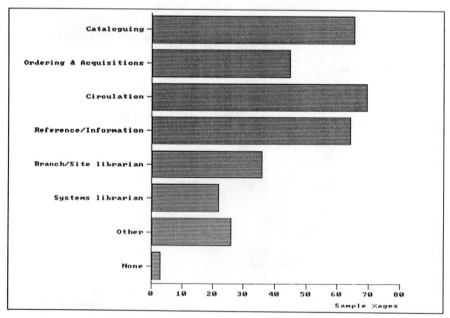

Fig. 1.11   Previous library experience

The relative merits of a library or a computer-orientated background is a subject that has been debated in the literature and about which respondents to the survey expressed opposing opinions in their marginal comments. The literature emanating from the USA seems to suggest that systems librarians there are more likely to have a background in computers or be dual qualified.[1, 2] Computer skills, in the narrowest sense of hard technical and programming knowledge, are not enough, but in the light of the systems librarians' evaluations of their education which are reported later, this is a trend which we in the UK would do well to follow through more appropriate education and training, and as part of an ongoing commitment to continuing professional development (CPD).

Any affinities between the detailed and sometimes complex work carried out in some specialist technical and support services posts and the technical and problem-solving skills required by systems librarians appear to be insignificant, as all areas of library work are equally well-represented in Figure 1.11. This is also supported by the spread of jobs which the respondents held immediately before becoming systems librarians (see Figure 1.12).

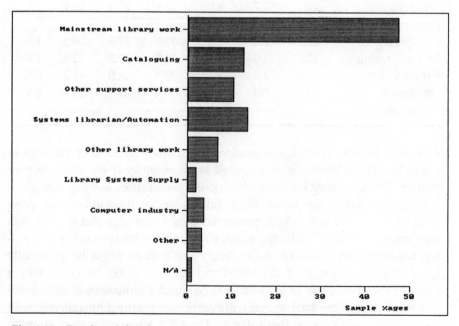

Fig. 1.12   Previous job title

Those who had been in mainstream library posts accounted for 47.3% of the sample, 12.6% had been cataloguers, 10.4% had been in other support services posts, and 6.8% in other specialist posts. Of the remainder, 13.5% had been systems librarians, 1.8% had come from a post with a library system supplier, and 3.6% had been in the computer industry. So there is no evidence to suggest that a technical services post is the most common route into a systems post, or even that it is a necessary prerequisite.

As well as asking systems librarians about their qualifications and experience, the survey also asked them to assess its relevance by rating seven separate components from their education, training, and work experience on a five-point scale ranging from 'not useful' to 'essential'. The results are shown in Table 1.5.

Table 1.5   Relevance of education and previous work experience

	n (100%)	Not useful (%)	Fairly useful (%)	Useful (%)	Very useful (%)	Essential (%)	N/A (%)
PG Dip/BLib	218	36.7	20.6	16.5	3.7	6.4	16.1
Other education	211	28.4	19.9	27.0	12.8	4.3	7.6
Previous library experience	226	2.7	8.0	23.9	23.5	38.9	3.1
Previous computer experience	225	2.2	8.9	19.6	27.6	26.2	15.6
External training	223	1.8	9.0	24.7	32.3	22.4	9.9
Supplier doc.	225	4.4	13.3	23.1	16.0	42.2	0.9
On-the-job training	221	0.0	4.5	10.4	23.5	55.7	5.9

Although library experience is considered important by most of the respondents, library qualifications are regarded as irrelevant by an equally large proportion. The low rating for other educational qualifications is significant given the arts/humanities bias noted above. Taken together, these low scores, along with the frequency with which greater technical knowledge and training was mentioned as a way of reducing stress, suggest that a background in computing together with familiarity with library applications might be an equally good preparation for this multifaceted and demanding job. However, with a considerable differential in the salaries for computer professionals and librarians, it seems unlikely that libraries will ever be able to attract suitable staff with computing qualifications. Returning to Table 1.5, although system supplier documentation was rated highly, it was also singled out by a number of respondents for its poor quality. As Thompson comments in her review of some of the literature on vendor manuals, 'these are seen as essential to have, even though they are often wrong, inadequate, and poorly organised'.[3] (Thompson's own survey of 29 New Zealand libraries indicated that libraries with 41–300 staff found vendor documentation more useful than did smaller libraries, and she speculates that this might be because these libraries have a systems librarian who is able to interpret and use the manuals properly, and rewrite them for general staff use, incorporating library-specific information.)

What conclusions can be drawn from these findings regarding the future education and training of systems librarians? The first point to make is that Table 1.5 probably paints an overly pessimistic picture of the current scene in library and information studies departments. Many changes have taken place in the curricula to accommodate IT since today's generation of systems librarians came through the system. As the chapters by Fisher and by Woodward and Meadows later in this volume show, most library schools now offer modules designed to increase students' expertise in automated library systems and in IT systems generally.

A second point concerns the content and structure of what is taught. There are few information professionals for whom the acquisition of, or at least an understanding of, system-related skills would not be beneficial, whether their post requires these skills or not. As was shown earlier, these skills are many and varied, and aspects such as hardware maintenance, programming, and the physical operation of the computer centre are considerably less important than those duties which cast the systems librarian in the role of mediator and which therefore required highly developed communication skills – liaising with system suppliers, providing support for system users, documenting the system and training staff, etc. This casts some doubt on the value of simply increasing the hard technology content in the curricula and strongly suggests that the teaching of IT should embrace not only a narrow technical expertise but also this wider range of related skills. At a practical level this might mean, for example, that students not only learn to use IT but are also taught techniques for training others;[4] or again, in addition to hands-on experience of parameter management and a knowledge of hardware and software requirements they might also be be familiarized with some of the areas (for example the complex formal procedure for going out to tender for the purchase of a new system and the management issues which such a project raises) described later in this volume by Fisher.

Structuring courses to deliver these extended skills presents further difficulties. The library schools are faced with the problem of providing a rounded and balanced education in the face of criticism from various groups that their own particular specialism is being neglected. Should IT be accorded special status in the curriculum by virtue of its all-pervasiveness and unparalleled importance for the future of library and information services? Should special provision be made for those who, like systems librarians, intend to pursue a career in IT? There can be no universal answer to this dilemma. In arriving at a solution, library schools will have to confront a number of related difficulties:

- lack of resources and time
- frequent changes in the technology itself
- the slowness with which changes in the curriculum can be implemented
- the variety of environments into which students will move when qualified
- the absence of a scientific background among library and information studies students
- the varied degrees of computer literacy among students from different backgrounds
- the shortage of teachers who are qualified and experienced in the relevant areas.

The trend towards modular courses and interdepartmental cooperation may be one way of overcoming some of these difficulties. Students are increasingly able to select modules from allied courses on offer in other departments within an institution. Using IT itself to deliver education can also help.[5] But the matter is too important to be left to the library schools alone. Library and information professionals usually spend from one to three years in a library and information studies department, and this short period can only prepare them for the first steps on what must be seen as an ongoing process of professional development involving other relevant organizations and bodies. Feather suggests this need for wider involvement in the provision of education and training when he states that the aim of the schools should be 'to produce well-educated generalists with a broad understanding of librarianship and associated activities. . . . and that the profession itself, through its various representative bodies, should accept the responsibility for continuing professional development . . . .'[6]

So the third conclusion is that the future education and training of systems librarians will require input from various groups within the information community, often working in partnership in new and creative ways. These groups would include:

1   The library schools: commenting on the need to provide ongoing library and information studies education for the IT environment of the future, Meadows quotes the following extract from a recent report on the job market

in the EC produced by IRDAC (Industrial Research and Development Advisory Committee of the Commission of the European Community): 'Universities and higher education establishments will have to develop much more fully the continuing education axis in a variety of formats. *Continuing education should become a mainstream activity of the higher education sector*, which will have to assume an increasing responsibility in this area.'[7] As noted above, this is happening with the spread of modular courses and credit accumulation, which opens the door to more flexible access to CPD, either in the form of free-standing modules or leading to a formal qualification.

2 Professional bodies and organizations: there are many specialist IT-related groups which could be included here. Some are mentioned above in the discussion of systems librarians' professional activities. The Library Association is in a unique position to lead the way as a more active provider of the specialist education required through its own Education and IT departments and also through members' special interest groups such as the Information Technology Group and the Cataloguing and Indexing Group. Several courses have already taken place or are being planned, ranging in level from elementary computer awareness to topics such as systems migration. This activity needs to be consolidated and built on.

3 Library system vendors: the 'added value' of providing ongoing training could become an increasingly attractive service for customers in an ever more competitive market. It is encouraging to note several cases of collaboration between system vendors and library schools, similar to those reported by Fisher in Chapter 11, which enable students to gain hands-on experience of using commercially available library management systems both as a learning experience in itself and to reinforce and support teaching across the whole curriculum. It is also encouraging to note a number of training courses organized under the joint auspices of the Library Association and some of the major system vendors. Again, there is room for further initiatives of this kind.

4 Systems librarians and their employers: Meadows again quotes from the IRDAC report on skills shortages:

> Individuals should realise that a basic diploma is no longer a guarantee, let alone a key for a successful professional development. *They will have to develop attitudes on the need to up-date themselves regularly in a more structured way than before*, since the acquisition of professional experience alone will be insufficient to be kept up-to-date.[8]

Systems librarians therefore have a responsibility to themselves and to their employers to maintain a current awareness of developments in technology and a general market awareness of the library supply and computer industries as part of their own personal professional development. The LA's recent moves to formalize CPD should provide support and encouragement for systems librarians who wish to update and extend their skills and qualifications, but this can only be achieved with the support of employers, for whom there are clear benefits.

To sum up, the future education and training of systems librarians – indeed of all information professionals – will be a continuous process requiring imaginative and creative solutions which involve contributions, either singly or in partnership, from the various interested parties together with a commitment to CPD from systems librarians supported by their employers.

6   STATUS

6.1   Perception of status

Status is the outcome of an often complex mixture of objective and subjective variables. It is not easily measurable, and meaningful comparisons are difficult to find. Asked directly if they enjoyed more or less status as a systems librarian than in the last post they held, 75% of respondents said more, 20.8% the same, and only 4.2% less (see Figure 1.13).

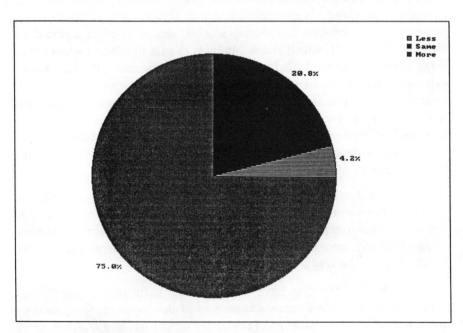

Fig. 1.13   Status compared with previous post

This perception of increased status may be due in part to the fact that for some systems librarians their appointment will have been a real promotion to a higher grade. However, there are also less tangible reasons inherent in the nature of the systems librarian's job which are relevant here. As the sole repository of what can sometimes seem to be abstruse wisdom, the systems librarian is often invested with a certain mystique. In so far as the systems librarian is responsible for the smooth running of the library system and the maintenance and repair of equipment, large numbers of staff are dependent on him/her to be able to carry out their duties, as well as for minimizing any stress associated with using IT.

6.2 Position in the organizational structure

Turning from the systems librarians' own perception of their status to more objective measures, the evidence is conflicting and much less conclusive. Figure 1.14 shows that 66.1% of systems librarians report directly to either their director/chief librarian or his/her deputy rather than to a head of section which, taken in isolation, is encouraging. This both recognizes that IT is no longer confined to any one domain but has penetrated all areas of library and information services, and also enhances the status of the systems librarian and his/her influence in decisions which are of service-wide importance. This figure is roughly the same as the results of an Association of Research Libraries

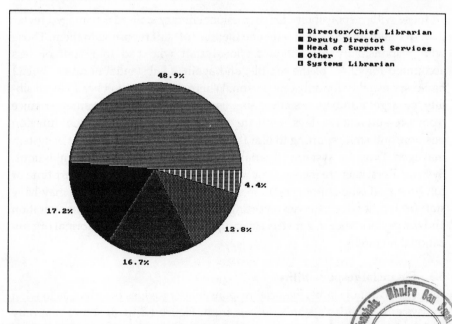

Fig. 1.14   Line manager of systems librarians

survey of organizational structures, which found that 39 of 76 systems officers reported to the director of library services, 6 to the associate director, and 4 to the director/associate director jointly.[9, 10]

On the other hand, 48.2% of systems librarians were not members of their senior management team. (Apart from any issues of status, this can have important consequences for organizational communications. As Dickmann points out,[11] policy decisions often have implications for the system, and systems staff need to be consulted before any such decisions are finalized. Membership of the senior decision-making group avoids issues like this becoming a problem.) And while it is true that almost the entire library staff depend on the systems librarian, 29.6% of respondents said they had no line management responsibilities for other members of staff. Table 1.6 shows that of those who did, the numbers of staff reporting to them were relatively small.

Table 1.6   Percentage of systems librarians with line responsibility

	n (100%)	Number of staff		
		<5	5–10	>11
Paraprofessional	138	72.4	16.6	11
Professional	100	84	13	3

Of those with responsibility for professional library staff, 84% managed fewer than five staff and 53% had only one member of staff reporting to them. Those with responsibility for paraprofessional staff who had four staff or less accounted for 72.4% of the sample, and again, a substantial number (39.1%) had responsibility for only one person. Where there is section head responsibility for larger numbers of staff, again this is more often than not an inheritance from pre-automation days, with the postholder occupying a dual-function position, and staff reporting to him/her in a capacity other than that of system manager. Thus the systems librarian's authority is complex and ambiguous. Systems librarians are increasingly responsible for small teams of part-time or full-time staff who support them in systems work. In addition they may have staff from other departments reporting to them in matters of system operation and/or performance in a matrix structure which cuts across the formal organizational hierarchy.

6.3   Financial responsibility
As an indicator of status, financial responsibility provides few clues as to what the systems librarian's status derives from. Figure 1.3 (p. 8) shows that only 44.7% of respondents said they were responsible for a budget, and in many

cases much of their budget will be committed from year to year, giving them only notional financial control.

6.4 Salary

The final indicator of status in the questionnaire was salary. The salary bands used were those used by the LA's Membership Department. One consequence of this choice was that these broad categories do not permit any detailed analysis of the often quite telling differences between salary scales within given library and information sectors. For example, public library staff on APT & C SO1/SO2 grades and those at the lower end of the PO range would all be included in the £15,000–£20,000 band used in this survey. Also, with hindsight it would have been wiser to have omitted the two lowest bands, which were unused, and extended the top end of the range in order to discover how many systems librarians were earning more than £25,000. On the other hand, by adopting these bands, it has been possible to make comparisons with the profession as a whole, and across sectors where different pay scales are used.

Table 1.7 shows a comparison of systems librarians' salaries with the 1991 salaries of the entire LA membership, excluding overseas, retired and student members.

Table 1.7 Systems librarians' salaries compared with salaries of LA members

Salary	LA members[a] (as % of UK with salaries)	Systems librarians %
20,000+	10.8	37.2
15,001–20,000	20.5	47.8
12,001–15,000	23.3	11.5
10,001–12,000	17.7	2.7
8,001–10,000	9.7	0.9
6,001–8,000	5.9	0.0
<6,000	12.1	0.0
Total (100%)	15,816	226

[a] Based on figures taken from an LA Membership Department internal report.

Even allowing for a margin of error due to the difference in sample size, the top-heavy appearance of the right-hand column indicates that systems librarians are enjoying above average salaries by comparison with this broad spectrum of library and information service professionals. However, further analyses revealed significant differences within the sample of systems librarians. As Table 1.8 shows, sector is one of the most important determinants of salary.

Table 1.8   Cross-sector comparison of salaries

	n (100%)	Salary (£'000s)				
		8–10	10–12	12–15	15–20	20+
University	49	0.0	0.0	2.0	22.4	75.5
Polytechnic	29	0.0	3.4	6.9	65.5	24.1
College	17	5.9	11.8	23.5	58.8	0.0
Public	81	0.0	2.4	13.6	58.0	25.9
Special	28	3.6	0.0	17.9	46.4	32.1
Government	18	0.0	5.5	11.1	44.4	38.9
Other	4	0.0	0.0	25.0	0.0	75.0
Total	226					

Systems librarians in university libraries tend to receive the highest salaries: 75.5% were earning over £20,000 (representing 44% of this salary band), and a further 22.4% earned £15,000–£20,000. Of those systems librarians working in public libraries, 25.9% were earning in excess of £20,000, accounting for 25% of the top earners. However, the importance of this latter figure lessens in view of their numerical superiority: as Table 1.8 shows, higher proportions of those in the special and government libraries fell into this category (32.1% and 38.9% respectively), while the proportion of public librarians earning £15,000–£20,000 (58%) was roughly the same as the proportion of polytechnic and college librarians in this category (65.5% and 58.8% respectively). College libraries were the only group not represented in the top salary band, and tended to score more highly across the middle ranges.

Predictably, gender was found to be a significant factor in relation to earnings, but only in the highest salary band. Of this group, 71% were men, which, even allowing for the the fact that men accounted for 57.1% of the total sample, shows that the 'glass ceiling' that obstructs the progress of women to senior management in libraries generally is an equally effective barrier in the case of female systems librarians.

The significance of other variables in determining salary was less clear. Of those who supervised paraprofessional staff, only 13% were earning less than £15,000 (10.1% were earning £12,000–£15,000), 47.8% earning £15,000–£20,000, and slightly less, 38.4%, earning over £20,000. No one on a salary of under £12,000 was responsible for supervising professional staff, and only 6% of those with this responsibility were in the £12,000–£15,000 band. The remainder were equally divided between the two highest paid groups, with no noticeable differences in the number of staff in their teams.

It was evident from the reply sheets that a number of systems librarians also had section head responsibility for an operational unit of their organization. An analysis of these 59 dual-function posts revealed only a minimal difference in their earnings compared with the sample as a whole: 43.6% were in the £15,000–£20,000 range (compared with 47.8%), and 38.2% on over £20,000 (compared with 37.2%).

These analyses of salary seem to point to a number of conclusions. Systems librarians do earn above average salaries, but there is variation across the library sectors, and (among the highest salary earners) between the sexes. Thereafter, local factors such as management's appreciation and understanding of the systems function, and the resources at their disposal to fund it may well be as important in determining salary as are the duties performed, or position in the organizational hierarchy. It is also worth noting at this point that a number of systems librarians used the questionnaire to express the feeling that their salaries were not commensurate with their responsibilities. This complaint certainly seems to be justified if one compares their salaries not with those of other information workers, but with those employed in the field of computers and data processing. Although more work would have to be done comparing qualifications and job duties before one could state categorically that systems librarians are underpaid by comparison, the substantial differential in salary between the two sectors does seem to suggest that this is in fact the case.

7 STRESS

Stress, like status, is not easy to pin down. It is the result of an interplay between societal, organizational, and interpersonal forces, and manifests itself in a variety of physical, psychological, and behavioural symptoms. Added to this, there is a purely subjective dimension. The salutary influence of limited exposure to pressure is generally recognized, but the point at which this changes from being a stimulus to a source of distress will vary from person to person.

However elusive the notion of stress may be, it has very real consequences in the workplace. This is as true for library and information services, where it has been rather unkindly dubbed 'grey stress', as it is for any other employment sector, and there is an already sizeable literature on stress and burnout in libraries.

The growing dependence on IT systems in all areas of library and information services, and range of duties and responsibilities undertaken by systems librarians would seem to suggest that they might be especially prone to stress. This survey set out to discover whether systems librarians do in fact feel themselves to be under stress, and if so, what the main stressors are. On a more positive note, it also asked how their quality of work life could be improved, and what the rewards of their job are.

7.1   Perception of stress

Asked to compare the levels of stress in their present post with that in their last post, almost 80% said they were now under more or much more stress, and none replied that they were now under much less stress (see Figure 1.15).

One specific and measurable example of the kind of pressures systems librarians are working under is the fact that 62.8% of respondents in the survey said they regularly worked beyond their contracted hours, and a further 32.3% said they did so occasionally. It would be rash to interpret this as indicating that systems work is inherently more stressful than other areas of library and information services, or that the effects of this stress, personally for the individual and operationally for the organization, are always negative or detrimental. Moreover, the perceived increase in stress may be due to quite irrelevant factors: promotion to a higher tier of management; the steep learning curve associated with any new appointment – 45.4% of respondents had been in post for two years or less; a more straitened economic climate; or simply the immediacy of their more recent systems experience compared with experience that is more remote in time.

7.2   Stressors

Rather than constrain respondents to force their own unique experiences into a preconceived matrix, it was decided to allow them the freedom to describe

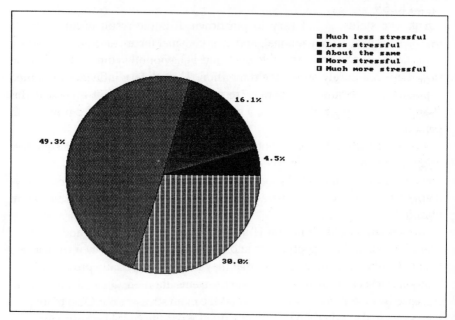

Fig. 1.15   Stress compared with previous post

their sources of stress in an open question. A total of 175 systems librarians responded to this question, generating a vast quantity of raw data. Because of the sheer range and quantity of stressors cited, and because in many instances the stress was not a result of one single factor, the responses resisted easy categorization or straightforward comparison. With the constraints of time and money available, therefore, a detailed quantitative analysis was not possible. However, a number of concerns emerged quite clearly in the replies: workload (sheer quantity of work/insufficient staff, responsibility for a widening circle of IT applications, conflict between need to maintain the existing system and the demand for enhancements and new developments), time (lack of time and having to work to strict deadlines, time management), 'technostress' (high profile of systems work, urgency of system problems, high-level dialogue with system, complexity of work and lack of training/computer knowledge, pace of change), people (lack of understanding by management, intermediary role, demands of users/staff), and a variety of external factors (for example institutional politics, changing organizational environment, etc.).

7.3 Quality of working life

The suggestions for how matters could be changed for the better were to a large extent a positive image of the sources of stress. For example, one solution to the problem of increasing workloads was to allocate more staff to the systems unit. This was frequently qualified by a desire for staff with appropriate skills and in a few cases it was seen as a way of allowing the systems librarian to concentrate on a narrower range of activities or to develop a more strategic role. Other suggestions related to training (both for the systems librarian and for staff generally), status, finance, better external communications, more dependable hardware, more support from senior management, and other miscellaneous factors to do with the organizational climate and the work environment.

7.4 Conclusions

The measures of stress used in this survey clearly do not do justice to a multidimensional concept like stress, which merits more sophisticated and detailed research. Many questions remain unanswered in quantitative terms: What are the levels of stress and burnout among systems librarians? Are these higher or lower than for other occupational groups (that is, other library and information workers, and computer/data processing personnel)? What are the main sources of stress? What can be done to improve this situation? To address these would require a comparative approach, possibly over time, employing what Fisher calls a 'triangulation of research methods', that is a methodology which focuses not just on the psychological measures of stress and burnout, but also uses a variety of other techniques (for example diaries, observation, questionnaires, interviews) to investigate the problem in its broader organizational and societal context.[12]

The main value of this section of the questionnaire was to allow systems librarians to speak for themselves about the problems encountered in systems work. The stressors mentioned are in many ways similar to those which occur in other studies of stress among library staff,[13, 14] however, as Bunge's studies of stress in public and technical services librarians show, these stressors manifest themselves in different ways in different environments. Two notable characteristics of systems librarians' work lend a unique aspect to the way stress is experienced by this group.

The first is that many systems librarians are working as one person units, with a minimum of support from colleagues. This in turn creates problems of overload, time management, and a feeling of professional isolation.

Secondly, as mediators, systems librarians move between a number of contiguous but non-communicating milieux, each of which presents its own problems. For example, systems librarians often feel there is a communication barrier between themselves and colleagues within the library. This might manifest itself in a resistance to IT, unreasonable demands for new developments or management reports, or simply a failure to report system faults promptly and accurately. The demand for system enhancements can also come from library management, but without sufficient resources to make these possible. And again, because they are caught in the middle between the computer system and front-line staff, systems librarians are constantly the focus of negative feedback. They are heavily dependent on system vendors and other external support to resolve these problems, and when this support is poor the inevitable result for the systems librarian is tension and a sense of not being fully in control.

Remedies to the problem of stress often focus on the individual and embrace a variety of techniques for stress management. It is possible that some systems librarians would benefit from these. However, as Fisher points out, stress is more than just a narrow problem for the individual concerned; it also has an organizational dimension, with implications and lessons to be learned for all the parties involved – senior library management and staff, computer personnel, system vendors, and systems librarians themselves. From a purely library perspective, what can be done realistically, with limited staff and resources, to tackle these problems in the short term? One obvious area where much can be achieved is through training and education initiatives. For example, the diffusion of basic systems knowledge to a core of interested staff is one way of promoting a greater understanding of the systems role, easing the systems workload, and ensuring greater operational efficiency by reducing dependence on one individual. For systems librarians themselves the training should focus on reducing dependence on external organizations, and increasing confidence in technical skills by creating opportunities to gain further qualifications and experience in these areas. Employers should be doing all they can to facilitate this process. In the long term, though, the only solution, for the well-being of the organization as well as that of the systems librarian, is for automated systems to receive increases in staffing proportionate to their increased importance as a corporate resource.

8 JOB SATISFACTION

'All systems librarians have the problem of trying to supply a technical service as well as a strategic planning function. Difficult to cope with both – Best job in the library!' This quotation from a senior member of staff in a university library sums up well the paradox that despite the pressures, being a systems librarian can be immensely rewarding. What makes the job a passion for some, and for others at least tolerable? In the survey satisfaction derived from three aspects of the job.

Systems-related duties were often spoken of in terms of intellectual challenge/problem-solving, learning opportunities/new skills, breaking new ground/pioneering, keeping the system running smoothly, sense of achievement, and IT strategy/policy-making/management skills. Contact with people was a second area of job satisfaction. This could be contacts with library staff (collaboration, staff training, providing advice/support), library users (user education), other departments, and a variety of outside suppliers. Thirdly, many systems librarians were conscious of their role as service providers and derived satisfaction from being able to give direct benefits to their colleagues and to library users. It is worth remarking that technology was rarely mentioned as a reward in itself. Being a systems specialist is a high-profile job where the satisfaction of providing a service to people is as important, if not more so, than the enjoyment that comes from the technical and problem-solving aspects of system management.

Previous studies have suggested that the rewards and stresses of library work often have common sources.[15] The above comments seem to confirm that this is also true for systems librarians. System faults are stressful, but they also give the satisfaction of solving complex problems. The high profile of systems work makes it of critical importance to deal with problems urgently; it also means that the benefits of new enhancements can be seen and appreciated at once by staff and users. Encounters with other staff can sometimes be uncomfortable, especially where there is resistance to technology; they also provide an essential source of positive feedback. The range of responsibilities is a burden to some, while others find variety a source of great satisfaction. One person's chaotic working day is another's flexible and creative time management.

9   CONCLUSIONS

In the course of this chapter, the overall picture which has been built up is a positive one. Systems librarians emerge as extremely competent and hard-working individuals, not only performing a key strategic and operational role requiring many skills and abilities, but also contributing to professional affairs beyond their employing organizations. If their duties frequently place them under undue pressure, this is balanced by the stimulus and fulfilment provided by these same factors. This positive image is amply demonstrated in the contributions which follow, where the themes and issues which have been introduced here are taken up and amplified in real situations.

REFERENCES

1   Webb, T. D., *The in-house option: professional issues of library automation*, New York, Haworth, 1987.
2   Martin, S. K., 'The role of the systems librarian', *Journal of library administration*, **9** (4), 1988, 57–68.
3   Thompson, V., 'Training staff for newly installed automated circulation systems', *Library management*, **11** (5), 1990, 18–23.
4   Meadows, A. J., 'Training and education in IT', *ITs news*, **25**, 1992, 12–17.
5   Meadows, A. J., 'Education and training', in Smith, J. W. T. (ed.), *Networking and the future of libraries: proceedings of the UK Office for Library Networking Conference, April 2–5, 1992*, Westport, Meckler, 1993, 151–6.
6   Feather, J. P., Letter to *Library Association record*, **94** (7), 1992, 449.
7   Meadows, see ref. 4.
8   Ibid.
9   Association of Research Libraries, Office of Management Studies, *Systems office organization* (SPEC kit 128), Washington, DC, ARL, 1986.
10   Association of Research Libraries, Office of Management Studies, *Organization charts in ARL libraries* (SPEC Kit 129), Washington, DC, ARL, 1986.
11   Dickmann, J., *Introducing IT in the library: some management issues*, London, The Library and Information Technology Centre, 1990 (Library and information briefings, 22).
12   Fisher, D. P., 'Are librarians burning out?', *Journal of librarianship*, **22** (4), 1990, 216–35.
13   Bunge, C., 'Stress in the library', *Library journal*, **112** (15), 15 September 1987, 47–51.
14   Hodges, J. E., 'Stress in the library', *Library Association record*, **92** (10), 1990, 751–4.
15   Bunge, op. cit.

Appendix: Systems librarian questionnaire and guidance notes

GUIDANCE NOTES

1. The questionnaire is in three sections. Section One should be completed by all libraries, <u>regardless of whether or not they have a systems librarian </u>(see note 5 below). Only those libraries in which there is a systems librarian should complete the entire questionnaire.

2. The questionnaire should be completed personally by the systems librarian. Where there are more than one professionally qualified systems librarians, it would be extremely helpful if a separate questionnaire is completed by each of them individually.

3. In the case of libraries with no systems librarian, Section One should be filled in by an appropriate member of the senior staff.

4. All information will be treated with <u>ABSOLUTE CONFIDENTIALITY</u>. If, however, you would prefer to remain anonymous, or are unwilling to disclose certain information, please return your part-completed questionnaire – the responses will still be valuable.

5. For the purposes of this questionnaire, systems librarians are specialists whose <u>principal </u>responsibility is the management of automated library systems. The term is used to embrace a variety of job designations – Library Systems Manager, IT Librarian, Assistant Librarian (Systems), Systems Development Librarian, and Systems Administrator are a few examples – and it does not exclude those who have additional line or other responsibilities. If you are in doubt about whether or not you qualify under this definition, please assume that you do, and complete the questionnaire as instructed above.

6. 'Paraprofessional' (see Q18D) is here taken to mean staff who are variously referred to as library/clerical/administrative assistants, library technicians, and non-professionals.

7. Completed questionnaires should be returned to the address below by 13th December 1991 at the latest:

> **Graeme Muirhead,**
> **Systems Librarian Survey,**
> **Central Library,**
> **Homer Road,**
> **Solihull,**
> **West Midlands B91 3RG.**

A stamped addressed envelope has been provided for this purpose.

SYSTEMS LIBRARIANS QUESTIONNAIRE

Please read the 'Guidance notes' before attempting to answer the questions.

All information will be treated with ABSOLUTE CONFIDENTIALITY.

Name   :   _____

Position   :   _____

Organization :   _____   Tel.No. : _____

SECTION ONE: YOUR LIBRARY

To be completed by ALL respondents.

Q1   Type of library?

1	University	( )
2	Polytechnic	( )
3	College	( )
4	Public	( )
5	Special	( )
6	National	( )
7	Other (please specify)	( )

Q2A   Are any of your library housekeeping procedures automated?

1	Yes	( )
2	No	( )

        If the answer is no, please go to Q3.

Q2B   If yes, which system(s) is (are) used (e.g. BLCMP, Dynix, Geac, etc.)?

Q2C   Please indicate which modules are available:

1	Cataloguing	( )
2	Ordering & Acquisitions	( )
3	Circulation	( )
4	OPAC	( )
5	Serials	( )
6	ILL	( )
7	Other (please specify)	( )

Q2D   Total number of terminals?

Q2E   Where is the computer situated?

    1   Library premises   ( )
    2   Central computer section   ( )

Q3   Are any other forms of IT use in your library (e.g. online, CD-ROM, micro-based applications)?

    1   Yes   ( )
    2   No   ( )

If yes, please give brief details:

Q4   Does the post of Systems Librarian (as defined in Guidance Note 5) exist in your organization?

    1   Yes   ( )
    2   No   ( )

If the answer is no, please go to Q7A.

Q5A   If yes, how long has the post existed?

Q5B   How many post holders have there been in that time?

Q6   If the post was created after the installation of your library system, what was the job title of the member of staff who led the automation project?

If you answered yes to Q4, you have now completed Section One. Please go to Q10A.

Q7A   If you do not have a Systems Librarian, has this post **ever** existed in your organization?

    1   Yes   ( )
    2   No   ( )

Q7B   If you answered yes, why does this post no longer exist?

Q8A   If you have an automated library system but no Systems Librarian, what is (are) the job title(s) of the member(s) of staff responsible for system management?

Q8B   On average, how many hours are spent on systems work?

                       _____ hours per week

Q8C   Is any support provided by a central computer section or DP unit?

1   Yes   ( )
2   No   ( )

Q9A   Are you planning to automate your library or upgrade an existing
        system within the next 2 years?

1   Yes   ( )
2   No   ( )
3   Possibly   ( )

Q9B   If you answered yes or possibly, will this lead to the creation
        of a Systems Librarian's post?

1   Yes   ( )
2   No   ( )
3   Possibly   ( )

**If you do not have a Systems Librarian, you have now completed
the questionnaire. Please go to the end of Section Three.**

SECTION TWO: YOUR BACKGROUND

To be completed only by libraries which have a Systems Librarian.

Q10A   Sex?

1   Male   ( )
2   Female   ( )

Q10B   Age?

EDUCATION & EXPERIENCE

Q11A   Formal education (please tick and state subject where
        appropriate):

1	First degree	( )
2	B.Lib. (or equivalent)	( )
3	PG diploma in Librarianship	( )
4	DMS	( )
5	Higher degree	( )
6	Ph.D.	( )
7	Other (please specify)	( )

Q11B   Are you currently studying for a further qualification?

1	Yes	( )
2	No	( )

If yes, please specify:

Q11C   Previous experience in library or information work (please tick all those which apply):

1 Cataloguing	( )
2 Ordering & Acquisitions	( )
3 Circulation	( )
4 Reference/Information	( )
5 Branch/Site librarian	( )
6 Systems librarian	( )
7 Other (please specify)	( )
8 None	( )

Q11D   Before taking up your present appointment did you have any previous work experience in computers or data processing?

1	Yes	( )
2	No	( )

If yes, please give brief details:

Q12A How long have you been in your present post?

Q12B What was your job title immediately before this appointment?

Q12C Were you appointed to your present post internally?

1	Yes	( )
2	No	( )

Q12D If no, how did you learn about it (please tick one only)?

1	Word of mouth	( )
2	Professional press	( )
3	National press	( )

    4   Recruitment agency (e.g. TFPL, INFOmatch)   ( )

    If you ticked 2, 3, or 4, please specify:

Q12E   What job did your predecessor (if any) move to?

    Please give the general occupational field if you do not know the exact job title.

PROFESSIONAL ACTIVITIES

Q13A   Are you a member of any of the following professional organizations and groups?

    1   LA   ( )
    2   IIS   ( )
    3   Aslib   ( )
    4   BCS   ( )
    5   Special interest groups (e.g. LAITG)   ( )
    6   System supplier user groups   ( )
    7   Other   ( )

    If you ticked numbers 5, 6, or 7, please give brief details:

Q13B   Are you actively involved in any of these bodies (e.g. committee membership)?

    1   Yes   ( )
    2   No   ( )

Q13C   Other professional activities (e.g. research, publications, etc.):

Q14   Please state the three journals which you find most useful to you as a systems librarian:

    1.
    2.
    3.

	Regularly	Occasionally	Never
Q15A Do you use ever use email (please tick)?	1	2	3

If yes, please give brief details:

Q15B Do you subscribe to any electronic distribution lists (e.g. PACS-L, LIS-INFO, etc.)?

1 Yes ( )
2 No ( )

Q15C If yes, which do you find most useful?

Q16 What is your primary source of information and support regarding the special problems and interests of systems librarians?

SECTION 3: YOUR JOB

Q17 What is your present salary (including local weighting where appropriate)?

1 Under £6000 ( )
2 £6001-8000 ( )
3 £8001-£10000 ( )
4 £10001-£12000 ( )
5 £12001-£15000 ( )
6 £15001-£20000 ( )
7 £20000+ ( )

Q18A Who do you report to?

1 Director/Chief Librarian ( )
2 Deputy Director ( )
3 Head of Technical Services ( )
4 Other (please specify) ( )

Q18B Do any staff report to you?

1 Yes ( )
2 No ( )

Q18C If yes, how many professional staff?

Q18D   How many paraprofessional staff (see Guidance Note 6)?

Q18E   Do you have a designated deputy who is trained to manage the routine
        running of the system in your absence?
        1   Yes   ( )
        2   No   ( )

Q19A   Have you ever been involved in the purchase of a new library
        system?

        1   Yes   ( )
        2   No   ( )

Q19B   Have you ever been or are you currently involved in planning a
        system upgrade?

        1   Yes   ( )
        2   No   ( )

Q19C   If you answered yes to 19A and/or 19B, please give brief details
        of your role:

Q19D   If you answered yes to 19A and/or 19B, were you the project
        leader during the implementation/installation phase?

        1   Yes   ( )
        2   No   ( )

Q20   Does your present job include any of the following (please tick
        all those which apply)?

        1   Physical operation of computer centre   ( )
        2   Computer programming   ( )
        3   Actual hardware maintenance/repair   ( )
        4   Staff training/documentation   ( )
        5   User education/documentation   ( )
        6   Generation of management information   ( )
        7   Responsibility for a budget   ( )
        8   Other library system related duties   ( )

        If you ticked no.8, please specify:

Q21   Are you the designated contact within your library in
        communications with the following organizations (please circle
        the answers which apply):

		Yes	No	N/A
Q21A	System suppliers	1	2	3

Q21B	Hardware maintenance contractors	1	2	3
Q21C	British Telecom	1	2	3
Q21D	Central Computer Section/DP Unit	1	2	3

Q22   Are you involved in any IT developments within your organization additional to the administration of the automated library system?

    1   Yes   ( )

    2   No   ( )

    If yes, please give brief details:

Q23A   Do you have any non-automation/IT duties?

    1   Yes   ( )

    2   No   ( )

Q23B   If yes, please list these briefly:

Q23C   On average, how much time do you spend on these duties each week?

                              _____ hours per week

Q24   Please rate each of the following in terms of their value in equipping you with the skills necessary to carry out your job as a systems librarian (please circle the answers which apply):

	Not useful	Fairly useful	Useful	Very useful	Essent- ial	N/A
PG Diploma/ B.Lib	1	2	3	4	5	6

Other formal education	1	2	3	4	5	6
Previous library experience	1	2	3	4	5	6
Previous computer experience	1	2	3	4	5	6
External training	1	2	3	4	5	6
Supplier documentation	1	2	3	4	5	6
On-the-job training	1	2	3	4	5	6

Comments:

Q25A   Are you a member of your library's senior management team?

1   Yes   ( )
2   No   ( )

Q25B   Are you a member of any other teams, working parties, committees, etc.?

1   Yes   ( )
2   No   ( )

If yes, please give details:

Q25C	In comparison with your last job, do you enjoy more or less status as a systems librarian?	Less	Same	More
		1	2	3

Q26   Can you give two examples of changes which you have initiated since taking up your present post?

	Never	Occasionally	Often

Q27   Do you ever work beyond
      your contracted hours?   1   2   3

	Much less	Less	Same	More	Much more
Q28A In comparison with your last post is being a Systems Librarian more or less stressful?	1	2	3	4	5

Q28B   If you answered more stressful, to what do you attribute this?

Q28C   What single factor would most improve the quality of your work life?

Q29   What aspects of your job do you find particularly rewarding?

Q30A   In what ways have technological or other developments changed
       the nature of your job since your appointment?

Q30B   In what ways do you think new technological or other developments
       will affect your role in the future?

Q31   If you have any views about being a systems librarian which you
       have not been able to express in the questionnaire, please
       summarize them below (continue on a separate sheet if
       necessary):

Q32   Would you be willing to discuss your answers in more detail?

1   Yes   ( )
2   No   ( )

Thank you very much for your assistance.

Please return the completed questionnaire to:

Graeme Muirhead,
Systems Librarians Survey,
Central Library,
Homer Road,
Solihull
B91 3RG.

by 13th December 1991 at the latest.

2 Dazed and confused: system management at Hillingdon Borough Libraries*

❖ Duncan Westlake

IN THE BEGINNING WAS THE SPECIFICATION

Because everything has its historical and geographical context, it might be useful to devote a few lines to the authority for which I work. The London Borough of Hillingdon was formed at the time of the reorganization of Greater London government in 1965. Situated on the north west edge of London, it currently has a population of about 235,000, and covers an area of 42 square miles. As an area it is a mixture of light industrial, offices, dormitory suburbia (part of John Betjemen's Metroland), and considerable open space.

The library service is provided from 17 static and 1 mobile library. The main town, Uxbridge, is the home of the Central Library, where all the support and administrative functions are also located.

Throughout the history of the borough, computerization had been considered with varying degrees of enthusiasm, but apart from the sporadic production of the catalogue on microfiche after 1975, no progress had been made. Indeed, we feel that this was to act in our favour, for when we finally did come to automate we were able to do so unencumbered by the shortcomings of systems based on older technology. (Even this advantage has been eroded of course; the technology we currently use is now comparatively old-fashioned).

Eventually, it was decided to buy an integrated online system. The key, and at the time by no means automatic, decision was taken to create a new post of Library Systems Manager. Equally crucially, the postholder sat on the library service's policy-making body, the senior management team. My predecessor Graham Morris was appointed to this post, and his initial task was to write a specification for the planned system. This he did, in considerable detail, which has stood us in good stead ever since. Tenders were received from three companies, with Geac being the eventual winners of the contract. Naturally, Graham had a considerable role to play in the negotiations and eventual selection of the supplier. We had agreed to automate all our service points, includ-

---

*All opinions expressed in this chapter are those of its author and do not necessarily reflect the policies of the London Borough of Hillingdon.

ing the mobile library and a particularly small branch, even though on purely economic grounds this might have been difficult to justify. In 1991 the Geac 8000 mini was upgraded to a much more powerful 9303, with many new terminals and greatly enhanced performance and functionality. The specification for the upgrade, and much of the negotiations, this time fell to me.

The original contract included not only the traditional bibliographical packages of Circulation and Catalogue, but also Geac's embryonic Local Information system. Having previously experimented with a small local viewdata system we already saw that there was considerable potential for providing the public with access to networked, fully up-to-date information about their locality. The Local Information system was not originally very suitable for our purpose, but it was at least a recognition of the need for such a system, which had not been addressed by other suppliers at the time. After much rewriting the package was greatly improved by Geac and we went live with it in November 1985. As one would expect, much of the improvement evident in this package was due to the efforts of the system manager, in conjunction with colleagues both within Hillingdon and at other libraries using Geac as their automation supplier. At that time automated local information did not seem to have a very high priority, so whatever progress was made was owing to the foresight of those system managers working together to create something from scratch. It is a matter of some concern and amazement to this author that even now neither Geac nor most of their competitors seem particularly interested in developing these systems, choosing to endlessly refine the more traditional bibliographic systems.

The system manager in Hillingdon was originally appointed to specify and implement the online 'housekeeping' system, but since that time there has been an intense growth in the use of information technology in libraries, such that the running of the Geac system now comprises perhaps only one half of the work of my team at Hillingdon. The rest of our time is given over to installing and supporting PC-based applications, such as word processing and desktop publishing, spreadsheets, and providing access to other systems for online searching, financial information, electronic mail, etc.

Once the chosen system began to be implemented it quickly became apparent that the system manager (the only new post) could not do everything himself, and that help was needed. This was achieved by diverting library staff, some professional and others not, from their normal duties to work in what became known as 'the computer section'. It is still called that to this day, although it has never officially been given this title.

One of the staff asked to join the computer section on a temporary basis was myself. I was working as a reference librarian, and was told I would be back at the reference desk after six months. In fact, every professional librarian at

Hillingdon now spends some time on a public enquiry desk, so in a sense that prophecy came true. As the senior professional working for Graham Morris I became known as his deputy. I must acknowledge the help Graham gave me at this time, which I feel was an invaluable apprenticeship.

During this period, the system was developing rapidly with branch libraries 'going live' at the rate of one every six weeks or so. At its peak our team had grown to about five in number, to allow us to operate a system we called 'Guardian Angels'. The idea was that for the period leading up to a library going live and a short while afterwards, one of our team would work at that library, helping to enrol the borrowers, training the staff, making sure that installation of terminals and counters was accomplished on time, and acting as the main link between the library staff and 'the management' at a very difficult and stressful time for them. It worked very well, and the entire system was fully live within 18 months of the first borrower being enrolled. It also seemed to help the members of the team: Graham Morris joined Geac; Melvyn Evans went to another supplier, ALS, via a spell at Hertfordshire County; Cathy Perry moved to an important job in Birmingham; and I was lucky enough to take over as systems manager when Graham left.

THEN CAME THE NEW STRUCTURE

The computer system did not exist in a vacuum of course. Part of the justification for having it was to allay extra staffing costs that would be incurred when our new Central Library opened in September 1987. This allowed management to look anew at how the work of librarians was best organized, especially in view of the fact that we had never been particularly well-staffed and were now beginning to feel the effects of local government cut-backs. Coupled with the changes to working practices brought about by the computer system, the time was right for reorganization.

This proved to be a fairly dramatic affair, upon which our subsequent reorganizations have been built. The key to it was to remove full-time professional staffing from branch libraries, allowing librarians to use their professional skills in the Central and two area libraries. Branches from now on were to be run by paraprofessional library managers. Professional librarians would have their time spread across three teams — a public service team staffing enquiry desks on a rota; a stock team responsible for all the stock functions in a fairly broad area of stock; and a 'function team' covering such aspects of library work as local studies, services to the housebound, reference provision, or the computer section. Apart from the most senior managers, no staff were therefore dedicated to one area of work, and this was felt by the structure's architects to be a strength. As far as I was concerned as the manager responsible for computing (job title now 'Coordinator for Automated Systems Development'), it had its drawbacks. However, the Senior Management Team still existed as the policy-forming body, and I was still part of it. I felt this to be very important, for in our service the rapidly expanding computer systems for which I was responsible were of crucial strategic significance.

By 1991, this structure was under intolerable strain as a result of continuing reductions of staff numbers, and so another reorganization was carried out. This time professional staff had their time split across two teams, one of which was the one providing the public enquiry service. Therefore, staff continued to spend some time working directly with the public, and worked for the rest in one of a number of stock or functional teams. My team consisted of myself (job title now 'Information Technology Manager') almost full-time, and two team librarians spending half their time with me, and half on the enquiry desk.

Further even more drastic cuts forced yet another restructuring exercise in 1993, with, for the first time in Hillingdon, library staff being made compulsorily redundant. The principle that everyone should come into contact with the public (new job title 'customers') has survived, with every professional, including the highest level of management, doing their turn on the desk.

I have always argued that to be most effective, the system librarian should be dedicated to that task. We have extremely specialized skills, which have been developed, trained, or bought at considerable expense to our employers. In Hillingdon at least, and I suspect in the majority of other organizations, the systems librarian is reasonably well-paid in relation to most of the other staff. My post has, over the years, been regraded several times. It is now paid on the same grade as one of our four Heads of Area, or put another way, it is graded higher than any post other than the top layer of library management.

Given the cost to the employer, and we would hope the essential nature of our work, it therefore comes as a surprise to me that employers sometimes do not make the fullest use of our skills. In Hillingdon, I and my team spend 800 hours per year away from information technology, on the information desk. In other organizations, systems librarians spend time cataloguing, or taking their turn working in branch libraries. There are of course arguments in favour of such arrangements. It is undeniable that systems librarians working for some of their time on mainstream library services maintain contact with their profession, and with the customers of the library service. It is true that direct contact of this kind is good for managers, in that it constantly reminds them of what they are working towards. I believe that in the Disney organization managers of all levels spend a small, some might say token, amount of time on front-line duties. I have also heard of the chief executive of a London borough working on the council's main reception desk.

These initiatives are laudable, and I fully acknowledge the benefits that can accrue from reminding staff of the purpose of their service. It would be nice to think of many 'faceless bureaucrats' having to come face-to-face with the public, and changing their approach as a result.

That said, I do feel that such service away from the main job should be limited, and not looked upon as part of the normal establishment for the part of the service to which staff are seconded. There are times, as all system librarians know, when to be away from the current crisis is simply unthinkable. However, if you are timetabled to be doing something else when the system goes down, life can get a little fraught. In such extreme circumstances, colleagues are usually understanding, as they need the system too, but when a BT line to another branch library goes down, they do not always see the problem in the same light.

I have one other worry about taking system managers away from managing systems, and having them do some mainstream librarianship. That is that unless they do significant amounts of the other work, which I have just argued against above, they will inevitably have a reduced level of competence. Either their work, perhaps cataloguing, will be of a poor quality, or it will be slow, so making them less productive than a full-time worker in that field, as well as their productivity being reduced as system managers. If they are put into contact with the public, unless there are other, fully competent full-time staff also on duty, customers themselves will suffer, receiving a very variable level of service.

In Hillingdon, throughout the years, there have been variable amounts of time required of the system manager in other areas of work. In the very early days systems management was unquestionably full-time. There was a specification to write, and then a large system to implement quickly. Once that was done, however, time on stock and enquiry work began to be required. At some stages I felt that too much was being taken away from information technology, albeit for excellent reasons as outlined above, and that I had to try to mitigate the effects of staffing cut-backs. I am happy to say that at present the commitment to the enquiry desk required of myself and my team is not onerous, and achieves the aim of keeping us in touch with the 'real world' without drastically reducing the effectiveness of our information technology work. We are expecting a major new release of software soon, which will take us back to the stage of almost having a new system to install, so it will be interesting to see how the arrangement works in that situation.

From our latest reorganization the Information Technology Team has emerged in a stronger position than recently. My job title is now 'Service Manager – Information Technology'. I have a deputy – job title 'Coordinator', and a third professional, still called 'Team Librarian'. From the three of us I have to provide some 16 hours per week to the information desk, which is a considerable reduction of the previous commitment. I can only assume that the growth of our commitment to information technology reflects the organization's realization of the amount of work involved.

As I have already said more than once in this chapter, I firmly believe that where appropriate the system manager should be included in the library's key decision-making body. This is particularly important when implementing new systems, but can bring continuing benefits throughout the life of the system. Information Technology has become so pervasive in library services that it seems to me to make sense to be able to call on input from the person responsible for it when considering policy changes. This is a position I have come to from my experience at Hillingdon, where both I and Graham Morris sat on the senior management team.

Having said that, situations change with time, and in common with many other organizations, Hillingdon's structure appears to be evolving to a 'client/contractor' arrangement. It is now no longer appropriate for the Information Technology Manager, with very much a 'contractor' role, to formulate policy with the 'clients', and so I, and the managers of other services, am now called upon for advice when required, rather than having constant input. I cannot pretend I find this arrangement ideal, as spontaneous responses to suggestions can no longer occur, but it is a change made inevitable by new approaches to management provoked by the forthcoming round of compulsory competitive tendering (CCT).

As a manager providing a service to clients each responsible for the full range of library services in a geographical area, I am now in the process of drawing up specifications of service they are entitled to expect from my team. As part of this process, budgets could be disaggregated to our four areas, and used by them to buy (or in theory at least, not buy) my service. While this may in the end result in broadly the same service being provided in more or less the same way, it has led to considerable thought about what it is we do, and why, and how much it all costs. If nothing else good comes of it, this alone will be a great benefit.

Having referred to it so often, it might be of some interest here if I were to expand a little on the current structure in operation at Hillingdon, since it does not have the traditional shape of many other public library organizations. Reference to the organizational chart (Figure 2.1) may prove helpful in reading this section.

My team consists of myself and two others: a team librarian, and a team coordinator. I work almost full-time for Information Technology, and the other two spend all but about seven hours per week in the team. Clerical work, such as tape backups and printing of overdue notices, is carried out from a pool of paraprofessional staff provided by the Central Library. This work only takes a couple of hours per day; the rest of their time is spent as library assistants.

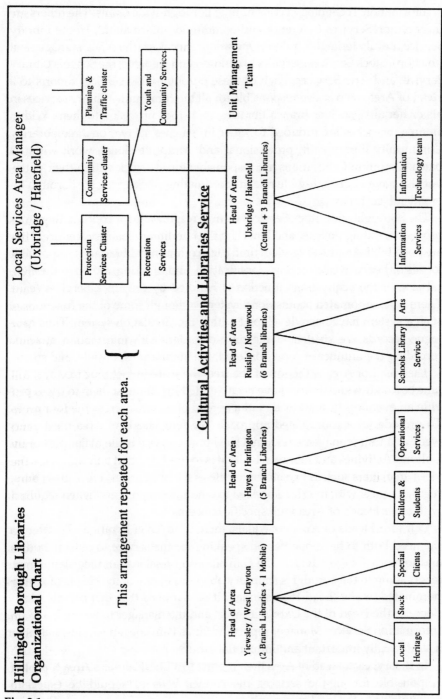

Hillingdon Borough Libraries Organizational Chart

Local Services Area Manager (Uxbridge / Harefield)

Protection Services Cluster

Community Services cluster

Planning & Traffic cluster

Recreation Services

Youth and Community Services

This arrangement repeated for each area.

Unit Management Team

Cultural Activities and Libraries Service

Head of Area Yiewsley / West Drayton (2 Branch Libraries + 1 Mobile)

Local Heritage

Stock

Special Clients

Head of Area Hayes / Harlington (5 Branch Libraries)

Children & Students

Operational Services

Head of Area Ruislip / Northwood (6 Branch libraries)

Schools Library Service

Arts

Head of Area Uxbridge / Harefield (Central + 3 Branch Libraries)

Information Services

Information Technology team

Fig. 2.1

Information Technology is one of nine borough-wide teams. The others are Information Services (reference and community information), Home Library Service, Local Heritage Services, Operational Services (the office management function), Stock Services, services to children and students, the Schools Library Service, and Arts Services. Each of these borough-wide services reports to a Head of Area, who is also responsible for all the community library services in his or her area, such as branch libraries, and stock provision to them. Within an area, branches are grouped together in 'patches' of two or three libraries. Community library staff, professional and paraprofessional, work within a patch. Community librarians are responsible for the stock within their patch, but also have a borough-wide role in coordinating stock across the borough for broad subject areas.

The borough-wide Stock Services team is responsible for coordinating stock provision, setting policies, and handling the interlibrary loans procedure. They are not a bibliographical services unit: each community librarian is responsible for his or her own cataloguing, classification, and ordering, although the clerical side of the acquisitions function is handled by the Stock Services team. There is no automated acquisitions system, although some of the functions of such a system have been developed within the circulation system. Thus catalogue records are created at the time of order, with information attached recording the number of copies ordered, the librarian responsible, and so on.

The Head of Area is the top of the tree; there are in fact four treetops. The nine borough-wide services have been divided up amongst them to try to provide an evenness of workload, and a spread of services across the four areas. To provide for a coordinated approach, the four Heads of Area meet every week as a unit management team. (The library service is the major part of the Cultural Activities and Libraries Unit). It is to this body that borough-wide services' managers such as myself contribute as the need arises. We also of course regularly meet with the Head of Area to whom we report, and when required, with other Heads of Area with specific concerns.

Our four Heads of Area are equals; there is no 'chief librarian'. To cater for the need both to have one person speaking for the service to outside bodies, and to have a voice advising the council on professional and legislative matters relating to the borough's statutory obligations, one of the Heads of Area is nominated as the 'Lead Professional'. It so happens that this person, Harry Boote, is the Head of the Uxbridge Area, and the manager to whom I, and the Information Services Manager report. As far as I am concerned, this makes for a strategically important and influential group.

In theory, each Head of Area then reports to a Local Services Area Manager, responsible for all the services the council believes should be especially accountable to the local communities in the four areas. These include Planning and Transportation, Highways Management, Trading Standards, Environmental Health, Refuse, Recreation, Adult Education, and of course, Libraries and other cultural activities. In practice, this led to overload on the Area Managers, so each area has a number of 'cluster managers' who take some managerial control of three of the services in their area, reporting upwards to the Area Manager. Like Lead Professionals, being a Cluster Manager is simply another layer on top of a person's job. Someone can be a Head of Area, Lead Professional, and Cluster Manager all in one. If they are, they have a lot to do. In our case, one Head of Area is also a Cluster Manager, and one, as already described above, is Lead Professional. Clusters each contain three service disciplines. Libraries share the Community Services clusters with Youth and Community Services and Recreation. As there are four areas, so there are four community services clusters, each with their Cluster Manager reporting to the appropriate Area Manager, along with the Cluster Managers for Planning and Traffic, and Protection Services (covering environmental health, trading standards and building control: despite the title, the mafia are not involved). Of the four Cluster Managers overseeing the management of libraries, one is a librarian, but equally all or none could be. Interestingly, two of the four Area Managers are previous chief librarians of Hillingdon.

As may be appreciated from the above, relationships between borough-wide services, whose approach is similar to how it used to be, and the areas, whose prime focus is on the services provided to their own community, are complex. Because the structure is still new and subject to fine tuning, these relationships are still evolving. The work I have recently been doing on specifying levels of service to the areas, and determining the costs of those services, is an early stage in redefining how we will all interact. In placing matters on a quasi-contractual basis it has been illuminating to see just how much we do provide for our colleagues. My challenge now is to ensure that they want me to continue to do so.

THE SPICE OF LIFE

In discussing my contribution to this book with the editor, it was felt that a description of the kind of work undertaken by one systems manager might be interesting. Of one thing I am convinced; there is as yet no standard for a job such as this. Colleagues I know do some elements of what I do, and I do some of the things they are responsible for, but I doubt if any of the systems managers of my acquaintance have easily interchangeable job descriptions.

If variety is the spice of life I often get a burned mouth. Just as I love spicy food, I generally greatly enjoy the range of duties I can be expected to perform. As the manager of the team, I am expected to set priorities and work on a more strategic level, rather than being completely 'hands-on', but by a combination of pressing need, a lack of available expertise at precisely the moment urgent work is required, and no doubt my inability to delegate properly, I still manage to do some concrete 'real' work amongst all the meetings.

My team is responsible for the operation, support, and administration of maintenance requirements for everything falling under the heading of 'Information Technology'. I have loosely interpreted this as 'anything with microchips', although I have managed to avoid any contact with photocopiers or microfilm reader/printers. (Why is it, incidentally, that every member of library staff has a relative who is a particularly knowledgeable computer genius, and who would be only too happy to come in and sort out your thorny problems, but no one knows anyone who can stop photocopiers from jamming – least of all the supplier of the machine?)

Under this broad heading we are responsible for the day-to-day operation of the Geac minicomputer, and all the associated networking. Tape backups and printing are carried out on a daily basis by paraprofessional staff from the Central Library. Faulty equipment and software is reported to us, and we then ensure the appropriate help is called. Support for users of the various systems, both Geac and PC-based, is an increasingly important part of our work. In most cases it seems to result from our inability to fully train users in the first place, owing to lack of funds. Included in the 'anything with microchips' category are fax machines and the Central Library's telephone system. Since these need periodic reprogramming, which is something we are very used to, these seem logically to be our problem. I am happy to say that tills, which have recently been introduced, and which also require periodic reprogramming, are someone else's problem.

The work I do as a manager can be split into two areas; the management of my team, and the contribution I make to the running of the library service by dint of my seniority and specialist expertise. Managing the team consists of chairing team meetings, setting priorities and assigning work to my staff, and the drudgery of working out timetables to ensure work continues in times of leave and sickness. At some stage, evaluations of performance will also have to be carried out.

The other work I do by virtue of my position is associated with strategy and special projects. As the manager of what is still one of the largest computer implementations in the borough, I sit on the Information Technology Strategy Group. This is a body of council officers charged with setting an information technology strategy, and monitoring its suitability and effectiveness. We seek to advise people planning new implementations, but have no power of veto if this advice is rejected. With the council's latest reorganization the library service has become part of a very large department called 'Local Services', the aim of which is to bring accountability and management of many services down to four fairly small areas. It is a policy that needs information technology to make it work, and I am part of a small group looking at how this can best be achieved.

The other work requiring specialist expertise coupled with seniority in the organization covers such areas as assessing workstations for conformance to the recently introduced Display Screen Equipment Regulations, writing specifications for new systems, business planning, writing reports, meeting suppliers, and taking part in special projects. Examples of the latter include: a team to improve our success in book recovery, the setting up of a new community school incorporating a public library, with immense technological implications, and the reorganizing of open plan office accommodation following our most recent restructuring, with the minefield of office politics to negotiate.

I also greatly enjoy the day-to-day work of my team whenever I get the chance. This will include such tasks as altering system parameters and settings, administration of the electronic mail system, training staff, troubleshooting and fault reporting, fault fixing – including sometimes wielding a soldering iron, programming of overnight batch jobs, production of management information, perhaps by writing a program to answer a particular query, and installing equipment or software.

While I was writing this chapter I decided to note down all the work I performed in a week. Although this may not be a typical week – none are it seems – it does broadly reflect the range and amount of tasks I might expect between one Monday and another. They are enumerated here in no particular order.

- After several attempts, succeeded in configuring a new Windows-based word processing package to be used by the Personal Assistant to the Heads of Area. This will enable her to use a range of fonts on her laser printer which had just been returned from repair, and had to be fetched from a central collection point and reinstalled.
- Took a telephone call from a system manager working in another borough asking how we obtain reservation supply time statistics, and what our fines policies are. In return, learned from him something about the system we both use that I did not know before. Informal interchange of information like this is something I find very valuable.
- Assisted our office manager in selecting a workstation for a PC, and once it arrived installed the PC on it. Ordered a cable to allow this to share a printer, and once it was received fitted it through the cable management system.
- Wrote a report for the Unit Management team on word processing and desktop publishing policies for the unit. Completed the first draft of Specification of Service provided to users and passed it to the Unit

Management team for inclusion on a future agenda.

- Advised on cataloguing policy for donated fiction. Ran a report on youngest borrowers registered on the system. This was required for a promotion for National Library Week. As a result of changes following the staff restructuring I updated distribution group lists for all members of staff on the electronic mail system.
- Answering our helpline, talked a member of staff at a branch library through resetting a terminal's configuration. Reported several faults to Geac hardware centre for engineering attention. One of these transpired to be a British Telecom problem, so reported it to them, and subsequently tested the line and accepted it back into service. Backed up the system software and operating system – a weekly job usually performed by the Team Coordinator, but he was on holiday. Sent a faulty cable off for repair so that a new PC can be installed as a public terminal in a branch library.
- Completed negotiations with British Telecom for putting the majority of our leased line circuits on long-term contracts, thus securing savings for the borough. Completed a project appraisal form as part of a bid for capital to replace several library counters in order to bring them up to the standards required by the new Display Screen Equipment Regulations. Apart from the mortgage application forms I also completed that week, this is without doubt the worst form ever devised.
- Completed two spells on the information desk; one in my own right, and one to cover for the Team Coordinator, who was still on holiday. Made mental note not to authorize any more holidays for anyone. In the few quiet moments here managed to clear up some records on the system prior to a 'garbage run' of redundant data over the following weekend.
- Took a telephone call from a company selling EDI services – the cutting edge of technology. By way of contrast, advised office manager on how many date slugs stamped '94' he should order. Spoke to the teacher lumbered with project managing the ambitious community school project regarding access to a network room for installation of BT lines and network gateway equipment. Arranged to ring back again when there may be some news.
- Showed PA to Heads of Area how to convert ASCII files, brought in by one of said Heads of Area from home, into her word processing package, and arranged for simple instructions to be written. Helped with access to a bibliographic database which was refusing to talk to us. In the process showed a school student on work experience with us some of the wonders of online information retrieval and the virtual library. Don't think she understood. After the search was completed, retrieved the resulting

downloaded data, which had been 'mislaid', and printed it, after fiddling with the printer to persuade it to feed paper properly. While this was happening, to fill the time checked that our own dial-in facilities were working properly. Checked my electronic mailbox on the borough's mainframe system. No news – probably this equals good news.
* Finished the week with a contemplative pint with colleagues.

Almost the only predictable thing about the work of myself and my team is that regardless of what is written in the diary, the day is unlikely to turn out as planned. It then becomes a matter of prioritizing what gets done when, which can lead to tension and frustration, but it also makes for a very interesting time at work.

THE FUTURE

There are two sides (at least) to the work of a library systems manager likely to be influenced by the future trends emerging now. It is in the interests of all working in this field that these trends are recognized so that strategies for surviving them can be adopted. That may seem negative, and there certainly is a large element of self-protection involved in planning for the future, but there is also a positive side. We are the kind of people organizations need in times of dramatic change: simply by doing the work we do we have demonstrated that we are adaptable, capable of analytical thought and planning, are not frightened of technology and the new ways of working it brings, and we should have some understanding of the way information technology can be used to further the aims of our organizations. It is to be hoped that our organizations recognize these facts also.

The first area of dramatic change that concerns library system managers is in the technology itself. We will nearly all have learned our trade in one of the earlier generations of computer technology. Some will be fortunate enough to have had formal education in computing, some will have 'sat next to Nellie', and some will have simply picked it up as they went along. However they have developed their expertise, most will now have to be learning about new developments as best they can as part of their work. This is a big responsibility and can be rather frightening: I know I find it so. As has been pointed out so often before, the pace of change is accelerating, and system managers are not immune from the effects of 'future shock'. As with many other walks of life, it is most unsettling to find that your area of expertise is rapidly becoming obsolete.

If Hillingdon is anything like typical, and I think it has similarities to many other organizations, the technology that was adopted for a particular job has now become something of a handicap. This is not because there is something inherently wrong with the technology; it still seems remarkably well-suited to the original task. Rather, it is that the task itself has changed. We are now demanding different attributes from our computer systems than we did when we originally specified them. To colleagues in the organization who do not understand this, 'the system is no good', but in reality what is needed is to define precisely what it is that systems are now needed for. Once that is clear, we can respecify for new systems. At the start of this chapter I wrote 'In the beginning was the specification', and now, at the start of a new approach to the delivery of services, we need to be very clear again about what we want technology to do for us.

The second area of change that concerns us is closely related to the first; indeed to a large extent it drives the first. Organizationally, British public libraries are undergoing fundamental changes, largely at the behest of the Government, but not necessarily unwillingly. Some of the new attitudes are also appearing in the academic sector too, again with varying degrees of enthusiasm.

In Hillingdon, service charters, customer care and our approach to decentralization are attempts to make services more locally accountable. New relationships have to be worked out between providers of services such as ours, and the managers responsible for the different areas of the authority. The question 'who is the customer?' constantly arises, and the answer can change from day to day.

The opportunities for information technology to help with the process of localization as it is called in Hillingdon are immense, and part of my role at present is to help to work out ways in which this can be achieved. We hope that more people than ever before will be using the information services of the library, so appropriate computer facilities are essential.

One of the options open to Hillingdon is for the development of libraries as some form of 'one stop shop', as has happened elsewhere. Technology will be essential if this is to be done properly, and again, the library systems manager should have a big part to play.

Competitive tendering, compulsory or otherwise, is becoming increasingly likely. Many authorities may wish to apply the principles involved in CCT2 to many services, regardless of whether or not they are included in the legislation. Libraries in general are among these, and support services such as Information Technology particularly so. In my situation it is currently unclear whether my work is likely to be included as part of the Government's minimum target of 80% of the IT element of a local authority's work to be contracted out. It still remains unclear whether the 80% applies to the Authority as a whole, or whether each department, or perhaps each service, has to identify 80% of its IT work and offer it up for competitive tendering. It is therefore very difficult to formulate a view, or a strategy for survival.

Even if for the time being at least we avoid the dangers of CCT, our work is being put on a more business-like footing. Service level agreements, or the specifications of service I have referred to above, can be thought of as internal contracts, and are being reached with many 'customers'. Given the changing conditions, this is no bad thing, and may well prove essential when there may be pressures to change priorities from managers of different areas. If we are to be subjected to CCT we should be in a much stronger position to win contracts having already discovered the true costs and had some practice in forming and adhering to contracts.

One of the choices to be made, over which we may have little influence, but which will have a great effect on us, is whether the system manager is to be a client, directly employed by the organization, or a contractor, possibly employed by someone else. For anyone who is able to choose, it will probably turn on whether you prefer fun, or some element of security. I leave the reader to decide which applies to the contractor role, and which to the client.

Only one thing is certain: the next few years will continue to be interesting, exciting, quite often very worrying, and far from predictable.

3 A life in the week . . .

❖ *Gordon Dunsire*

SUNDAY: 'ABOUT A LUCKY MAN WHO MADE THE GRADE'*
I never intended to be a librarian, nor did I expect when I started my career as a non-professional Library Assistant in 1973 to be still working for the same institution 20 years later. With a science background and having an interest in the 'hard' side of libraries, dealing with information rather than mere books, and computers rather than customers, I imagined that information scientist was a much more attractive category of occupation than librarian. As a result, I did not balk when asked to type out catalogue cards, especially as I had access to my first piece of information technology in the shape of an electric golf-ball typewriter. When management realized that I was genuinely interested, I was encouraged to compose the information on the cards instead of just transcribing the handwritten notes of the professional staff, and even allowed to classify! As every other member of staff loathed cataloguing, the Chief Librarian endeavoured to prevent my moving on to pastures new by tempting me with a series of professional training and development opportunities: a postgraduate Scottish Certificate in Information Science; the Library Association external examinations for Associateship; a Scottish Higher National Certificate in Computer Data Processing. I was in the right place at the right time, for all of these courses were available from within the institution, and the first two were run by the library itself. Each course was part-time, taking a year or two to complete and thus ensuring that the cataloguing backlog was kept to a minimum for as long as possible! So I stayed.

While I was accumulating qualifications and experience, my employing institution, the then Napier College of Science and Technology, was busy accumulating students, courses, buildings and other institutions at such a rate that we now have eight or nine times the number of library staff that we had 20 years ago. What was a local authority further education college concentrating on scientific and technical subjects has become Napier University, located

---

*All section heading quotes from 'A day in the life' by John Lennon and Paul McCartney, © 1967 Northern Songs Ltd.

on three major campuses and a host of minor sites within the city of Edinburgh; it is now one of the five largest universities of Scotland.

The library purchased its first microcomputer in 1979 and over the next ten years followed the well-trodden path of in-house, standalone microcomputer developments: WordStar, dBase II, IBM PC, WordPerfect, dBase III+, small database applications, a little desktop publishing, embryonic management information. Large-scale system developments took the form of SCOLCAP, the ill-fated Scottish library automation cooperative which resulted in much experience of the advantages and disadvantages of doing it with somebody else instead of yourself, and a high quality MARC catalogue encompassing most of the book stock. In 1990, the library was able to buy a Dynix library system; at the same time the then polytechnic installed local area networks on the big campuses and linked them together, and suddenly it was the last decade of the millennium. The library finally had a system; all it lacked was a systems librarian.

It was, in any case, time for a reorganization of the library staff structure, to take account of the professional and institutional changes of the 1980s. When the dust had settled, my old post of Head of Central Services had mutated into Information Systems Librarian, and I found myself responsible for fewer staff, but one heck of a lot more computers, terminals, Ethernet cables, modems, and the rest. I now coordinate the Information Systems Team of myself, two professional Assistant Librarians, and a Senior Library Assistant. The main tasks of the team include day-to-day administration of the library housekeeping system and its development; coordination and management of personal computer applications for library staff, including office automation; system documentation and training; liaising with the University's Computer Services Unit; advising library management on automation developments and strategies; evaluating and implementing new automation products; database quality control; and keeping cool, but with our heads above water.

MONDAY: 'THEY HAD TO COUNT THEM ALL'

An immediate problem for the systems librarian is the perception and accepted definition of what constitutes the system, and in particular its components and boundaries, for this will determine the role and responsibilities of the job. In many libraries, the system is seen as the large-scale automated bit, the hardware and software used to support the basic operations and services of the library. It usually comes with a proper name, and is actualized as computer equipment in a well-defined location providing a well-defined function: what system have you got? – BookshelF, Dynix, Geac, URICA, etc.; where is it? – the processor in the basement, the circulation terminals on the desk, the PACs beside the stacks; what does it do? – circulation, cataloguing and acquisitions, and serials will be ready real soon now. If the library uses or offers other automated services such as CD-ROM, word processing, and electronic mail, they may be included in the definition on the understanding that these systems require hardware and software too. If the proprietary housekeeping package can integrate such additional services within itself, the system retains its commercial name and apparent definition while its functionality and boundaries expand. If not, the separate automated services may be given their own names such as 'the network', 'the company reports database' and 'the CD-ROM workstation', and the nameless collection of automated services becomes 'the system'; the boundaries are less distinct, but still defined for most librarians and their clients in terms of information technologies. Using this simple definition, the role of the systems librarian is perceived as being that of a technically-literate facilitator, ensuring the availability of the hardware and software tools required by colleagues in providing services to enquirers.

In the most basic scenario, these services are predetermined; the systems librarian is expected to anticipate and advise on the impact of technological developments on library provision, but is otherwise reactive. The systems librarian automates what is already there; the card catalogue becomes a PAC while Browne issue trays morph into circulation terminals and light pens. Functionality, and therefore the quality of service, is supposed to improve, of course; little purpose is served if the PAC merely provides the facilities of the card catalogue, such as fixed sequence single-term searching.

Changes resulting from automation cannot be confined, however, to enhancing the features and functions of a specific area of library services. In many cases, alterations to staff work-flows, tasks, and responsibilities may be indicated; the system should be capable of carrying out a number of tasks which were formerly labour-intensive but required little skill, such as circulation overdue notice processing. In other cases, the level of functionality might actually decrease: for example, the library managers could decide that it is better to integrate serials processing into the main housekeeping system to provide, say, an interfiled serials and books catalogue, even if this results in less flexibility in serials acquisitions or claiming. This applies equally well to existing automated services which may be upgraded as a result of underlying technological developments. It is clearly important that the staff involved in such changes are properly informed and consulted; established work patterns and relationships between colleagues will be disrupted, while long-cherished aspects of service provision may be degraded or abandoned for reasons which might be difficult to appreciate or understand. It seems reasonable, therefore, to include library staff as a component or subsystem of the 'main' system.

The other human subsystem to be considered is the library client. Similar factors apply: the client may have to learn new ways of using library services;

the client may perceive a degradation in individual provision and functionality, even if the overall service generally improves; the client may feel threatened or even abused by the imposition of the system; clients may have expectations and ideas of their own about automated information services. It should not be surprising that both staff and clients require similar consideration by the systems librarian: the system supplies tools to library staff to amplify their ability to supply services to clients, but it also supplies similar tools and services direct to the client. Needless to say, the systems librarian is also just as much a system 'user'; we are all 'fleshware', if not wetware, to the machine.

The final major factor influencing system effectiveness is the data which it contains. For a library system, data is perhaps the single most important component, for the primary goal of a library is surely to provide accurate and comprehensive information at a time and place convenient for the enquirer. The client is unlikely to admire the wonderful user-friendly PAC screens if they are full of spelling mistakes and other erroneous data, or if they indicate that the required material is available on the shelves when it is in fact missing, or on loan, or being rebound. Similarly, the best efforts of library staff to raise the quality of service and provide the human touch will be thwarted if the client detects a rottenness in the state of data, pretty smiles notwithstanding. The systems librarian must have a concern that data quality standards are being followed, and that transactions with the system are properly carried out.

Modern library and information systems allow a great deal of customization, offering many options for achieving the same level of service and functionality in any particular area of application; the best strategy chosen will take account of client requirements and expectations, staff perceptions of threats and opportunities, and management perceptions of strategic planning and development, while preserving system integrity and efficiency. In order to carry out an effective role, the systems librarian must be able to consider the system beyond its technological manifestations; responsibilities for personnel, data quality control, and strategic developments may lie with others, but the systems librarian has legitimate concerns in these areas. In many ways, the system librarian's 'system' must incorporate the entire library including its users, staff, services, equipment and aspirations. This is not very different to other professional library roles, where any specific consideration is usually made with regard to its impact on the general, but I suspect that the systems librarian is forced to perceive the interconnectedness of the various components in a more immediate and possibly clearer way. The systems librarian has a vocabulary and suite of concepts such as input, output, black box, feedback, and flow control which ultimately clarify the way in which the library actually works, but this 'systems approach' is still a very new idea for most librarians, and the jargon is more likely to obscure than enlighten. Most library staff and clients will have a narrower view: the system remains coextensive with its technological manifestations. When something goes wrong, however, perceptions may focus more specifically, with the system all too often being identified with the systems librarian. We are too smart these days to blame poor dumb hardware for failures, but anger and frustration have to be directed somewhere! This works both ways: the systems librarian may become so close to the system that genuine and proper attempts by colleagues to engender changes can be perceived as personal threats and consequently be resisted.

Like most real systems, the library system is not closed. Instead, it is open to interactions with external systems and environments; its boundaries are leaky. Three factors in the wider world may affect system effectiveness and planning: technological developments; system developments elsewhere in the institution; and changes in professional library practice. The systems librarian must be able to monitor and evaluate the impact of these influences; there is little mileage in purchasing and installing an interlibrary loans package whose supplier goes bankrupt three months later, or which will be incapable of handling the new arrangements being proposed for local library cooperation.

The systems librarian's 'system' might be graphically represented as a type of 'view from your town' postcard which distorts the geographical perspective so that your town occupies a large part of the foreground, with the rest of the world radiating away into the distance, detail becoming fuzzier the further out you look. As a sophistication, there may be some indication that things are really the same over there, out on the edge; the curvature of the horizon may hint that if you go out far enough, you'll eventually end up back where you started from. In an alternative, absolutist view, the system's location and sphere of influence is reflected in the primary account address: The Systems Librarian, The Library, That Street, This town, . . . The Earth, The Solar System, . . . The Universe! Is this what is meant by information space?

TUESDAY: 'I READ THE NEWS TODAY OH BOY'
Keeping up with developments on a stellar scale can be extremely difficult and frustrating. The systems librarian has to keep track in many different areas: the technological environment of the hardware and software; the application environment which includes the library clients, staff, resources, services, and professional practices; the political environment which determines policy and planning. The systems librarian may have direct control of these developments, or an indirect influence through colleagues; at the other extreme, changes can be a result of forces beyond anybody's control, such as the emergence of *de facto* data standards. Developments may occur solely within the library, or within the institution, or outwith the institution; they may affect a

small area of the system, or every part of it. Great technical expertise is probably not necessary for effective monitoring; it is more important that the systems librarian gains an overview or synthesis of the general trend of library system developments. In certain key areas, depending on local circumstances, much more detailed account of the potential changes will have to be taken; art libraries are more likely to be affected by a new graphic data compression standard than law libraries.

The usual means of staying informed are available: seminars, meetings, publications, personal communication. There are several significant differences, however, in keeping up-to-date with this particular field of librarianship. The library system is an amalgam of information management techniques, information services, and information technologies. It is a discipline emerging from the convergence of library and computing sciences; as such, it has no natural focus. The UK Library Association does not currently have a systems special interest group. Professional current awareness is supplied by whichever established group has an interest in a particular topic; at the time of writing, honours are shared between the Cataloguing and Indexing Group, concerned primarily with data standards, and the Information Technology Group, concerned with technological issues. As a result, the systems librarian in the UK often joins both groups in addition to any relevant sectoral interest groups.

There are several other national groups of which the systems librarian is likely to be a member: there will be a system user group if a proprietary housekeeping system is being used; there may be a users' group for each operating system in the library, and a hardware platform group for different pieces of kit. Not all are essential; I take a close interest in four or five of the eight or so groups with which I could be involved, while the others are of passing relevance. In addition, at any one time there may be several temporary working parties set up to exchange systems expertise and information on a geographical or sectoral basis; systems always seem to be the first consideration for library cooperation! This situation can only become worse in the near future; the trend towards open systems means that systems librarians will be assembling integrated systems from a larger number of separate software and hardware products, requiring even more of an overview and generating additional user group opportunities.

The field is subject to rapid technological change, and there seem to be enough new developments of interest to libraries to warrant several national and international exhibitions and seminars every year. The systems librarian may thus require a higher level of financial support for travel and accommodation expenses than other colleagues, to maintain an effective level of professional current awareness. A correspondingly longer amount of time will be spent off-site, bearing in mind that the professional groups may have three or four relevant meetings during the year. Electronic mail is an important facility for reducing the number of meetings required, in addition to giving access to communication on a global scale. As with most information technologies, telecommunications can be a two-edged sword, a tool allowing the systems librarian to cope with the pace while being a direct contributor to the rate of change. The bumf factor is very high. Hardware and software manufacturers seem to be front runners in the use of automation for marketing management, particularly with mailing-lists, and have the budgets to make those lists as comprehensive as possible. As a result, the systems librarian enjoys a larger proportion of unsolicited mail, along with assorted freebies and advertising gimmicks, than colleagues. Needless to say, visits to exhibitions result in huge quantities of glossy brochures, demonstration disks, and fluffy things to stick on your VDU, much of which gets filed away in case there's some extra capital money made available at the end of the fiscal year. Then there's the popular computing press: it can be very interesting checking out the advertisements on a regular basis, just to see what's available and how cheaply it can be obtained. The home computer magazine is also useful for providing a non-technical overview of developments, as well as indicating what the expectations of some of the library's younger clients might be.

There is a great deal of information to be digested, much of it apparently irrelevant, but all contributing to the overview essential for the with-it systems librarian. There is little point in trying to attenuate the input or ignore certain channels; it's a flux, a constant flow, and you don't learn to swim just by dipping your toes in the water. After all, once you've got your head wet and tried floating around for a bit, you can try surfing. Paddlers quickly reveal themselves at meetings: as well as metaphorically dry hair, they display blank expressions instead of nodding sagely when the latest buzz word or acronym is tossed into the conversation; of course, no one will actually know what the acronym means, but everybody who's anybody will have heard that it's the next big thing. It is better to have listened and misunderstood than never to have heard at all. The net should be cast wide, for we surf the sea of serendipity. Chance remarks can save a great deal of money, stimulate research, or simply reassure. At the same time, the emperor's clothes require careful inspection; it is easy to be dazzled. The danger of information overload is very real, but it diminishes in time as learning and experience ripen into intuition. Only connect?

WEDNESDAY: 'I'D LOVE TO TURN YOU ON'
The systems librarian has to act both as interpreter and evangelist, translating the body language of the screen into comprehensible instructions and encouraging the human component to believe that this really is a better way of doing

it. The systems librarian is the middleman, the go-between of the supplier and user: priest-like interpreter of the mysteries; hippy-like dealer in good vibes. Positive promotion of the system is essential: the users must be on your side because you'll need all the help you can get to survive the dreaded downtime. Downtime is inevitable, downtime is bad. Everyone suffers during downtime: the atmosphere is tense; emotions run high; feelings of paranoia, hostility, even rage, may be experienced. If they're not on your side, they're part of the problem. Downtime is the serpent of Eden, the revealer of knowledge, of fallibility. Downtime strikes at random: interrupting the training session, the demonstration of the right-on-ness of the rules, the rush; reinforcing prejudices, exposing weaknesses, confounding, confusing, chaotic.

Communication is essential, with all channels open and receiving on all wavelengths. The boundaries of the technological components of the system, the limitations of software and hardware design, must be explained to the library's staff and clients. Not only should they understand what part the package, the set and setting, the infrastructure, is capable of playing in the system; they must appreciate the options that are available, the reasons for the 'rules that must be obeyed', the usefulness of arcane rituals in ensuring a feeling of well-being (especially the invocation RTFM), the eight things to do to avoid the suffering of downtime and how to distinguish downtime from a momentary lapse of reason, and two fun things to do with bar-codes.

The communication subsystems available to the systems librarian typically include personal contact; group seminars, demonstrations, and workshops; documentation and training; reprographics; the internal mail system; noticeboards, posters, hand-outs and flyers; institutional publications; telephone systems; fax and e-mail systems; bulletin boards; static PAC displays, help screens, prompts, examples; audiovisual technologies, slides, overhead projection; computer-assisted-instruction systems, hypertext, interactive guides. That's a lot; all those accessible can be used in the final mix, assuming that where there's a medium, there's a receiver, and a message completes the loop. The message must be coherent, the same on all channels, the vibrations good. Others will be transmitting their own messages, wherever the system properties allow: library staff; library clients; traffic on shared systems resources such as the telephones and the local area network. It is important for the systems librarian to enable two-way communication where circumstances permit: the users will be the first to notice when there's a bummer going down, and the quicker the system librarian is told, the greater the chance of restoring harmony and avoiding the dreaded downtime. Things can go noisily wrong, resonant feedback loops howling: it might start with a system crash; half a dozen library staff immediately telephone the systems office, the first call indicating circumstance, the second, happenstance, and the third, enemy action; the systems librarian heroically identifies the cause of concern and rectifies it, valiantly ignoring the flood of incoming electronic mail alerts; the second wave of telephone calls comes through just in time to block transmission of the reset and go message; a dissatisfied client decides it's all too much or isn't cracked up what it's supposed to be or ought to be banned; and the following day a memo arrives in the post to ask if the system is down, or did I press the wrong key.

So, the systems librarian has access to the media, but what is the message to be? At the very least, staff and clients have to know how to use the system: which key to press, when to press it, what happens after it's pressed, what to do if something else happens, what to do if nothing happens, why it can't do this or that, when not to panic. Automation engenders changes in the way that the human and non-human components of a system interact; the systems librarian must attempt to explain why different approaches are needed, and what benefits accrue. Automation often enhances system flexibility, and there may be several different ways of achieving the same result; users must be informed enough to choose the appropriate method. It is not sufficient to communicate on a 'need to know' basis, or to pass on only the instructions required to carry out the particular task in hand. Integration of functionality and data, with a resulting increase in efficiency and effectiveness, is one of the principle benefits of automation. As a result, subsystems which formerly did not interact or share information are dynamically linked; operations carried out on one part of the system will cause changes in another. If users are not aware of this, serious problems can arise: existing data may be corrupted or spurious data created, confidence can suffer and performance will degrade. The personal downside of integration is the constraint on doing your own thing, particularly in an automated subsystem with rules that must be obeyed under penalty of capital punishment. Thou shalt not start the print without checking the paper alignment, nor restructure the search menus without consulting the library tutors! The systems librarian must explain the interconnectedness of all things, demonstrate the influence of individual actions on remote events, stress the values of group cooperation and personal responsibility.

All users must be treated equally; the system is no respecter of status. The systems librarian must tell the truth, like it is, the whole truth, no censorship, especially to those who would rather not know. White lies should only be used when exposure is unlikely. Even the systems librarian sometimes has to stand naked in the presence of downtime. The systems librarian must endeavour to remain neutral and objective in the face of differing conceptions, perceptions, and expectations of clients, staff, and managers. The dangers of disenfranchising or disillusioning any particular group of users must be recognized and understood by the users themselves, particularly managers, as well as the systems staff. The systems librarian has to try to help the users appreciate the 'vision thing' so they can accept the systems approach and gain the maximum benefit from it; the systems librarian must engender trust if the system is to continue developing. This can be difficult, especially when the system is influenced by external forces; the cataloguer might not be too happy when informed that insignificant initial title words will now be ignored in filing only when the MARC indicators are set, and not by a system stop-word list. The final complication, then, in communicating the system to its users is its dynamic: yesterday's rules are today's options and tomorrow's archaisms.

Communication should become easier once library staff and clients have started to interact with the system: the medium is the message. A successful system will draw users to it; queues will form at the autoteller while the bank staff practise smiling at each other. The power of the systems approach is self-demonstrating, augmented by the enthusiasm of acolytes and converts.

THURSDAY: 'HE DIDN'T NOTICE THAT THE LIGHTS HAD CHANGED'

The systems approach is necessary for the 'hard' components, the hardware, software and data of the system, the parts at the centre of the systems librarian's universe. The values of connectivity, integration, and generalization have been learned through past mistakes; flexible development strategies and a rapid response to environmental changes are to be preferred over super-specialization and too rigid a definition of goals, procedures and methods. The system boundaries cannot be fixed; the system is open. The system evolves, develops, and mutates under the influence of its users, its own subsystems, and external agents. In turn, the system affects its environment. Perceptions of the library and its purpose change. Systems techniques might be found appropriate or necessary for library tasks and procedures outwith the currently defined system limits. Systems tend to grow, first making powerful connections to other systems just beyond the pale, and then often absorbing them as subsystems. This works both ways, with the library system itself potentially a subsystem of the larger organizational system.

The systems librarian cannot afford to be solely reactive. Considerable forward planning is required if systems development is to be effective. Services which are to be incorporated into the library system must be made ready in advance through analysis, consultation, and agreeing on changes. The systems librarian is the expert, the one who can explain the options, their relative merits, the bigger picture. This often expensive expertise is wasted if the systems librarian is instructed to implement developments without prior involvement in their formulation, as big a mistake as planning without management or client participation. Systems cannot be implemented with reluctance, at least not properly. The systems librarian is the library system's bootstrap: something's got to start it going; and somebody has to keep it going in the face of ambiguous technological developments, misapprehensions and misunderstandings, techno-fear, future shock, system fatigue, the weariness of seemingly constant change. The system cannot do this for itself, no matter how well designed or constructed. The systems librarian therefore has to be proactive: alerting management to technological developments and their potential impact; convincing users of the efficacy of the systems approach; gaining converts; preparing for further integration; anticipating requests for system enhancement; constantly monitoring performance and usage.

While the prime directive for the systems librarian must be to avoid a meeting with downtime if at all possible and to keep the system up and running, there must be a concern about its long-term development. The luxury of completely replacing the library system every few years is becoming rarer because of the costs, the inevitable waste of suddenly incompatible or redundant equipment, and the stress it imposes on the people involved. Instead, systems are expected to adapt, to build on existing structures, and to recycle components for fresh purposes. Mistakes, when made, will persist; there will be few opportunities to get rid of them by throwing it all away and starting again. Today's acceptable development path may become tomorrow's dead end; careful consideration, tempered with blue-sky speculation, must be given to the direction and time-scale of change. Options should be kept flexible and open, even if it means accepting a less than optimal system in the meantime; red lights can be avoided by travelling more slowly between intersections, or taking a more circuitous route. These ideas can be difficult to put across, especially to clients and managers who may often be more attracted to short-term solutions which work than longer term maybes.

The immediate goal of any service-oriented system is to provide an acceptable level of service to the user; library housekeeping functions for managers, and information management functions for clients. The longer term goal is to always meet the immediate goal in spite of changes in user expectations and the nature of the services required. The systems view regards the service delivery infrastructure, operators, information resources, consumers and managers as components or subsystems of the bigger system. Each of these can also be regarded as a system, with its own properties, methods and goals; in isolation, it is quite possible that the properties and methods are incompatible and that goals lie in different places. Even within the library system as a whole, there will be differences of opinion in various human components as to what constitutes an acceptable level of service, or what services should be offered, and what the priorities are. Add to this technological developments in the world outside the library and its host institution, and developments affecting the non-human components of the library system, and the result can be a battery of incoherent forces influencing the choice of direction for the next big step.

Like it or not, the single biggest factor to be taken into account when resolving conflicting pressures for change has to be the technology. Developments in information technologies are not being controlled by information managers; this is the fault of the managers, not the technologists. Although there are some signs that librarians are becoming aware of this, we face an uphill struggle. We cannot agree amongst ourselves on what a library is, let alone what a good library system should be; the messages reaching proprietary system developers and the manufacturers of information products are as incoherent as those directed at the systems librarian. Other messages are being transmitted; there are experts closer to the technology, the computer professionals, who are turning to the consideration of information rather than data, now that they are required less for programming, operations, and maintenance. After all, information is just data embedded in natural language, isn't it? The systems librarian sits piggy-in-the-middle: in one ear, library managers asking why the system can't handle invoicing for overdue materials; in the other, library system suppliers asking why there are so many differing requirements for fines subsystems; and in the distance, out of earshot, a COBOL programmer is putting the finishing touches to the institution's financial management system.

Information technology drives the library system, not the clients, nor the staff, nor the managers. The direction of technological change is determined by scientific research, inertia and the need for backwards compatibility. Occasionally, a near-discontinuous jump can occur, when the value of compatibility is outweighed by the benefits promised by the change. The systems librarian should try to determine which technologies are ripe for reformation, and gauge whether a particular development represents a refinement or a revolution, equilibrium or punctuation. Users can then be alerted to prepare to think differently about how the system operates, to anticipate new facilities, and to plan for the effects that amending one subsystem will have on the others, even if there was no announcement on the six o'clock news. Conversely, users can be reassured that the system will operate as before, that existing facilities will be preserved, and that there is no need to panic, in spite of the newsreader's assertion that things will never be the same again. Systems librarians get the greatest satisfaction when they have been able to foresee changes, have prepared for them, and are able to say 'no problem' when the library manager asks 'what about Windows?'; they get the least satisfaction in saying 'I told you so' when advice has been ignored and there are half a dozen expensive, but non-standard, modems dumped in the trash can.

FRIDAY: 'NOBODY WAS REALLY SURE IF HE WAS FROM THE HOUSE OF LORDS'

A typical mission statement or job function of the systems librarian might indicate a role in leading and developing automated information services for the library and its clients. If the accent is on coordination and consolidation, passive rather than active, and there is no compensation elsewhere in the staff structure, then the mission will fail and the job malfunction. Coordination cannot be achieved without development, nor consolidation without leadership; if I were going to Tipperary, I wouldn't start from here. On the other hand, the library manager's mission statement will certainly emphasize the role of leading and developing information services in general for the library's clients. The only apparent differences in these roles are whether a service is automated or not, and the nature of the client base; as such, the roles would appear to be converging owing to the increasing prominence and dominance of automated services in the information environment. Is the systems librarian then threatening to make the senior manager redundant, either by leaving no service unautomated or by automating the management function itself, or is the library manager evolving into a systems manager by acquiring technical expertise and familiarity with systems concepts?

As yet, automation has not infected every aspect of library services. Indeed, there is, perhaps, an assumption that there will always be some library service which will resist attempts to automate it: an assumption reinforced by naïve ideas concerning customer care, despite the trend towards self-service and the evidence of the autoteller; by informed ideas about the truth of user-friendliness and the reality of artificial intelligence; or vice versa. If the automated system is not coextensive with the library as a whole, there are three possible modes of relationship between areas under the authority of the systems librarian and those controlled by colleagues. The automated system, the empire of the systems librarian, may be encompassed by, and therefore subject to, the realm of the library manager: this mode is traditional and well-established, but limits system efficiency and development potential by perpetuating too-rigid barriers and unnecessary subsystem interfaces. Or, the non-automated services are treated as anomalous subsystems, tolerated but threatened with eventual extinction or absorption by the system: this mode is currently unrealistic and is suitable only for cyberpunk dreaming. Or, the automated and non-automated components form a patchwork, apparently stitched together to provide best-fit coverage, but in reality more like a fractal, with automated subsystem embedded in non-automated subsystem embedded in automated subsystem, and so on: this mode will become the norm for the foreseeable future. It is neither possible nor desirable to separate automated and non-automated areas of authority for management purposes; all boundaries leak, and the property of 'non-automated' does not form a particularly natural or useful primary category.

The traditional relationship between systems librarian and library manager is hierarchical, with the authority of the systems librarian well-defined, clearly-bounded, and delegated by the library manager, just as for the chief cataloguer or circulation desk supervisor. While the influence of automation has spread both horizontally and vertically through library and information infrastructures, the need for systems control has increased. As a result, the status of the systems librarian has been steadily enhanced, so that in many libraries the systems librarian is regarded as a senior manager and is a vital part of the strategic management process. The focus of responsibility has moved from the specific to the general; automation affects us all and everything we do. At the same time, hierarchical approaches to management have become less useful or appropriate, partly as a result of automation, and are being replaced by team-based, goal-oriented, collective decision-making structures. It is essential that the systems librarian be a full member of the highest level library management team, and not merely co-opted when matters concerning automation and automated services are considered. Overviews cannot be comprehensive if the visual field is restricted; the systems planner cannot be effective if there are hidden agendas.

As the roles and responsibilities of the technologist and manager have converged within the library or information store, there have been similar changes in the wider organization. Information itself is becoming recognized as a prime focus, rather than the means of its storage, access or delivery. Thus computer managers, programmers, systems analysts, archivists, librarians, and indexers are increasingly seen as working in the same field, to the same goals. As the importance of efficient and responsive information management becomes apparent, so cooperation and coordination are encouraged by realignment of hierarchical management lines under an information supremo, and by merger of formerly separate units and divisions. Library managers have a particularly valuable role to play by virtue of belonging to an established profession, which has taken an objective view of information for many years, particularly with respect to the message rather than the medium, and the receiver rather than broadcaster. In the emerging information management paradigm, the chief librarian occupies a neutral, expert and strategic role which, with respect to the organization as a whole, is very similar to that of the systems librarian *vis-à-vis* the library. The clients of the information manager include not only the clients of the organization, but also the organization itself. As the library system has become a framework for structuring services for educational, leisure, and research information, so the library system is becoming a model for organizational information services, including office automation, management information, and data processing.

The jury is still out on whether the systems librarian and library manager are the same person. For as long as the roles are perceived as distinct, by the organization and the profession as well as the participants, then cooperation and partnership is the only viable model. The systems librarian and the library manager are now dependent on each other's roles, for technological and managerial expertise are essential to the evolving library. If either party attempts competition or restrictive practices, both will fail; the relationship is symbiotic.

SATURDAY: 'SOMEBODY SPOKE AND I WENT INTO A DREAM'

In the cyberpunk, blue-sky, virtual future, information users will have a great deal of control over the way in which they can search, retrieve, and manipulate information. The virtual library could appear as any of a number of familiar environments, the choice being the user's: Alexandrian with scrolls in cubby-holes; medieval with manuscripts in heavy leather bindings chained to the wall; public with brightly coloured dust jackets arranged in categories; academic with plain, dusty books arranged in classified order; office with documents arranged in filing cabinets. Or something more radical, perhaps; simulacra of the authors standing in a bus queue, ready to recite their works if asked? The underlying reality is information in some kind of machine-representational form, overlaid with expert retrieval and display systems, and herein lie the barriers on the way to our brave new world.

For information to be processed in a consistent way by computer, it must be machine-readable, standardized, and accessible. The virtual library depends on vast quantities of information being scanned or keyboarded into electronic format, according to internationally agreed standards, and stored in standard-format databases linked electronically on a global scale. Essentially, this requires fingers on keyboards and agreements in committees, difficult but not impossible tasks. The flexible, user-defined, self-service interface depends on getting more power for less kit and money, and the development of expert retrieval systems operating over-generalized knowledge domains. The former requires a continuation of existing trends; there is as yet no clear evidence that the latter is feasible.

While the hybrid library exists, the space that provides a physical focus for a mixture of electronic and non-electronic information resources and the tools to access them, then library staff will be required to organize, assist, develop, and manage it. As more and more of the non-automated information backlog is tackled, fewer clerical functions will be required; as better information manipulation tools are developed, less professional assistance will be sought by the enquirer. Automation upskills the paraprofessional and downskills the professional; many traditional library skills such as knowing the difference between letter-by-letter and word-by-word alphabetic sequencing or standing orders and serials are becoming irrelevant. The expertise of the subject librarian, marrying specific subject knowledge with professional training in the vagaries of language and the principles of cataloguing and indexing, will be an essential requirement for the uninformed user until artificial intelligence delivers the goods. There will be a role for the library manager for as long as there is a real library; when the boundaries dissolve, the library manager will seek firmer ground as the organization's information services coordinator.

The systems librarian will probably last the longest. Mutation into systems manager, followed by a struggle with other ex-library managers for the supremo's job, is one personal survival strategy. Continuation of technological developments, evolution of data standards, and changing expectations of users will ensure niche employment opportunities for some time to come, if not forever. Many areas of cyberspace will require policing, particularly where access is deliberately restricted or resources are vulnerable to information guerillas, providing job prospects for control freaks if not systems librarians; the image of a rogue virtual librarian, *à la* Westworld, stalking the corridors of information space, frightening the users, and sprinkling knowledge viruses around pops into my mind, I don't know why!

In the end, the true role of the systems librarian will emerge: it is to be the last person in the library, who, after a fond glance at the dust-laden shelves, microcomputers, and circulation desks, will step outside, lock the door, and turn the key over to the museum attendant.

4 Market influences and the role of the systems librarian

❖ *Janet Broome*

INTRODUCTION

Recently, I attended a system managers user group meeting to discuss system migration strategies with my system supplier. During the course of the discussions an interesting point came to light: that the role of the systems librarian/manager would fundamentally change with the implementation of 'open systems'-based library systems.

The migration to 'open systems'-based library systems is forcing systems librarians to reassess the library systems market-place in a way it has never been evaluated before. Suddenly, systems librarians are expected to acquire a whole new set of skills and knowledge they may not possess. The aim of this chapter is to show how a restructuring of the library systems market-place will affect the systems we choose and the future role of the systems librarian.

1 WHAT MAKES AN OPEN SYSTEM

For several years the library systems market-place has been oversaturated by suppliers who have been unable to deliver the functionality that librarians require. With the development of computer industry standards, such as UNIX, RDBMS (Relational Database Management Systems) and TCP/IP (Transmission Control Protocol/Internet Protocol) many library system suppliers are able to offer functionality which was previously unavailable because of technical constraints.

When selecting first and second generation library systems the logical starting-point was with the library systems supplier. The move towards open systems-based library systems was driven not by the library systems suppliers but by the technical advances in the computing industry. There are several building blocks that define an open system; this section intends to introduce these components. Library system suppliers to some extent are guilty of jumping on the open systems bandwagon. One only needs to read the glossy advertisements in the *Library Association record* – everyone seems to be offering an 'Open Approach'. Instead of evaluating the functionality of the various library systems currently available, we should assess the technical requirements of our various institutions and we should examine carefully our library system supplier's preferred supplier. Library system suppliers are selling open systems as a benefit of migration, therefore it is in our interests to determine on whom our suppliers are dependent.

1.1 Central site hardware

Library system suppliers have almost universally adopted open systems. As prospective customers, librarians should expect a choice of UNIX central site hardware. Is there greater freedom of choice? The whole point of open systems is greater freedom of choice, flexibility, and the ability to move applications from one machine to another. Suppliers who are tied into one or two hardware vendors are restricting customer choice and may be limiting their own future development path. It is for this reason that we should evaluate very carefully the library system suppliers' preferred hardware platforms for UNIX. We are dependent on the hardware vendor our supplier chooses for our central site hardware support (see Figure 4.1). As UNIX is the industry standard operating system, we should be looking at a hardware platform which is not only tried and tested in the library systems market-place but also in the UNIX systems market-place.

The UNIX market-place is changing, as is almost every area of computing, therefore one would expect any serious system supplier to be planning migrations to other types of UNIX machine. In early 1993, we saw the launch of Digital's new UNIX machine DEC ALPHA. How many library systems are

Supplier	Product	UNIX Hardware Platform Supported
BLCMP	TALIS	Data General, SUN, Hewlett Packard
Geac	ADVANCE	Motorola, IBM RS6000, SEQUENT, PYRAMID
Geac	LIBS100plus	SEQUENT, Motorola, IBM
ORACLE	ORACLE Libraries	SUN, SEQUENT, Compaq System Pro, ICL DRS6000, IBM RS6000
Dynix	Marquis	Data General, SUN, DEC ALPHA IBM RS6000

Fig. 4.1 Hardware platforms supported by a sample of system suppliers

currently available on DEC ALPHA? How many system suppliers have planned to migrate to DEC ALPHA? Library system suppliers are extremely reluctant to discuss future planned hardware platforms. The reason suppliers are reluctant to migrate to new or other hardware platforms is cost. Cost in terms of buying the hardware platform to port the library applications software to, but also cost in terms of staff resources to support another hardware platform. If suppliers have no plan to migrate to new platforms they are restricting customer choice. Remember, the main selling points of open systems are portability, flexibility, and greater freedom of choice.

1.2   Peripheral equipment

In theory open systems are supposed to give us greater freedom of choice with regard to the types of terminals, light pens, scanners, and printers we use. How many of us have terminals which are incompatible with other computer systems within our institution? The reason is that some suppliers have dictated the type of peripherals we use because of the central site hardware vendor they have been tied into. With the advent of open systems we are no longer dependent on our supplier for our terminals. We should be able to plug in any terminal which supports a standard VT emulation and find it works.

1.3   Maintenance

Peripheral maintenance and central site hardware maintenance have been to some extent the main revenue source for the traditional library turnkey system suppliers. With open systems we have the opportunity to shop around for the best deals on third-party maintenance, and to purchase hardware from elsewhere. This has significant financial implications on the suppliers' revenue. Richard Heseltine, in his paper 'Choosing in the dark',[1] discussed the effect of those suppliers who are financially reliant on maintenance from both central site hardware and peripherals. Ultimately, there will be winners and losers. Let us hope that the majority of systems librarians have the skill sets necessary to back winners.

1.4   Move to software-only solutions

Library system suppliers whose traditional source of revenue has been from hardware maintenance need to compensate for this loss. We are already seeing a move away from turnkey system solutions, with products like ORACLE libraries and INNOPAC. Software-only sales may become common practice. This in turn will put more strain on the library system manager, who will need to possess greater technical understanding of central site hardware operating systems and database management tools. With a move to software-only sales a restructuring of the library systems market-place is inevitable and has already started to happen – Geac took over CLSI in December 1992. Software licensing, maintenance and development will be the future source of revenue for the library system suppliers. Library applications software has traditionally been the least expensive component of a library system. For the first time, system librarians are having to plan software development in library budgets.

1.5 Operating systems

It would seem that for the time being the library community has fully adopted UNIX as the industry standard operating system. This is due to performance-related issues. UNIX boxes can give greater performance than their proprietary counterparts with regard to library applications and online transaction processing.

UNIX began life in the late 1960s. A research project was carried out in Boston to develop a multi-user, time-sharing computer operating system. The operating system developed was named MULTIX. Unfortunately, the project was abandoned, but one of the team leaders, Ken Thompson from Bell laboratories developed a cut down version of the operating system to play computer games. He named his version UNIX.

There has been much debate as to whether UNIX offers the solution for library systems. Arguments and objections are mainly raised by those institutions who have been locked into one supplier, that is, DEC, and one operating system, VMS. VMS has now been rewritten to become 'open VMS' to support UNIX applications.

There has been much debate as to the future of UNIX. This has largely occurred because of the various flavours of UNIX which saturated the marketplace. There were mainly two strands of UNIX: AT & T's System V-based UNIX and Berkeley-based UNIX. There was clearly a need for an international standard; this came in the form of POSIX. The current industry standard version of UNIX is System V.4. Therefore, any system supplier who is selling open systems, should be selling a product that runs on this version of UNIX. If System V is not present then the system is not truly open.

Another criticism of UNIX has been that it is unfriendly. Much work has been done to develop a friendly interface for the operating system. SEQUENT have developed a menu-driven version of System V and SUN have developed a Windows feature in SOLARIS.

1.6 Relational database management systems

Another key component of open systems is relational database management systems (RDBMS). Library system suppliers are divided on their choice of relational database management system. RDBMS currently used for library applications are ORACLE, INFORMIX, and Sybase (see Figure 4.2). What benefits

Supplier	Product	RDBMS Supported
BLCMP	TALIS	Sybase
Geac	LIBS100plus	INFORMIX
ORACLE	ORACLE Libraries	ORACLE
Dynix	Marquis	Sybase

Fig. 4.2   Relational database management systems supported by a sample of system suppliers

does a relational database management system offer over conventional database management systems? Data is stored once and is accessible across the system. The programming efforts for RDBMS are significantly less than for other database management systems. The advantage of this is that systems can be developed in a shorter time-span, hence software enhancements and bug fixes should be available in a shorter time-scale. This is only true if the systems supplier has the necessary technical resources in this area. As with UNIX, systems librarians should examine carefully the supplier's choice of RDBMS and examine how the RDBMS is performing in other market-places.

When choosing a relational database management system attention should be drawn to the structured query language (SQL) licence agreements. Structured query language is an excellent diagnostic tool available with RDBMS; it is the utility used to manipulate data. SQL can be used to get the statistics we have been struggling to get out of library systems for years. SQL tools include report-writing utilities and special query forms. Without report-writing utilities unsuspecting systems librarians may believe they can have any report they require out of the system. The ability to generate reports is not just dependent on what tools or utilities are available with the RDBMS, it is dependent on something much more fundamental – how the database has been designed.

Database design has so often been overlooked in library systems. How often have we heard users say 'why doesn't the system do this?' Bad database design has led many system suppliers simply to 'add on' features and functionality without integrating them fully.

Evaluation of database design is necessary. There are a number of areas that need to be evaluated, such as the time-span for product development. In theory, the longer the development period, the greater the finished result. Try to ascertain from suppliers how much money has been invested into development, what the future development plans are, and the skill sets of the development team. Traditionally, library automation companies have not matched the salaries of computer software houses. The size and location of the development team may be critical for your migration. A larger development team suggests a heavier commitment on the suppliers' behalf to the new product. The location of the development department could be a cause of concern, if you have to wait for new releases of software to fix bugs. However, with the advances of the Internet many suppliers are performing software application upgrades across the Internet. Companies offering this service include Innovative Interfaces and Geac.

1.7 Communication standards

Communication standards are an important part of an open system. The introduction of distributed client-server systems will have significant impact on existing networks. It may be necessary to replace whole networks if the institution has several client-server-based systems, as existing networks may not be able to cope with the download of information from the server to its clients.

In many ways the communications revolution we are currently witnessing is enabling us as librarians to rethink the way we store and retrieve information. In the future it is possible that OPACs will return to storing only bibliographical information and that library news-type information will be moved to campus or community wide information systems (CWIS). The library system or the CWIS may be used as a gateway to many other systems which hold information.

Introducing a service such as CWIS would have financial and resource implications. Some system suppliers are selling CWIS as part of the library automation system, others are selling it as a separate product. The systems librarian, although keen to implement a CWIS, would need extra resources to update information on the system. In some institutions the CWIS may be managed by departments other than the library.

Using CWIS and the library system as a gateway to other information services has been possible with the TCP/IP protocol. With the advent of the Internet there has been a need within the library community to develop retrieval tools and standards to interrogate the network. The Internet is a loose amalgam of computer networks connecting thousands of sites and millions of users all over the world. Any computer with TCP/IP has the capability of getting into the Internet.

There are three main information tools available on the Internet: Gopher, WAIS, and World Wide Web.

1.7.1 *Gopher*

The Gopher system was originally designed at the University of Minnesota as a campus wide information system. Gopher is menu driven and makes use of telnet to access OPAC information.

1.7.2   *WAIS*
WAIS (Wide Area Information Service) was designed by the Thinking Machines Corporation as a tool for full-text retrieval over wide area networks.

1.7.3   *World Wide Web*
World Wide Web (WWW) project was developed in Switzerland. It combines the techniques of hypertext, where links can be set up between documents of any kind (multimedia) and of text retrieval.

ANSI Z39.50 (ISO 10162-1: 1993 *Information and documentation – open systems interconnection – search and retrieve application service definition* and ISO 10163-1: 1993 *Information and documentation – open systems interconnection – search and retrieve application protocol specification*) is an international standard and is one of a set of standards used to facilitate the interconnection of computer systems. The aim of OSI (Open Systems Interconnection) is to allow the interconnection of computer systems. Z39.50 defines an OSI protocol within the application. With Z39.50 implemented on our machines, we will be able to interrogate other library systems' OPACs using our usual search methodologies. This is of course dependent on the other machine also using the Z39.50 protocol.

Although Z39.50 is not currently used in the UK, it is being used to develop a national library network in Ireland (the IRIS project). BLCMP, Dynix, McDonnell Douglas, ORACLE, and Fretwell Downing are involved in the IRIS project. Any future library systems must have this protocol.

1.8   The problem of functionality
One of the biggest problems at present is that the new library systems based on open systems technology are functionally behind existing library systems. When CLSI launched LIBS100plus it was functionally behind LIBS100 – it was missing an acquisitions module. BLCMP's TALIS system is functionally behind BLS – interlibrary loans and serials are incomplete. These companies are faced with difficulties when trying to sell the new system to existing customers. There has to be a point when the old product is not developed any further and all development effort goes into the new system. Otherwise, if development is continued in both products, what are the benefits of migrating systems? A systems librarian is faced with a very difficult problem here: how can you bid for money to replace an existing library system for a new system which is functionally behind the old? Open systems alone should not be the

reason for migration; the underlying reason for any migration is to improve library services, not to take services away!

2 PROCURING AN OPEN SYSTEMS-BASED LIBRARY SYSTEM

2.1 EC procurement thresholds

For central government and public bodies the threshold for tendering is 200,000 ECUs or £141,431 excluding VAT. Careful planning of a system procurement exercise could avoid these regulations by bidding for hardware and software separately or migrating costs across two financial years. Some system suppliers are actively encouraging this with their proposed migration strategies.

2.2 Evaluating system suppliers

Library trade shows are the only place where librarians can evaluate systems side by side. For the purpose of a visit to the Library Resources Exhibition I drew up an evaluative questionnaire which I used to interview the various suppliers before a demonstration of their system (see the appendix to this chapter).

2.3 The costings proposal

It is normal procedure for the systems librarian and senior library management to draw together a costings proposal to bid for funding for a replacement system. The purpose of producing a proposal is to sell the benefits the institution will gain by replacing the existing library system. The audience of the proposal are senior management within the institution. The management team may comprise staff who are IT illiterate, therefore technical jargon and arguments will need to be presented clearly. With proposals of this nature one needs to be wary of presenting a document which is lengthy and goes into too much technical detail. Costings proposals need to be succinct, brief and to the point.

There are real dangers in selling the benefits of open systems and forgetting the benefits to the library. The reason we wish to migrate is to improve library services. The costings proposal needs to contain a number of sections. The introduction should state clearly why the existing system needs replacing. The main body of the document should present a series of bullet points that list the advantages of replacing the system. In contrast to this, the disadvantages of not replacing the system need to be presented. Time-scales for implementation have to be presented together with detailed costings prepared by the designated suppliers.

The costings proposal should detail the hidden costs of migration. For instance, it may be necessary to replace existing peripheral equipment and upgrade telecommunication networks. Extra funding may be required for resources to manage the changeover to the new system. Therefore the costings proposal needs to form more than a ballpark figure for replacing central site hardware and software. You may wish to include a detailed analysis of maintenance charges. Some suppliers may deliberately submit low costings for system migration, as they intend to recompense a low cost migration for high cost annual maintenance on hardware and software.

The proposal should close with recommendations and a conclusion. The recommendations should be to write a specification of system requirements with other library staff and members of the institution. Once the specification is complete the institution is ready to begin the tendering process.

2.4   Specification of system requirements

It is standard business practice for any institution buying software to write a specification of requirements, so that suppliers can provide exactly what the end-user requires. The task of writing the specification for a replacement library system normally falls on the shoulders of the systems librarian in conjunction with other senior members of staff. In recent years, there have been demands for greater connectivity between computer systems within institutions. It is not beyond the realms of possibility that the institution may dictate the technical requirements of a library system so that it fits into an already firmly established IT strategy. Systems librarians normally find themselves in the position of negotiating and liaising with IT management committees. In this scenario the systems librarian needs to be fully conversant with current IT trends and be able to put forward a case for the library system going down a particular route. For instance, not all institutions have gone over to open systems and are still clinging onto proprietary systems. Systems librarians may find themselves in a position of having to justify the benefits of open systems to a reluctant IT committee.

For this reason it is desirable to establish a three-tier system-selection committee. The first level would comprise of a technical working group made up of IT staff, the systems librarian, and other representation from the library. One of the benefits of forming a technical working group is to build on the existing IT knowledge and experience within the institution. The technical working group could explore hidden costs of migration such as telecommunication network upgrades, and offer advice and additional resources during the migration process.

It may be vigilant to have a contracts expert as part of the technical working group. The role of the contracts expert would be to understand the software licence and hardware licensing agreements with the supplier. Librarians have traditionally been weak in the area of drawing up contracts with suppliers. Perhaps this is one of the reasons why so many system migrations have been unsuccessful. If the specification includes a series of contractual acceptance tests which relate to promised functionality being available before the migration takes place, we would probably see more successful migrations. All too often we are promised features and functionality as part of the next release. Suppliers must be forced to honour what they have promised; contractual acceptance tests are one way of ensuring this. The existence of acceptance tests gives the institution some freedom to decide whether to pay for software maintenance, or to defer payment until the specified functionality is present. A government body CCTA (Central Computer and Telecommunications Agency) produces model agreements for acceptance of computer hardware and software.

It may also be vigilant to build into the specification a section on damages. For instance, you may wish to specify a contractual expectation of system uptime – if the system fails as a result of supplier negligence, such as unforeseen problems with software upgrades, then maintenance reductions are compulsory. If more library authorities introduced measures such as these we would see better quality software.

The second tier could consist of a library functionality committee, comprising of senior library staff. The purpose of this committee is to establish how library services can be improved and to draw up a list of desired and essential functionality. One of the major problems facing librarians at present is that library systems based on open systems technology are functionally behind existing systems.

The third tier could comprise of end-users. 'End-user' could mean the staff on the issue desk as well as the end-information-user, such as the student or the partner in a special library. This group could provide details of how they wish to retrieve information in a more cost-effective way.

2.5   Supporting an open system

With the restructuring of the library system market-place due to the technological developments in open systems, the traditional turnkey system suppliers may be forced to rethink the support strategies offered to customers. Support for open systems-based library systems can be defined in three stages:

- Pre-implementation/conversion training
- Migration support
- Post-implementation support

2.5.1   *Pre-implementation/conversion training*

This support comes before the actual system migration. What does migration mean? In computing terms it means moving the users from one system to another. The other system is usually better than the system the users have migrated from. In library terms it means moving all the library housekeeping modules such as circulation, OPAC, acquisitions, cataloguing, interlibrary loans, serials, and community information to a system that looks and performs better than the old.

System migrations should be fast, accurate and cause minimum disruption to staff. In reality the library system suppliers do not have a proven success rate in any of the above. Before launching into a migration the systems librarian and other library staff should have received pre-conversion training. If this training has not gone ahead, the migration is likely to fail on the grounds of accuracy and minimum disruption to staff. The aim of pre-implementation training is to establish the requirements of library staff from the new system. The supplier and the customer need to be clear what data needs to be taken from the old system to the new. Most suppliers convert borrower, loan, MARC, and copy information. This is done by running a suite of data conversion programmes prior to the system migration. Data conversion may also be a hidden cost of system migration if you go to a new supplier, although some suppliers may be prepared to negotiate conversion charges depending on the size and structure of the database.

Accuracy of data conversions is dependent on two factors:

1   That the integrity of the data from the old system is good.
2   That the supplier has accurate data conversion programmes which have been tried and tested on a 'live' site.

How can a systems librarian ensure that data is accurate? Most suppliers will recommend a database tidying up exercise prior to conversion to iron out any data inconsistencies. It is probably worth scheduling for the data conversions to be run twice – once to test that the data has converted correctly, identify any problems, and ensure they are fixed by the supplier; a second time for real.

The more sophisticated the library system, the more problematical the system migration. Two problematical areas are the transfer of book acquisitions information and OPAC information. The conversions for these modules should be carefully scheduled with the library system supplier.

Many public and academic libraries use the financial processing features available with acquisitions modules. Supplier information on systems is extensive and it is unreasonable for any system supplier to propose that this information is not converted across to the new system. The planning of a system migration may have to be planned around the end and beginning of a new financial year. This will be dependent on whether the supplier has written sophisticated conversion programs to carry information such as outstanding orders, invoice information, and prior year financial information. If the supplier does not offer conversion programs that do this, then the logical time to migrate would be at the end of the financial year. This is not a desirable option but it may be a necessary one.

It is impossible to convert OPAC indexes from one system to an open system. OPAC data can be converted but not the indexes. This is due to the way that MARC information is stored in a relational database management system. Therefore, it will be necessary to build into the migration schedule a period for rebuilding the OPAC indexes. The estimated time to rebuild OPAC indexes varies with each library database – the more sophisticated the OPAC, the longer the rebuild will take. With open systems one consolation is that the indexes can easily be built online. This is dependent on whether the systems supplier has allowed for this in the disk space configuration.

For academic libraries the ideal time to migrate would be during the summer vacation. This should allow enough time for staff training, conversions and indexing. What options are available for large public libraries with OPACs? Some suppliers have quoted that a rebuild of indexes can take between five and ten working days. One option would be for the system supplier to rebuild the OPAC indexes in-house.

2.5.2 *Migration support*
Support is the most critical aspect of a library system. A library product may offer all the functionality we require, but if the system supplier does not have adequate resources to invest in support the migration is often a disaster. There are two aspects to the support issue. Does the customer's expectations from support exceed their ability to pay? Or is the customer paying far too much for support? Support is critical during the migration process. A systems librarian should expect on-site support during this period. Part of the process is for the supplier to put forward the best migration strategy for the library concerned. No two libraries are the same, and different criteria may affect the system librarian's and the supplier's choice of migration strategy.

There are three possible strategies for system migration:

- Big bang
- Gradual
- Gentle

2.5.2.1   *Big bang*

Big bang is an interesting migration strategy. It is the strategy where the library system you have loved, nurtured, and cherished for the past number of years has departed, and 'bang', a new library system is in place. There are advantages with big bang: the migration is over in one fell swoop and there is no hybrid system for us to cling to. (A hybrid system is where half the applications are on the new system and half are on the old.) Another advantage is that the money comes out of one financial year. The biggest disadvantage is staff reaction to sudden change. Many librarians have built whole departments around the way existing library systems work. Big bang has implications for time-scales and data conversions. There will be a great deal of pressure on the supplier to get the conversion right first time. Performing a data conversion in this scenario would involve freezing the database on the live system. While the database is frozen, libraries are still open for business and would be heavily reliant on their backup systems. It is not desirable to have libraries in backup for any length of time – users often tend to panic and delete data.

The essence of big bang is speed. It is unlikely there will be much time to test converted data, so responsibility lies with the systems librarian to have a clean database free of inconsistencies before conversion and with the supplier to have accurate conversion programs. In this scenario there is no scope for mistakes on either part.

One way of alleviating the problems of staff change would be to negotiate with the system supplier a training machine two months prior to the scheduled migration. If a systems librarian is forced by their institution to go for big bang they should insist that the supplier build a copy of their existing database in-house and run the conversion programs and test them for them. If necessary the systems librarian could draw up a list of test criteria to accept the data conversion. This could be arranged in advance of the migration allowing for mistakes to be corrected.

If the library system has OPAC implemented, remember these indexes will need to be rebuilt. It may be possible to negotiate with the supplier to do this in-house.

2.5.2.2   *Gradual migration*

The term 'gradual migration' conjures up images of moving over to a new system with gentleness and ease. Gradual migration involves moving one module of the system across at a time. This strategy has many benefits to both the supplier and the customer. It enables librarians to bid the cost of migrating a system across two financial years. In some institutions it may be desirable to bid for the money in phases rather than in one large amount. Therefore the cost of a system migration is gently spread, gradually avoiding EC procurement thresholds. However, be sure to evaluate whether the gradual migration costs more in financial terms than migrating the system in one year. Another deciding factor with regard to funding in this way is that the library needs to be absolutely sure that the money to complete the migration will be available for when the institution has promised. Otherwise, the library may find itself with a hybrid system for a number of years.

Gradual migration offers advantages for staff training as only one module is moved at a time. Moving modules in this way has a significant advantage for system suppliers eager to implement new customers and existing customers who may not have implemented all the system modules. The supplier can begin migrating without having written all the necessary conversion programs.

There are resource implications and technical implications for both the supplier and the customer. More support may be required for customers who gradually migrate as the customer has two systems to support. The old system is linked in some way to the new system allowing the flow of data from the old to the new, creating a 'hybrid' system. It is not beyond the realms of possibility that the link between the two machines will fail. Also, the architecture of the machines will be completely different. The old system will be based on proprietary architecture and the new on open systems architecture; both will be running on two completely different operating systems and hardware platforms. Hence, operations staff will need to support two machines. If the link fails, two library systems are down instead of one.

There are disadvantages with regard to staff training. Staff may not fully understand which system they are connected to and which modules reside on which system. In 1992, Coventry University went live with LIBS100plus. The acquisitions module remained on a separate UNIX box, together with the old system. The rest of the library went live with circulation, cataloguing, and OPAC on the new system. Staff were very confused in the early days of the system going live with the two systems running side by side. The Coventry scenario was an interesting migration strategy as the system was not a true 'hybrid' system as there was no flow of data between systems.

2.5.2.3 *Gentle approach*
Gentle migration offers a gentle approach to migrating the system. It involves purchasing the central site hardware and a number of peripherals eight to twelve months before scheduling to 'go live'. The reason for doing this is to build a training system in the library. The new database can be built well before schedule, giving the systems librarian and the supplier the opportunity to test the data conversion. It also gives library staff the opportunity to familiarize themselves with the new system. This approach allows the systems

librarian enough time to perform contractual acceptance tests, iron out functionality problems with the supplier, and check that the system parameters work in the way the documentation says they should work. This approach is costly in terms of financial resources as money is spread across two financial years. Gentle migration is also costly in terms of resources, as library operations staff will be supporting two systems in parallel.

2.5.3 *Post-implementation support*

Post-implementation support is offered after the system has migrated and 'gone live'. It varies from supplier to supplier but should include most of the following:

- help desk support
- software bug fixes
- software development
- implementation support for new modules in the form of on-site project management
- installation support in the form of software consultants to load new releases of operating and applications software
- central site hardware support
- peripheral support
- up-to-date documentation for various modules
- customer training

CONCLUSION

Changes in the computer industry are forcing system librarians to acquire new skill sets. Greater technical knowledge of networking, central site hardware and operating systems are being demanded by employers. Suddenly, systems librarians are having to become all things to all men – contracts expert, EC threshold expert, and systems expert to name but three. Traditionally, systems librarians have been librarians who have drifted into systems. With the move towards open distributed systems, greater systems knowledge is required. Systems librarians can only gain technical skills by their employing institution investing in them. We may see a move away from the systems librarian having divided loyalties, for instance managing bibliographic services and the system. Only by training and keeping up with the technical developments in the computer industry will the systems librarian be able to cope with the issue of system migration and the future! Without employers investing in the skills of the systems librarian, ultimately we will be 'choosing in the dark' when it comes to system replacement.

REFERENCE

1 Heseltine, R., 'Choosing in the dark', *ITs news*, **27**, May 1993, 13–18.

Appendix: Evaluative questionnaire

LIBRARY RESOURCES EXHIBITION SYSTEM SUPPLIERS QUESTIONNAIRE

SUPPLIER:

PRODUCT:

1.0 GENERAL
Number of UK installations
Smallest UK installation (terminals)
Largest UK installation (terminals)
Number of European installations
Smallest European installation (terminals)
Largest European installation (terminals)
Number of US installations
Smallest US installation (terminals)
Largest US installation (terminals)

2.0 HARDWARE
Preferred hardware platform
Hardware platforms supported
Future hardware platforms planned for migrations

3.0 OPERATING SYSTEMS
Operating systems supported
Versions of UNIX supported

4.0 RELATIONAL DATABASES SUPPORTED
Which RDBMS supported
Version

5.0 MIGRATIONS
Number of UK system migrations
Number of US system migrations
Number of European system migrations
Estimated time to migrate a system with 300,000 titles

6.0 COMMUNICATION PROTOCOLS
Does the system support Z39.50?
Could you explain what you think Z39.50 means?

7.0 OPERATIONS SIZE
Size of Development Team
Size of Implementations Team
Size of Project Management Team
Size of Help Desk

8.0 APPLICATIONS – OPAC
Average speed to index a database of 300,000 titles
Support of multiple catalogues
JANET access

9.0 APPLICATIONS – Acquisitions
Support of EDI
Fund account management
Year end reporting facilities

10.0 MIS
Are Management Information Statistics available?
Does the system have the ability to download statistics to spreadsheets?

11.0 MARC
Cataloguing demonstration
Ability to download bibliographic records
Plans to download bibliographic records electronically from book suppliers

12.0 COSTINGS
Average cost of 130 terminal system
Annual software charges based on a system of this size
Central site hardware maintenance charges based on a system of this size
Peripheral charges based on a system of this size.

5 The quest for the Son of Deep Thought

❖ *Michael R. Schuyler*

Cardboard boxes are piled high near my desk in a remote corner of the Central Library. Inside are parts for the new computer system – cables, cartridges, CRTs of all sorts. There are several new microcomputers still in their boxes awaiting configuration. On tables nearby are old and dirty terminals ready to replace the next failure somewhere in the system. Yellow Post-It notes are glued to the screens: 'May work locally', 'Screen scrolls when warm', and 'Use as a last resort'. A toolbox sits open on a chair to reveal esoteric looking pliers and wrenches along with a volt/ohm meter and a pile of wire and connectors. An open box of network interface cards is on the floor beside the chair. Various circuit cards and hard disks are piled into the next box over. A poster tacked on the end of a nearby bookshelf reads, 'Dynix tames Wilde's Irish rows'.

Life has come full circle. When Deep Thought rolled through the door of the newly created computer room ten years ago I had no idea what we were in for. Far larger than my coveted Apple, the new minicomputer included three massive 300 Mb disk drives the size of washing machines, connections in the back for dozens of terminals, and a huge reel-to-reel tape drive that made any cassette player look like a toy. When the computer started up it sounded like the Enterprise reaching warp speed. A five-ton air conditioner swept the massive waves of heat away through the roof. Rows of red lights blinked an esoteric pattern hinting at feverish activity deep within.

As we began to learn about this new machine we discovered he used programming languages such as ZOPL, Ugli, HUGO, and Glug, not exactly household words like BASIC and Fortran, not that we had any familiarity with those, either, but at least we'd heard of them. It turns out ZOPL stood for 'Our Programming Language' with a 'Z' in front of it to 'make it sound cool'. 'Zed' meant 'Zee', 'Splat' was an asterisk and 'Bang' was an exclamation point. 'Dyna' was what we now know to be a root directory, the sub-directories continents floating in this worldwide sea; 'And God bless all who sail her' with an ASCII picture of a sailboat (the HMS *Dyna*) greeted us every time we entered this new world.

Without an academic computer department to take away the bliss of our wonder, we in a public library were forced to learn the intricacies of the 'system' ourselves. In fact, this new system behaved suspiciously like DOS. Its batch programming language was very similar, and the directory structure was very much like the smaller micros, wasn't it?

Then one day, early in its life, we had some problems with Deep Thought. He would crash at odd times, then start up again without a hint of the cause. Eventually the Geac corporation flew in an expert who refused to work on our machine unless we allowed him to smoke in the computer room. After we reluctantly agreed he proceeded to wrap the cables of the processor with aluminum foil. After each failure he would hit our big, red panic switch to halt the machine.

Still cowed by the big machine I suddenly realized he was treating it like I treated my Apple. He had developed 'creative contempt' for the machinery. It was as if a weight was lifted from my shoulders. I had the clue that would help me overcome my feelings of inadequacy before the monster. If I, too, could develop creative contempt, we could use this machine as the tool it was intended to be. I voiced my concern to this expert and told him he treated it like a micro. 'Yeah?' he said. 'The replacement for this thing will *be* a micro!' He told me it would fit on top of one of the disk drives. He told me it would be faster. He told me I could close the door of the computer room and walk away. Then he did.

Ten years later the Son of Deep Thought has just been installed, a RISC processor that would, indeed, fit on top of one of the old disk drives. And in the intervening ten years we went from 25 terminals running a circulation system to over 100 running anything you can think of except track. Rather than a couple of micros, we have 50 or more. We have more CPUs (by far) than people. The computer revolution is over. They won. It took ten years. In the business office ten years ago we had one Apple. It ran Visicalc and an ancient word processor from Australia called 'Zardax', the commands to which I am only now learning to forget. Today, we are very close to a computer on every desk. We're moving to Novell from Lantastic, to Windows from DOS, to open systems from proprietary, and to UNIX from, well, whatever it is: three point something.

Not to dwell too much on the past, but this has been an exciting time, much like it must have been when electricity began sweeping throughout the world, with entrepreneurs inventing yet more gadgets that ran with electrical motors, and farmers awaited rural electrification projects to bring hot water to their newly installed indoor plumbing. People like Nikola Tesla were theorizing about electricity transmitted through the ether, and George Westinghouse was making a fortune.

Although there was indoor plumbing ten years ago, there were no systems librarians. Position announcements did not require networking and CD-ROM experience. Automation meant machines that stamped due dates on three by five cards. We who now call ourselves 'systems librarians', probably grew into the title accidentally, perhaps adrift from the shores of the humanities or social sciences. I know one who nearly flunked mathematics, but had an interest in the trigonometric functions necessary for astrological calculations. It's like the computers were out there all along just waiting to grab us anyway.

Today, a systems librarian not only has to have the requisite library knowledge, but also be an expert (and this is a relative term) in minicomputers, micros, DOS, Windows, applications programs, networking, and data communications. Oh! And don't forget faxing documents from Windows to a fax machine with an Ethernet port, copy machines running DOS 6.0, and translating between cc:Mail and the Internet.

So what's it like being a systems librarian? Busy. But rather than proclaim any more definitions, the easiest way to depict this emerging profession is simply to tell you what we're doing over in my corner and how we fell into it.

That's right. It's not as if this was all planned, really, no matter how many times someone lauds us for our forward thinking. I suspect most large things that happen to us in life are accidents, the result of turning left instead of right.

Take using PCs as terminals, for example. Everyone says this is the smart thing to do these days. Don't buy any more dumb terminals, they say. Dumb terminals are a dead technology. They display only ASCII characters. They don't do Windows. They can't do anything. They are really dumb.

All the terminals on Son of Deep Thought will be smart terminals: all 486 PCs with 4 megabytes of RAM and VGA screens. They'll all hook to an Ethernet hub by level 5 copper twisted pair and be transported between libraries via frame relay technology. We're the first library in the State of Washington (top left corner, about half an inch south of British Columbia) to do this, and, due to my constant running off at the mouth, I suppose, there's a certain amount of attention directed our way at the moment. This may very well be our 15 minutes of fame because it won't take long for the stampede to overrun us.

But there's a minor confession to make about all this; it's all an accident. I guess I can admit to sort of knowing dumb terminals were not a good idea, but I never thought we could afford to do anything other than yet another typical system: dumb terminals running to ports in the back of a CPU. That's what all the systems vendors were proposing to us. They all proposed using Wyse dumb terminals, an oxymoron at the very least, to hook to a character-based software program. When we 'went out to bid' I composed two different requests for proposal (RFP). One was for a library system to replace Deep Thought; the other was for a data communications system. I did this only because I knew some systems vendors made it a habit to ignore data communications. I reasoned that if we liked one of those vendors, we had better be ready with a data communications proposal of our own to merge with whatever our favoured vendor was proposing.

So we set this up so a library vendor could bid on the data communications portion – or not: their choice. Then we sent the data communications RFP to many local firms, including lots of folks who set up in their garage with a cheap telephone system and considered themselves data communications experts. They tended to propose microcomputer modems and mysterious multiplexers from firms we'd never heard of. They wondered why we didn't choose them. One of them proposed all the multiplexers, but forgot the modems.

When the proposals came back to us we discovered, much to my surprise, that US West, the huge telephone company that served us since the breakup of AT & T, had proposed an innovative system called 'frame relay'. The *really* interesting thing about all this was that it was not only innovative, it was inexpensive compared to the other proposals. I had been told, and I assumed, that the phone company always bids high. I sent them an RFP as a courtesy.

It was really unfair of me to hit up the vendors in the way that I did. I told them I had no idea what kind of library system I was going to wind up with. I sort of thought it might be UNIX, but I wasn't sure. I suspected they would bid dumb terminals, but I wasn't sure of that either. So please work up a proposal for data communications taking these hardened facts as gospel.

Most vendors had proposed straightforward digital approaches using 56K circuits point-to-point between our Central Library and all nine branches. The cost was substantial, and so were ongoing costs, the monthly tithe to the telephone company that we would pay for the life of the system. But US West said their new frame relay service could be used to reduce ongoing costs. It works especially well with a wide area network concept using routers and hubs on an Ethernet backbone system. And it works very well with PCs. Indeed, lots of companies are moving to frame relay to hook their Novell networks together.

The ongoing costs were reduced because with frame relay, wherever you go, there you are. Cryptic? Perhaps, but they explain it using a cloud metaphor. The idea is that you hook up to a frame relay 'cloud' along with all your sites. Once you do, unlike a traditional analogue or digital approach, there are no distance-sensitive prices. The cost is in the connection to the cloud, and that's all you pay.

Further, the system is set up using 'permanent virtual circuits' that allow you to use as much bandwidth as you need. In our case, branch libraries are connected through 56K links and the Central Library is connected using a T-1 link. (T-1 in North America is 1.544 megabits per second. In Europe, the standard is 2.0 megabits per second.)

This system not only makes it cheaper for us to connect our own sites, but anyone else using frame relay can connect to us via the same cloud, organizations such as the Western Library Network, our bibliographic service provider, other units of local government, or even private organizations. All these scenarios are involved in the scenario discussed below.

But the bottom line is that the frame relay system was based on using smart terminals, PCs instead of dumb terminals. If we did choose to use dumb terminals, we needed 'terminal servers' at each branch location, and terminal servers began to drive the price up.

As far as I can tell, terminal servers are just another magic box that sits between an Ethernet hub and the terminals themselves. They are sold in chunks of 8 or 16 ports each, so if you only have three or four terminals per site, then you 'waste' half or more of the available ports. This means your 'per active port' price goes up.

Indeed, a dumb terminal currently costs about $500. Yes, you can get them more cheaply, but if you do that a typical vendor will balk and say, 'Fine, but unless you buy the whole enchilada from us you don't get the discount'. Since the discount was upwards of $100,000 we figured saving a hundred dollars per terminal was not an especially good idea.

Of course, dumb terminals need terminal servers, and when we figured out how much, on average, a terminal server port would cost us, we discovered it was $500, that magic number again. So that meant each dumb terminal would cost us $1,000 to implement. So we asked, 'How much for a PC that can do the job?'. Answer: $1,000.

Back to the astrological calculations again. Hmm. We can spend $500 plus $500 for ancient technology dumb terminals, or we can spend $1,000 for a state-of-the-art PC hooked to an Ethernet backbone. So we went back to a couple of our favourite vendors and said, 'Figure this out using PCs instead of dumb terminals, and don't forget our discount'.

That's how we got 486 PCs used as terminals on our new system. That's not the entire story, though. Once we had made that decision I was still trying to figure out what made all this work, so I put on a tie that matched my Levis and boarded a ferry to the big city, Seattle. There I met with the telephone gurus who sketched out the frame relay system on a blackboard. They showed me the wonderful network analysis software included with the system and how you could actually view the data coming across the wires, isolate troublespots, and actually see pictures of the remote hardware on a Windows screen.

This was an astounding leap forward for us. We were used to data communications analysis done by looking at the blinking lights on the face of the modems. If the lights went out, we had a problem. In certain rare cases we would hook up a stereo headset to the wires and actually listen to the data transmitted. You can actually tell the speed of the transmission. 9600 sounds a lot different than 2400, and you can even hear the polling of the computer, very much like a sweep of a radar screen. But with this new analysis system, called Optiview, you can see data on a Windows screen. So instead of looking at the red blinking lights, you can see pictures of the red blinking lights in full colour VGA graphics.

This was just a part of the overall frame relay demonstration. I understood that frame relay was cheaper. I understood how the cost of a PC was the same as a dumb terminal, sort of. But I was still having trouble conceptualizing how I could hook this stuff up, since undoubtedly it would be me who had to pull all the cables, strip all the wires, and actually use a little screwdriver to make it all work.

The phone company had proposed using Synoptics brand hubs to hook to the Ethernet system. In a branch library I would take wires from the PCs and hook each one up to a hub. The hub would then hook to a Nile router which would itself hook to a CSU/DSU unit that hooked to a 56K frame relay circuit, and out into the cloud all that data would stream. Each branch would be the same. The hubs were 16 ports each, minimum. There's a certain amount of waste there, but we're also poised for future growth without an entire redesign. At the Central Library the only difference was that the frame relay circuit was a T-1 line coming into T-1 equipment. There was still a 16-port hub sitting there for it all to hook up to.

'Okay,' I said, 'I see how this all hooks together, but how do I get the terminals hooked up to the CPU?' Here was Son of Deep Thought sitting here atop one of the old disk drives sporting all this RISC power, not to mention the entire library system software. Wouldn't I need a rack of ports back there somewhere for the terminals to plug into?

'You just plug it in,' he said.

'Plug what in?' I asked.

'The server,' he said.

'You mean Son of Deep Thought plugs into the hub?'

'Yes,' he said.

'With one wire?'

'Well, one cable. But, yes.'

'But I've got 16 plug-ins.'

'Right.'

'So what do I do with all those extra ports on the hub?'

'Anything you want,' he said.

'Like all the PCs in the central building?'

'Sure,' he said. 'Any PC you want.'

'Even the Novell PCs?'

'Yes!' he said. 'I think you're getting it.'

Yes, it's a different way of looking at things. Compared to the old way of ports and terminals, it's a paradigm shift in data processing. Sun Micro Systems has a saying about all this: 'The network *is* the computer.' Not only could we plug in the UNIX terminals-which-are-PCs, we could also plug in all the PCs on our network to the same Ethernet backbone running on the same wires as everything else. This means our network software could govern access for every computer in the library, not just those remote to the central facility. It means the PCs running Novell's IPX transmission protocol could run on the same wires as TCP/IP and the UNIX system. Thus, in spite of ourselves, we're winding up with an interconnected computing plant for the entire library system. And, no, we have no intention of using OSI, even if it comes free with the package.

I don't pretend frame relay is the final answer in data communications for us. It clearly won't do well transmitting video images. That may be left to a future cell relay technology called 'ATM' (Asynchronous Transfer Mode), and right now we won't go faster externally than our 56K and T-1 links, and internally at 10 Mbps. But at least the wires are ready for an exponential increase in speed (that's what level 5 copper will do for you), so I may never have to rewire the buildings again, I hope.

All this potential speed is nice to talk about, but what will be speeding, what kind of data will we be transmitting? I suspect and trust much of the data will be bar-codes spewing back and forth. We want the data to travel so fast that we never hear the words 'response time' in the same breath again. Right now, in the afternoons when all libraries are open, the response time is so slow that patron cards will time out before the first response returns to the terminal.

But that's all internal data. High on the agenda for us are external sources for data. Parallel to our search for a new data communications system and a new library system vendor we were also looking for an Internet feed. Around here a public library on the Internet is still a rarity. Academic institutions, big government, and large corporations all have Internet feeds, but public libraries have not until recently even had the opportunity to apply to this exclusive club.

Even to find out where to get an Internet feed is an exercise in determination. The basic Internet system works off a backbone run by the National Science Foundation. This organization has contracted with an IBM/MCI consortium called Advanced Network Services (ANS) to run the backbone. ANS then provides an Internet feed to more regional consortiums, such as NorthwestNet, which provides services to regional academic institutions. Any of these groups can resell Internet feeds.

NorthwestNet will provide a 56K feed to us for a mere $25,000 for the first year, then $15,000 every year thereafter. The start-up fee includes a router and other costs associated with getting us going. ANS will provide us with a 56K feed for $15,500 per year, and that's all. The difference between the two appears to be that with NorthwestNet you're eligible to attend a three-day conference once per year, and they say they'll help you out. With ANS, they hook you up, you get a connection, and you're expected to figure it out from there.

Our basic idea is to connect to the Internet and provide Internet accounts to the citizens in our service area. But we soon found out that it was unwise to proclaim this intention too openly. That's because those wise in the ways of the Internet are not anxious to have this collegial institution invaded by hordes of unsophisticated users. We've also been accused of attempting to circumvent private enterprise and its right to make money off the Internet.

Our attitude is that the unsophisticated users are the ones that actually paid for this national data highway and have a right to access. The data highway is like a national motorway system. Would we allow the government to erect a motorway system without any entrance ramps, then allow private enterprise to build the entrance ramps, complete with toll booths? Unlikely. It's the same with the Internet. The public paid for it; the public deserves free entrance ramps so everyone can use the product with equal ease.

ANS didn't seem to care too much one way or the other as long as they got their $15,500 per year. NorthwestNet was a little more inclined to suggest regulated access. But then I got a call from Clay Burrows down at the Western Library Network (WLN).

WLN is our local bibliographic utility, a public non-profit making corporation, which is a relative rarity. The North West is the only area of the country not completely dominated by OCLC for bibliographic records and interloan services. Our library, Kitsap Regional, is one of the founding seven members of the network, since grown to encompass hundreds of libraries. WLN has a number of products, including one of the world's first CD-ROM products, dubbed 'Lasercat', a set of disks depicting the holdings records of WLN participating libraries. WLN also includes an acquisitions system and a number of other products.

WLN also sees the handwriting on the wall. It's very much mainframe and central system based in its older products. It must branch out into other areas to survive.

'I hear you guys are going frame relay,' said Clay.

'That's right,' I said. 'It'll save us about seven thousand a year compared to straight digital.'

'We're on frame relay, too,' he said.

'Let's hook up,' I said, and so did he.

The advantages are several. First, hooking up via frame relay will instantly drop normal line charges we currently pay to WLN for terminal access. Secondly, a vast array of options will now be before us. One is full-text access to periodical information, such as that offered by Information Access Corporation, rather than restrict ourselves to a few CD-ROM units in the libraries. This means we will be able to hook up to the databases via the Internet and obtain access directly. Considering the immense popularity of these services with the public, we were anxious to provide access at all branches and all terminals, rather than just a few standalone devices.

'Where are you getting your Internet feed,' asked Clay. I told him I was pretty frustrated with the whole ordeal and that it looked expensive no matter where I turned.

'How about $500 per month?' he asked.

Magic number. I thought that was a fine deal. A feed through WLN would be a little over a third of what we were expecting to pay originally. I hadn't realized how good a deal it was until Patty Lewis, our US West contact, also stopped by for a visit.

'I hear you're wanting to hook to the Internet,' she said.

Indeed we were. I told her about the Internet advantages, including the full-text periodical information, and the fact that we could create a 'virtual' WLN terminal at any of our PCs. I told her of our plans to get full Internet connections for staff and perhaps even the public.

'Will your traffic be 10% Internet if you add it all up?' I thought that it would easily be that.

'Then you qualify for FCC tariff rates on your entire frame relay system,' she announced. This is in contrast to the intra-state tariff rates, which are much higher. And how much would we save compared to the regular rates? 'About $500 per month,' she said.

The FCC is the Federal Communications Commission, whose governance applies between state lines. If you're within the state, local regulators have jurisdiction, but once you leave the state with your network, the FCC takes over, in this case with cheaper rates that extend not just to the traffic which crosses state lines, but to every component of a network that is connected to the system. Looks like we outsmarted ourselves again – accidentally. None of this was planned.

This all rather begs the question of what the role of a public library ought to be. Here we are talking about Internet connections and all this high-tech stuff to spend money on. Meanwhile, we're busier than ever checking out books, and lots of video tapes, to many people who don't even have the foggiest notion of what the Internet is. Already, some of our own staff are wondering aloud why we're spending so much money on computers. Well, it just isn't so.

I looked up the budgets for the last ten years. It looks bad only when you look at the one-year periods where we shell out for a new system, but when you spread it all out over a decade, including capital costs and maintenance items, the total spent comes to about 3% of our budget. I hardly call that concentrating on technology. Yet we know from experience that once we install computers for public use, the few complaints are drowned out by the clicking of keyboards throughout the county. Those saying no tend to be people within the organizations who try to protect the public from this onslaught.

I've worried about this myself. Several years ago our vendor stopped making the wonderfully simple keyboards for their public access catalogue terminals. All they had were the typical QWERTY keyboard and a big, red SEND button. It was hard to miss. The new terminals were generic dumb terminals made for the minicomputer market. They had 16 function keys across the top plus several dozen strangely labelled keys with no apparent function. I was forced to install several, and I did so cringing. But, not one complaint, ever.

The fact is, our public is ahead of us. Consider: a student in college gets an Internet account and has a computer in the dormitory room. He graduates, moves out into the world, and loses his Internet access. Unless he has it at his place of employment, accounts are expensive and still problematical to obtain. He comes to the public library asking for Internet access, and we don't even have it for ourselves. This person doesn't want us in the way; he just wants to hook up. Can we justifiably deny this person access to the 'information highway'? And if we won't give him access, where will he go?

Compuserve has a couple of advertisements reflecting the reality of the market-place. One has people valiantly trying to enter an old-style public library. They are knocking on the door, crawling on the roof, parachuting from the sky. The caption reads: 'Ever try to get into your library at 3:00 am? Come to Compuserve.' The second has a prissy looking Mrs Wiggins, hair in a bun, staring over bifocals at the information desk, daring someone to ask a question. 'Sometimes it's easier to ask a machine', says the caption. That's one we have glued to the computer room door next to our 'No Whining' sign and the one that says 'You want it when???'

This is the competition talking. When it's easier to ask a machine, and when distance is no longer a barrier, the local public library will not be in a position to ask for more tax dollars to run an outdated institution. It doesn't matter that we can check out thousands of mysteries and science fiction books to people who still want them, or who can buy the same paperbacks at the grocery store.

That's why we're attempting to position ourselves right in the middle of the information revolution. And how we're doing it is a little basic community outreach. We've contacted all the local service organizations such as community theatre groups, chambers of commerce, and other local government. And what we've said is this:

'We're getting this new computer, and we want to help you with your information needs. We'll give you space on the new machine to store all your information. We're especially interested in community calendars, directories, land use planning documents, and city council meeting minutes and agendas. We're interested in anything that is of interest to the public and that will help our local economy. If you'd like to use our computer, we'll give you special access and make sure our citizens have access throughout the county. Further, we can hook up to you and provide your organization with the full range of library services, including full-text business information, census data, and other information you need to do your job.'

How do we hook up? Through frame relay when that's appropriate, through the Internet when that works (as a telnet session), through more conventional permanent hook-ups, and through dial-in lines and modems. We also have a hundred or so public access computer terminals strategically located at every branch library in the county, and anyone can come in and use them.

This last is a crucial point for it answers an oft-heard criticism of computers and dial-in access. Every time I mention dial-in access I hear, 'What about people who don't have computers?' Though often said in an accusatory manner, it's a valid point.

In the USA according to the latest surveys, computers are in 30% of all households nationwide. As you might expect, computer ownership rises with income so that a typical middle-class enclave might enjoy a 50% rate. Modem ownership is from 25–50% of computer ownership and rising fast as modems have become so inexpensive.

Is this enough to justify dial-in access? It depends on your point of view. From one perspective this is well less than half the population; we can't forget the majority. On the other hand, a small percentage of VCR ownership didn't stop video tape publishers from flooding the market-place. As it turned out VCR ownership exploded and today it has reached saturation: everyone has one. I've heard statistics that indicate there are more VCRs than telephones.

Nevertheless, how do you answer the criticism? In my view, quite easily. The public library is ideally suited for this sort of activity. With ten branches strategically located in every urban growth area designated by strategic planning documents, the library has free access to buildings with many terminals available for access. Anyone in the county can have access to the same online information as a person with a computer at home. You might not be able to get into the library at 3 a.m., but no one else even pretends to provide free public access to an equivalent system.

Further, online access is important not just for public access, but for access by the information providers themselves. By allowing special access for information providers we are allowing them to place their own data online (and be responsible for it) and also allowing them to find data to transmit to their own clientele who may not have as direct access. The advantages of hooking to the library are many. First, we provide the management of the computing facility. We also provide training on how to input and format data. And we provide access in the ways mentioned above. We've already seen one of the local cities try and fail to put up a local bulletin board system – twice! And we know other government units are grappling with the same problems. How do we provide access to the public? By letting the library help. Why? Because that's our job.

Already we've had some very good reaction. The local newspaper came to us and suggested we place their entire newspaper online, including such things as classified advertisements, keyword searchable. Thinking of the heavy resource hit I politely declined and suggested the newspaper might want to control access to its files by placing their newspaper on their own computer, and hooking to us via frame relay. That way they control their own data while we become a conduit for it. That's an example where a permanent connection might benefit both of us. For the Chamber of Commerce, keeping a data file on the library computer would be more appropriate. This is one of the advantages of a wide area network approach. Put the computing power where you need it, put the data where it is accessible. Because the network is the computer, an information server can be anywhere; it is not restricted to a single central location.

The schools also would like to hook up. We've had terminals in the secondary schools for years, but with only one terminal in one location, access was problematical. But a hook via the Internet, or a more permanent and faster one via frame relay, means the library can be a menu appearance on every computer at the school district. Right now one school district has a 386 on every teacher's desk. They do all their attendance, report cards, and electronic mail via a network in every elementary school. Because they have their own wide area network on Ethernet, a frame relay connection means the library can become a menu choice on every one of those computers. If the library is menu choice, so is the newspaper archive, and that means every classroom has immediate access to the largest two information sources around.

In the last few pages we've been using the words 'hook up' with abandon. All you have to do is hook up, as if hooking up is as easy as dialling a telephone or walking through a door. All this is theoretically possible, of course. Many places have already done it. But how do you 'hook up'? We're back to the life of a systems librarian, one minute with a suit and tie talking before the Chamber of Commerce, the next minute in jeans and a T-shirt pulling twisted pair wires through a conduit, attempting to make that last bend somewhere beneath a concrete slab floor, cursing the fellow who pulled the last wire without leaving a pull-string for you to follow. It's a bit of a schizophrenic existence, being a hacker one minute and an administrator the next.

In our request for proposal, the quest for the Son of Deep Thought, I specifically asked for pin-out diagrams. When you say 'hook up', which wire goes where? Where is pin one? Which wire is ground? How many wires do you need, total? It's these small details which can throw you completely when it comes time to actually make this stuff work and carry data properly. Just one example of this happened when we attempted to install frame relay into one our newest buildings.

We were having one of these 'get acquainted' meetings with the phone company where I was the lone library representative surrounded by a dozen phone company staff members. They were laying the groundwork for installing the frame relay system, and since this was a relatively new technology for them as well, they needed to meet each other. That's because the phone company is so huge, with so many different departments, that many of them had never met. They spent 15 minutes exchanging business cards with each other before the meeting actually began.

The conversation eventually meandered to wire availability, and one person from 'engineering' announced we had a problem at the Silverdale site. It seems we had only four wires entering the building.

'Then how come you're charging us for eight?' I asked. As it turns out she really meant four pair. And it was true, at least almost so. We had one telephone line taking up two wires. We had a fax line, also taking up two wires, and we had four wires connecting our older analogue data communications system on the still running, but ancient Deep Thought, Senior. Eight wires, four pair, that's all.

'So we'll need you to dig a trench. We don't do trenches,' she said, all too gleefully for my taste.

Of course, we did have these four wires for the old system, and our telephone company (telco) representative suggested we should 'hot swap' these wires at the very moment we switched from one system to the new one. Our plan had been to run the new system and the old system concurrently, at least for a little while, to allow staff members to become more familiar with the new system prior to cutting off the old one entirely.

You can imagine staff reaction to the 'hot swap' plan. I began thinking I needed to dig a trench for new wires anyway. In looking over the site I discovered the ground was open dirt clear to the street, so it looked like an easy trench. But when I called up engineering, I found out differently. It seems we were in an historical district where all the wiring was underground, so there weren't any nearby telephone poles. Further, the nearest 'point of presence' for the phone company was halfway up the block in the middle of a nice, green lawn owned by the school district. And there was at least one wide sidewalk between the library and that little green wiring box sticking up out of the ground.

'That's all county right of way, so you'll have to dig your trench to the box. Oh, and in the building we need a cold water ground, an isolated electrical outlet, and the appropriate wall space sufficient for a standard backboard. And we'll charge you for all this work. The only other choice is to trench across your own asphalt parking lot.'

'I'm sorry, but all we have is hot water in that building,' I said. But I had noticed a pay phone in front of the building with a conduit sneaking back under the rafters. Obviously, we had five pair, ten wires, into that building, which is a normal residential feed. So I called up the telco again.

'Tell you what,' I said. 'Let's steal the wires from the fax machine for a couple of months. Then we'll also borrow the two wires that hook up the pay phone outside, those other two wires you guys forgot to mention, and that'll give us four wires for the new system. Then when we cut off the old system, we get our fax back and you get your pay phone back. Pretty cool, huh?'

'Well, I'll check into it,' he said. 'But this may be beyond our control.'

Sure enough, a few days later he called back to say the pay phone was actually a gratis phone that didn't make any money, so the phone company left it there in the public interest. They didn't want to disconnect it at all. Sorry, no deal. And why couldn't we hot swap the lines anyway? What was the big deal for half a dozen staff members? Couldn't they learn the system at another library?

By this time I had an idea what those six staff members were going to do to me if they didn't get the system in concurrently. These are the same people who raised an incredible fuss with me, the director, and anyone else who would listen just because I once replaced a terminal with one that didn't have a ten-key numeric pad, thus stifling their manual bar-code entry patterns and making their lives so miserable they were all going to quit.

'Wrong,' I said. 'Those ten wires are our wires, not yours. You stole two wires for a pay phone that makes money. All I want to do is borrow them for two months. Then you can have them back. Thank you.'

Later, Patty told me how her group actually managed to talk the pay phone group out of the two wires. It seems the head of that group used to be on Patty's softball team. Since they were friends (who did hit in that winning run?) the pay phone graciously agreed to let us borrow the wires, and that's how engineering lost the pleasure of seeing us dig a trench underneath asphalt for half a block to their 'point of presence'.

In essence what we are trying to do here between running wires and sparring with the phone company is position ourselves for survival. Already there are quite a few libraries that have been invited to become a part of a computerized public information system. Often they are part of the National Public Telecomputing Network, which is an organization devoted to placing 'free-nets' across the world.

But in each case these libraries are a single-menu choice to a larger system. They have allowed themselves to hook up to someone else's system. I'm sure they feel justified and full of forward thinking in their decision to do so. Indeed, they are a menu choice, and that is good for all of us, citizen and librarian alike.

The difference here is that rather than hook up to someone else's system, we would prefer to be the system and to have other organizations hook up to us. We see ourselves as a primary information provider to the community; it makes sense for us to take on this role. Considering some of the expertise we've observed in some of these other activities, the library may get it by default anyway.

It also makes sense for our survival. For better or worse we are going through an era of retrenchment. Citizens are questioning every tax dollar spent. In many places initiatives are being passed which devastate local government spending. Proposition 13 in California was the most famous, but it was only the beginning of a tide that continues.

The library doesn't take much tax money compared to other areas of spending (it's about 5% of the local property tax bill in our area), but it's visible and lumped in with the rest. As information becomes less and less bound by location, people are finding other ways to find crucial information, sometimes leaving the library as an increasingly quaint and irrelevant institution hopelessly behind the times. In a relatively recent situation where the fire department and the library were unfortunately thrown into competition for the same tax dollar, the fire department placed an advertisement in the local paper: 'Next time your house is on fire, call up the library.'

A push to tl.e centre of the information revolution is central to libraries' survival; for better or worse, the systems librarian is thrown into the middle of this fray. We are often faced with pulling a reluctant institution into the twenty-first century in spite of ourselves, attempting to explain a vision of the future that isn't quite here yet, justifying a budget request before the Board of Trustees for what appears to be another project, and pulling yet another wire, all in the same day.

It's an exciting job.

6 The system vendor's perspective

❖ *Arthur Brady and Sally Ryan*

Over the years, it has become evident that the role of the systems librarian is as vital to the successful implementation of a library system as is that of the system supplier, and is pivotal to successful operation of the system thereafter. The first part of this chapter will outline what the supplier sees as the systems librarian's role, with particular focus on how it has changed in the past few years and continues to change now, as well as the characteristics of the 'ideal' systems librarian from at least this supplier's point of view. The second part will report and comment on a survey of former systems librarians who are presently working or have worked at Dynix, giving their views on the systems librarian role as well as on the transferability of skills between that role and working for a supplier.

Dynix Library Systems has been a supplier of automated library systems since 1983. With over 2,000 systems installed worldwide in 27 countries we believe that we have a great deal of experience in all aspects of library automation. This chapter will refer mainly to experience in the USA, Canada, and UK since that is the authors' principal sphere of knowledge. With a combined total of nearly a quarter of a century of direct involvement with library automation, working for both libraries and suppliers, the authors welcome this opportunity to convey impressions and opinions on what is certainly one of the most critical decisions a library makes in preparation for the implementation process and for ongoing system operations. A library's ultimate success with automation is inextricably linked to the systems librarian's commitment, preparation, professionalism, patience, and capacity to stay focused on the goal in the midst of the storm.

1 THE 'IDEAL' SYSTEMS LIBRARIAN

In the USA, Canada, and the UK, the responsibilities and tasks that make up the role of an individual systems librarian looking after a Dynix system are as varied as the libraries they work in. In addition to the obvious variables like size (200 users in one building versus 10 users in five buildings), type (academic versus public versus special, etc.), or experience (first-time automators versus third-generation system implementors), there are less obvious, but equally relevant, variables which in large measure shape the role and duties of the systems librarian.

For example, in the case of system backups, in some libraries the systems librarian who may also be the college librarian will physically do the file-save as well as organize the tape rota. In others, the systems librarian will ensure that the backups are done but delegate the task to an assistant. In the case of larger systems, the IT department or the facilities maintenance company may take on the task, either following procedures set out by the systems librarian or undertaking to provide a complete service with little involvement from the libraries department who only need to know that backups are being taken care of.

Another common example is the degree of networking present in the institution, and to what degree the systems librarian has responsibility for it. At one end of the spectrum, the network consists of simple ASCII terminal connections to terminal servers or serial cards on the host. At some mid-point, the network may consist of point-to-point multiplexer pairs from branches to the CPU site. At the opposite end of the spectrum (and here is where the two-dimensional spectrum model breaks down quickly), the network may consist of a variety of LANs connected over a variety of WANs providing access to a broad set of local and remote hosts and services.

It could therefore be seen as difficult, if not impossible, to define the ideal systems librarian from the supplier's point of view in terms of their role. However, broad areas of responsibility can be defined and since the characteristics of the ideal systems librarian are an integral part of the work that they do, the following discussion also covers both the role of the systems librarian and these characteristics. It has been divided into *before*, *during* and *after* an installation since different responsibilities and personal qualities are seen to be linked with these different stages. It should be emphasized that, even where not explicitly stated, the views given below are always that of the supplier.

1.1   Before the installation
In the vast majority of automation projects these authors have experienced, in calendar days at least, far more time is spent getting ready to automate than is actually spent in the process itself. From building the case to automate, to gathering the necessary data from which to create specifications, to the drafting, redrafting, re-redrafting (you get the point!), and issuance of the specifications, to the selection process, to contract negotiation, to pre-installation activities, to the start of the actual implementation, the process is measured in years. Our own studies show that the average 'buy cycle' exceeds 18 months,

and that clock only starts once we are invited to participate in the library's investigation. One consistent predictor of success of the automation project is how influential the systems librarian has been throughout this early process.

There certainly are examples of successful automation projects wherein the libraries reached the contract signing stage before appointing or hiring a systems librarian. These are the exception, however, and almost always result in some combination of extra time consumed in bringing the new appointee up to speed, and extra work for all parties involved in reconfirming or modifying decisions reached at various stages in the specification, selection, and contracting processes. When the systems librarian has taken the lead in these processes, which thankfully is more and more common, there is a continuity and a 'buy in' which allows events to proceed more smoothly than would otherwise be likely.

Again, aside from the obvious benefits of continuity and early agreement on the project's basic objectives and premises, a systems librarian appointed at the beginning of these key processes enjoys other benefits which flow directly to the success of the project. For one, a sharp systems librarian will seize the opportunity to observe carefully how staff react and contribute to the specification and evaluation processes, and thus to identify and classify specific staff and staff types with respect to training requirements, the development of decision-making procedures, and the possible need for attitude adjustment/enhancement efforts. Put more candidly, this is the best time for the systems librarian to identify who among staff will be assets and who liabilities at crunch time. Another of the less obvious advantages of early involvement of the systems librarian goes directly to the question of client expectations. Our experience – as well as common sense – suggests strongly that a customer with clearly defined, measurable expectations is likely to be a happy Dynix client. The early stages of project planning present the best opportunity for the systems librarian to: (1) get library staff and administration to understand the criticality of forming 'reasonable' (not to be confused with 'moderate') expectations, clearly defined and readily measured; and (2) develop formal as well as informal channels for communicating with them as to how closely the project is approaching those expectations. When this assessment role is left until the project goes live, or worse, left unaddressed altogether, the prospects for a successful implementation are greatly diminished.

As suggested above, the typical library spends far more time getting ready to automate – or to replace one automation system with another – than in actual automation implementation. To the extent that the systems librarian is in place and driving the pre-purchase, pre-installation processes, the tone and personality of the entire experience are improved. In this fashion many of the traditional 'people' challenges in projects of this magnitude and complexity can be predicted, planned for, and minimized, if not avoided altogether.

1.2   During the installation

Implementing a new library system, whether replacing an old system or automating for the first time, is a stressful situation. Dynix try to make it easier by providing experienced project managers as well as professional training and consultancy services, but there are a number of areas where the supplier cannot venture, and it is here that the role of the systems librarian comes to the fore.

1.2.1   *System responsibility*

One of the most important characteristics of a good systems librarian from the supplier's point of view is the ability to take responsibility for the new system and the decisions that will be necessary as part of the installation. In our experience systems librarians' ability to take such responsibility will be determined to a large extent by their position within the hierarchy of the organization and the support given to them by those in charge of the service as a whole as well as by their individual personal characteristics.

Unlike many other posts in libraries, that of systems librarian does not appear to fit easily into the overall management structure. In a small college library the post is often combined with that of college librarian. In this case the person who will be running the system will also have pushed to secure the funds for automation and has a vested interest in its success. In larger systems the systems librarian may have no staff but a direct reporting line to the chief of the library service or his or her deputy. This arrangement works as long as senior management are wholly behind automation. In the past, we have seen problems arise when the head of the library service has appeared unwilling to involve him or herself in the automation project or has ignored the advice of the systems librarian and the supplier with resulting problems for the implementation. Training of all staff, for example, is critical to the acceptance of a new system as well as its successful use after the live date. This means that the head of the library service needs to ensure that all library managers are both willing and able to release their staff for the training course which may take them away from their normal duties for one or two days at a time. The systems librarian is not usually in a position to be able to take such decisions in isolation.

While the systems librarian may report directly to the head of library service, this does not necessarily mean that he or she will be empowered to have the final say in all system decisions. Evidently a systems librarian has to seek the views of other users, and the chief cataloguer, for example, will often be responsible for signoff on the data-load specification or the library's MARC requirements. Where such delegation has been agreed this works very well as long as both the systems librarian and the supplier are kept informed of progress. Complications can arise when library departments are in conflict with each other or indeed when individuals within the same department do not agree with each other. The systems librarian's role here will be very much one of conciliation and arbitration but, again, s/he must have the backing of the head of service to enable him or her to take a decision that may be unpopular with one group of staff. If not, then decisions are often delayed indefinitely making progress on the project slower than both parties might wish.

The ability of systems librarians to make decisions may also be compromised by the amount of time they can spend on the task. Often they have had the title of systems librarian added to their existing job with no account taken of the amount of time required. A systems librarian survey carried out by Dynix Inc. in December 1990 and reported in *Dynix dataline* showed that nearly 75% of respondents saw their systems librarian role as part-time.[1] In the same article, Joanna Tousley-Escalante (Head Librarian for Technical Services and Automation at Austin Community College in Austin, Texas) stated that: 'All too often it appears that library directors decide that a manager (usually Head of Technical Services) can assume the new and additional duties of System Administrator. . . . I've not met one who had a reduction in existing scope of responsibilities.' Where these other responsibilities are heavy, the time that can be allocated to implementing the system can be severely reduced and this can lead to project delays. At Dynix, we are very aware of the pressures that such systems librarians can be under as well as the financial pressures on the library service as a whole which may result in posts being combined. However we do prefer that, where possible, the postholder be seconded full-time to the project, at least during those crucial early months.

1.2.2 One point of contact

We have referred so far to the 'systems librarian'. Occasionally a library service may decide to share the role among several staff with no one person being given overall responsibility. This may be owing to internal political reasons or, simply that, as above, no one person has the time to devote solely to the task. For the supplier, this is one of the most difficult situations to work with since it can be unclear where responsibilities lie and who knows what. This can lead to confused communications with the supplier caught in the middle. It can also lead to similar problems internally.

As a supplier, then, Dynix's preference, is for a 'one point of contact' systems librarian who has a recognized position within the library's management structure and is empowered to give final decisions on all aspects of the installation.

1.2.3   *Organizational ability*

The systems librarian should not only be personally well organized but also able to organize others. Installing a system requires good project planning and management skills from the systems librarian as well as the supplier. The supplier will usually take on project management of the overall project but, again, there are areas where they can only be involved in an advisory capacity. Examples of this are third-party suppliers (often another internal department) and planning for equipment delivery. Like other suppliers, for example, Dynix will arrange cabling for a library service but it may be that this is carried out by the internal IT department. In this case, the systems librarian will need to ensure that cabling is completed as required by the project plan and will need to ensure that all parties are kept updated on progress and any change in requirements. In the case of the equipment, the supplier will ensure that terminals and other equipment arrive on time, but the systems librarian needs to ensure that the right number of peripherals are delivered to each area, that they can be accommodated on the counters or desks as planned and that they can be plugged in. As stated by Duval and Main, 'ultimate success of the automated library system depends on the time, effort and informed decision-making that goes into the planning process. The project manager must be a skillful planner and problem solver who is capable of overseeing the dynamics of the project'.[2] Good systems librarians know that taking responsibility for their system includes good planning as a prerequisite for the project's success.

1.2.4   *Communication skills*

It is vital that the systems librarian has good communication skills since liaison and negotiation both internally and externally will be a major part of their role.

1.2.4.1   *Internal communications*

Implementing any new system whether into a greenfield site or the second or third time around is a major change for all staff, not just those most closely involved with the supplier. The systems librarian needs not only to keep all staff informed of progress but also to negotiate with section heads on many issues, including positioning of new equipment, shutting the service point, and releasing staff for training. S/he also needs to keep managers in touch with the project as well as ensuring their support for more unpopular decisions. In such a situation, tact and diplomacy as well as good negotiation skills are just as important as the ability to organize. While the supplier aims to give the systems librarian the support needed to implement the system, the supplier often does not meet other library staff at all or, if they do so, for no more than the length of a training session. To a large extent, therefore, the supplier is dependent on the systems librarian's communication and diplomacy skills for ensuring that library staff view automation as a positive step forward.

1.2.4.2 *External communications*
The systems librarian will also have to maintain good relationships with all suppliers external to the library. These may include, for example, the organization's computer department, the telecommunications company, and the barcode supplier. It will also include the automation supplier.

The supplier's relationship with both the library service in general and the systems librarian in particular should be one of partnership. Both parties are, after all, working towards a common goal, that of the successful implementation of a new automated system. From a vendor's point of view, the systems librarian needs to understand the library's requirements well enough to be able to communicate these in a clear and unambiguous manner. If the systems librarian is not clear when the library wants to go live on a particular module, then the supplier also finds it difficult to proceed. It is also important that the systems librarian lets the supplier know of any perceived problems before a problem becomes a crisis. In other words, while the supplier must communicate regularly and clearly, so must the client via the systems librarian.

1.2.4.3 *Systems librarian as intermediary*
The systems librarian will need to act as an intermediary between the supplier and other library staff. This will mean not only communicating library staff's needs to the supplier but also relaying the supplier's response to library staff in language that will be understood. From the supplier's viewpoint it is important that the systems librarian is able to do this well since s/he is often the supplier's only means of communicating with library staff.

1.2.5 *Library knowledge*
In order to be able to communicate with the vendor, it is essential that the systems librarian has a good working knowledge of all departments within the library. For example, if the catalogue is MARC-based, the systems librarian does not have to be a MARC expert, but should understand the concepts behind MARC and how the standard is being applied by the library's cataloguers, and have access to a MARC manual which s/he should preferably have read. S/he will also need to get to know how the new system handles MARC records in order to ensure that the cataloguer's requirements are met as far as possible.

From time to time we have had experience of systems librarians who are only interested in specific modules and do not get involved in the other, equally important modules. This can lead to frustration for both the supplier and the members of the library staff who are using the neglected modules. It is frustrating for the supplier since they are aware that the systems viewpoint is not being communicated to staff and frustrating for library staff since their needs are not being correctly communicated. The two following situations illustrate these issues.

Occasionally, a vendor finds that individual departments within a library want the automated system to work the same way as their previous system or like their manual system. A good systems librarian from the supplier's point of view would be one who was able to see further than current practice and use his or her knowledge of the library's policies and procedures creatively in order to exploit the new system most effectively.

Sometimes the combined requirements of different departments may be incompatible in terms of the system. The supplier may be able to advise on different solutions but ultimately the clients will have to decide for themselves on what will work best for them. The systems librarian should be best placed to understand all parts of the system and how they work together so that they can implement the best solution for all parties, including the library users.

1.2.6 *Training of other staff*

Training of library staff is vital in the successful implementation of a new automation system and it is essential that the systems librarian is aware of this.

The systems librarian is usually expected to carry out the majority of the training as well as organize it. The supplier normally provides training to core staff in larger institutions although in smaller libraries they may train all staff. In both cases, the systems librarian needs to ensure that all members of staff who should receive the training are available on the days set aside and that the training area is ready and, if necessary, booked. We have occasionally arrived on site to discover that staff have not been told of a training course or that inappropriate staff are attending the course.

In larger systems, there may be a number of staff who are already trainers or have been assigned to the project specifically for that purpose. In this case, the systems librarian is still responsible for organizing the training overall and may need his or her full range of negotiating skills to ensure that staff across the system are released for training (although they will need management backing for this as discussed earlier under the section headed 'System responsibility').

Often, systems librarians undertake the majority of training themselves. The supplier can provide consultancy on how to organize cascaded training programmes and what each group of staff need to know but they are reliant on the systems librarian to train successfully so that when the system goes live all staff are confident about using it. Good trainers share several of the characteristics that distinguish good systems librarians (competence in their subject, organizational ability, good communication skills) and indeed, our experience is that many systems librarians are also good trainers.

1.2.7 *Personal qualities*
The personalities of Dynix systems librarians are many and varied. However, the best of them share certain characteristics.

1.2.7.1 *Interest and willingness to learn*
The systems librarians who get the most out of their systems are those who have taken the time and the effort required to learn as much about the system as possible. When the system is first installed, Dynix provides courses on system administration and housekeeping as well as on specific modules. A good systems librarian will attend all the courses provided in order to gain an overview of the system and, often, to decide how s/he will train other members of staff. Frequently, they are also the ones who have already read the manuals before training takes place!

As well as learning the software, the systems librarian will need to become familiar to a certain extent with the hardware. This can include the CPU itself as well as the communications equipment and peripherals. While the supplier can give courses on all these, it will be the systems librarian's task to look after all the equipment on a daily basis and help troubleshoot should the need arise. S/he will also normally be ordering more equipment during the life of the system and need to know how to set it up. Even where the equipment is looked after by an internal IT department, it is still important that the systems librarian is familiar with the kit so that s/he can liaise effectively between library staff, the IT department, and the library supplier.

1.2.7.2 *Ability to cope*
The systems librarian needs to be someone who remains calm and confident in a crisis, albeit only outwardly. When the system goes down two days before you are due to go live because the electricians have suddenly switched off the power without warning or the bearcats you needed to start take-on last week have not yet arrived, calmness is essential. Good systems librarians know that problems are inevitable and concentrate initially on how to resolve them rather than on who or what was to blame. This can be sorted out once the system is back up or the project is back on schedule. The supplier needs to know of the problem as soon as possible in as clear and as concise a manner as possible. They also appreciate a systems librarian who does not take out his or her frustration on the supplier (where the supplier has not caused the problem, of course) as, unfortunately, a minority do.

1.2.7.3   *Flexibility*

During any project there will be times when external factors cause timelines to slip or when concessions have to be made to prevent slippage. Though they are rare, there are systems librarians who find it hard to adapt to such situations and react badly to any deviation from the original plan. As stated above, a good systems librarian needs to be someone who is able to cope with pressure, and ability to handle a change in plan is vital.

1.2.7.4   *Willingness to get involved at all levels*

It is vital that systems librarians be prepared to take on not only the 'clean' planning and training parts of the role, but also the 'dirty' parts to do with peripherals and cabling. In the installation phase of a new system, they need, for example, to be able to set up equipment, such as terminals and bar-code readers as well as to troubleshoot new cabling. When they are supporting the system in the future it will be important that they understand the equipment fully so as to be able to give the supplier as much information as possible on any problems that arise. The only way to gain this knowledge is to set up and test the equipment.

1.2.8   *Conclusion*

The characteristics of the ideal systems librarian in the installation of an automated system from the supplier's point of view are that: s/he takes responsibility for the system and the decisions required to progress the project; that s/he is well organized and good at organizing others; that s/he has good communication skills and is able to negotiate with staff at all levels, as well as the supplier; that s/he knows the library and its procedures well; that s/he is good at training; that s/he is interested in the new system and willing to learn; that s/he is able to cope under stress; and that s/he is adaptable, flexible, and happy to get involved at all levels.

1.3   After an installation

Once an automated system is fully installed, the focus of the systems librarian changes. The skills required in the initial installation are still required but in different ways.

1.3.1   *System responsibility*

Once the initial installation is completed there is occasionally a tendency to assume that the supplier will now take over all support for the system as well as the day-to-day decisions that are required. Systems librarians now working at Dynix were surprised at how some systems librarians appeared to want to abrogate responsibility for their system to their supplier. Suppliers still expect to be involved with the system but see responsibility for running that system as the clients'. The supplier would define responsibility for the system as including ensuring that all housekeeping tasks were done, that problems were reported promptly with all error messages and examples documented, and that some troubleshooting had been done, as well as taking on the task of fully understanding the system and the advantages it could offer to the library service. It should also include reading supplier's literature, such as user manuals and upgrade information as well as attending user groups.

Occasionally, some library authorities determine that a specific systems post is not required. From both the library's and the supplier's point of view, this is a retrograde step since to get the best out of system and supplier someone on the client site needs to take on this responsibility.

1.3.2 *One point of contact*
Ideally, the systems librarian should be the single point of contact with the supplier since there can be a breakdown in communication if the same query is reported by different members of library staff. Occasionally, we have found that the systems librarian tries not to get involved in a particular module, with the result that an overview is not taken, which can cause internal problems at the library.

1.3.3 *Organizational ability*
Organizational ability is still required, from ensuring backups are taken, to logging and tracking queries, to the introduction of a new module with associated training. Disorganized systems librarians are rare but can be difficult for a supplier to work with when they appear to take no notice of recommendations, with resulting problems for the system.

1.3.4 *Communication skills*
These are essential skills in the ongoing relationship with a supplier. The supplier needs to communicate clearly with the client, usually via the systems librarian, but the systems librarian needs to ensure that the supplier understands the client's requirements. Once an answer to a query has been received from the supplier, the systems librarian needs to be able to interpret the response and tell users of the results. The supplier is dependent on the systems librarian to do this well since systems librarians are the ones who combine specific site and technical knowledge.

A former systems librarian now working at Dynix also made the point that systems librarians need to market their services to other library staff to ensure that their users know that they can approach them on all system matters.

Both supplier and systems librarian need to build up a good relationship based on realistic expectations on both sides, as well as a sense of partnership. The old computing adage 'garbage in, garbage out' can also be applied to supplier/client relationships. Again, both sides have to take responsibility for maintaining good relationships.

1.3.5   *Library knowledge*
In the same way that library policies and procedures change over the years to accommodate change, so a good library system should offer added features and enhancements over the life of the system. The systems librarian is best placed to interpret the system implications of both sides of this coin and needs to keep up with changes in the library as well as changes in the system. A former systems librarian working at Dynix described the systems librarian post as being a 'jack-of-all-trades' in terms of knowing how each area of the library works.

1.3.6   *System training*
Although the need for training on a large scale will have passed once the system is installed, ideally, systems librarians should be building ongoing training into their future plans. One of the systems librarians at Dynix said that this was one of the main lessons she had learnt from working with a supplier. Not only will new staff join after the installation date but new features and new modules will need to be explained. Once the system has been installed for a few years, top-up training from the supplier could be considered to ensure that both old and new features are being used and understood.

1.3.7   *Personal qualities*
Asked what they considered to be the most important skills for a systems librarian, several former systems librarians working at Dynix identified common sense and logical thinking as very important, more so than in-depth technical knowledge. As well, all the qualities required during installation – interest in and willingness to learn about the system, flexibility, and an ability to cope – are still required during day-to-day running of the system.

1.3.8   *Conclusion*
The post of the systems librarian changes after installation but is still essential in ensuring that the system is giving the library the service it requires.

2   SYSTEMS LIBRARIANS AT DYNIX
The second part of this chapter will look at whether the skills of the systems librarian are transferable to the world of the automated system supplier. Although librarians are employed in the product and sales departments of

Dynix as well as customer services, the majority of former systems librarians are employed in the latter and this section concentrates on their experiences.

Of the 22 staff employed in October 1993 in the UK and European customer services departments of Dynix UK, half are qualified librarians. Of these, seven are former systems librarians or deputy systems librarians. All these staff were interviewed as well as one former member of staff who had worked with systems both before and after being employed with Dynix. The questionnaire used covered both the interviewees' posts before working with Dynix and their current roles at Dynix. In the case of the former employee, questions covered her former role with Dynix and her new role.

2.1 Roles before joining Dynix

All types of libraries were represented in the survey. Of the eight interviewees, three had previously worked in academic libraries, three in special libraries and two in public libraries. Their average length of service as a systems librarian or deputy systems librarian ranged from ten months to three years. Job titles ranged from Acquisitions Librarian to Systems & Evaluation Coordinator.

As has been discussed earlier in this chapter, our experience is that the post of systems librarian is often added to an already existing role. Of the eight people interviewed, none had been a full-time systems librarian. Typically, they had been involved in either cataloguing or acquisitions or both, in, normally, a supervisory role, and the role of systems librarian had been added to this existing responsibility. In two cases this was known before the role was accepted. The only interviewee who had been able to work on system responsibilities full-time had a part-time post of 20 hours a week and had to put aside the other part of their designated responsibilities until the system was fully installed. For most others, the systems part of their role took up between one-third and half their time, although one reported that during initial systems installation at least 75% of their time was dedicated to systems.

A number of reasons were given for their selection for the role of systems librarian or that of deputy. Not surprisingly the main reasons were either previous experience or that they had shown an interest in systems. When they got involved in the automation project ranged from before the selection process began to after the system had been installed for 20 years. All reported a moderate to good relationship with their supplier. This might have been expected given their later decision to work with a supplier.

Several reasons were given for why interviewees had decided to work for a supplier. All cited an interest in systems and the desire to develop their technical skills. Other reasons ranged from discontent with either the content of their previous post or its lack of potential for personal development or promotion, to a desire to apply skills already acquired in a different environment. Several interviewees saw working for a supplier as an opportunity to change their existing career path. All interviewees found that their status at Dynix and their status in their previous role were too different to compare.

2.2   Roles at Dynix

The staff interviewed ranged from support librarians in both the UK Ongoing Support and New Installations teams through to the European Support Manager. They had worked for Dynix for between six months and seven years with the average length of service being 2.75 years.

2.2.1   *Transferable skills*

Asked what skills gained as a systems librarian had been useful to them in their work at Dynix, four main sets of skills emerged.

2.2.1.1   *Library knowledge*

Most interviewees cited their knowledge of how libraries work generally as well as their own specialist areas of library knowledge as important transferable skills. They used this knowledge in several ways. Firstly it helped them to understand the implications for work-flows and the pressure on library staff if there were problems with the system. In other words, they could relate to the situation from the users' point of view and knew what level of response they would have preferred in that situation. It also helped them to explain the technical aspects of the system in a non-technical way using their shared library experience and the common language of librarianship.

2.2.1.2   *Communication skills*

Whether as systems librarians or deputies all interviewees had found that communication skills gained in their previous posts transferred directly to their new role at Dynix. Clients reporting problems can range from the chief librarian to an operator in the computing department with the degree of technical knowledge being equally varied. Previous systems librarians already used to speaking to people with different levels of technical knowledge in their previous post found it easy to make the transition to talking to clients. Indeed, one interviewee saw the job of a support librarian at Dynix as very similar to that of a systems librarian, with the library staff and users of the latter post being replaced by Dynix clients and staff. As well, most were used to talking library staff through system problem-solving over the telephone, also an important medium of communication between client and supplier. One interviewee said that building relationships with clients was similar to building relationships with library users. Most interviewees had also undertaken training in their previous post which not only helped them communicate with clients when advice on using the system was required but also provided a basis for learning how to train clients on Dynix.

2.2.1.3 Technical skills
As might have been expected, all interviewees considered that their previous knowledge of systems had been advantageous. However, several remarked that it was their general understanding of how a system fitted together (hardware, operating, and application systems) rather than an in-depth knowledge of any particular software or hardware that was important. The three interviewees who had worked on a Dynix site previously, found that they had an obvious advantage when they started since they already knew the system from the user's point of view and this made learning the support side quicker and easier.

2.2.1.4 Other skills
Three interviewees cited project management skills as important both in their previous post and at Dynix. Several interviewees gave experience of troubleshooting and problem-solving as other important skills that they had been able to use.

2.3 Return to libraries
Of the eight interviewees, all but one would consider returning to libraries in the future and all expected to get a better post than before joining Dynix. Interestingly, only half would consider a systems librarian post again, mainly because they would see it as returning to their previous post, rather than as an advancement. This may reflect the lack of homogeneity in the status and salary of the systems librarian and the lack of definition of the role. The former member of staff who had gone back to libraries had, in fact, returned at a higher, more strategic level than her previous systems post which had been combined with other responsibilities, and would not have considered a return otherwise.

In view of the fact that most interviewees would consider returning to libraries, they were asked whether they had learnt any new skills at Dynix and, if yes, if they could identify these. As might have been expected all interviewees cited a considerable increase in their technical skills since working at Dynix. Since this was the reason most gave for joining a supplier, it seems that this expectation has been met. Several staff felt that they had learnt much more about libraries in general since they dealt with all types and sizes of libraries at Dynix, a variety of experience that would be difficult to obtain anywhere other than with a supplier. Most respondents believed that Dynix had allowed them to build on and improve skills that they already had, in particular communication and project management skills. One respondent also remarked that her Dynix experience had honed her time management skills, owing to the importance of meeting client deadlines.

Interviewees were asked what they would do differently if they became a systems librarian again having worked for a supplier. All except one believed that they would feel more empowered to undertake the systems librarian role since they knew far more about what was involved both in introducing automation and in running a system. The one who did not believe that they would do anything differently had a computing qualification and experience of all stages of installing a system from selection to ongoing maintenance and believed that they had run their system well. Having worked for a supplier most interviewees believed that they would feel more confident about what they could and could not expect in terms of service from a future supplier. They would also be more likely to be more demanding in terms of future developments. Overall they would be likely to be more proactive in their relationship with their supplier than before.

They were asked if their view of the supplier/library relationship had changed while at Dynix. The overall impression was that they now understood how a supplier worked and the pressures they were under. One interviewee made the comment that they now knew that neither the supplier nor the library knew everything but that there should be a partnership between the two so that together they could work it out.

2.4   Conclusion

The skills required by systems librarians to do their job well – library knowledge, communication and training skills, troubleshooting and problem-solving – can easily be transferred to the requirements of a post with an automation supplier. Indeed, it could be argued that a combination of both experiences is a good preparation for a senior strategic management role.

REFERENCES

1   Dynix Inc., *Dynix dataline*, **8** (2), March 1991, 4–6.
2   Duval, B. K. and Main, L., *Automated library systems: a librarian's guide and teaching manual*, Westport, Meckler, 1992, 79.

❖ **Part 2**
Alternatives to the systems librarian

7　More by accident than design, or, The rise and rise of a chief cataloguer?

❖ *Angela Warlow*

INTRODUCTION

This chapter gives a personal view of the role of the Systems Librarian/Database Manager at the Manchester Metropolitan University Library formerly known as the Manchester Polytechnic Library. It describes the development of a centralized Technical Services Division where the role of a chief cataloguer is transformed into a post with a dual responsibility for both management of the library housekeeping system and the databases which it supports. It then argues the view that close involvement of this system manager in all areas of the service is fundamental to the success of the library operation.

The somewhat imposing job title referred to above was designated as such in 1986 and was a recognition of the enormous changes that had taken place in the development of this and many other academic library services in the late 1970s and early 1980s with the introduction of large-scale automation and 'new technology'. The development of a Systems Librarian/Database Manager from Chief Cataloguer is probably not unique but is most likely in this instance a product of particular circumstances, personalities and situations as they existed at the time – 'more by accident than design?'

TECHNICAL SERVICES – BACKGROUND AND DEVELOPMENT

A Technical Services Division was set up in January 1974 to coordinate all technical service functions in the newly established Manchester Polytechnic Library. This institution had been formed from three college libraries (two more were added in 1977, a third in April 1983 and the latest in October 1992) each of which operated independent systems. The inheritance then was one of three different acquisitions and ordering systems, catalogues on cards, and, of course, classification. The subsequent mergers each time brought their own systems with them but by then the Technical Services Division was well rehearsed in 'assimilation'. It was felt that to centralize and standardize all technical service functions would make the most efficient use of staff time and resources and provide an environment in which new methods and procedures could be established.

The staffing for the Technical Services Division consisted of a Head of Technical Services who was, and still is, a Joint Deputy Librarian together with Chief Cataloguer, Acquisitions Librarian, Serials Librarian, assistant librarians responsible for cataloguing and classification and library assistants (see Figure 7.1). The assistant librarians spent half of their time involved in Reader Services activities and half in the Technical Services Division doing cataloguing, classification, and subject indexing. This equal division of their time between the two areas of library work underpinned a commitment to ensuring that a consistently high standard of service was offered throughout the steadily expanding library. This type of post tended to attract young, recently qualified staff often entering their first professional jobs.

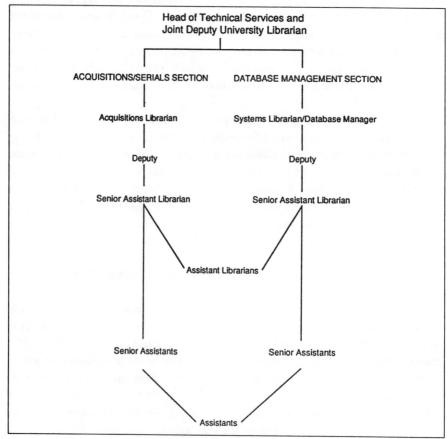

**Fig. 7.1   Manchester Metropolitan University Library
Staffing Structure – Technical Services**

The role of the Chief Cataloguer was to establish a well-ordered flow line through which material would pass in ordered stages from delivery, through accessioning, cataloguing, classifying and processing to completion. Cataloguing and classification became standardized for all libraries. The cataloguing rules chosen were AACR and the classification, DDC18. In both cases British Library interpretation was followed. This use of the national agency as an authority enabled a set of standards to be maintained at all the site libraries and also allowed the consistent training of staff amongst whom there was already a fairly high turnover. Thus the stage was already set for a Database Manager to emerge later.

A first venture into automation by the Technical Services Division concerned the creation and maintenance of a subject index file on the Polytechnic ICL mainframe computer. It seemed most appropriate for this file to be managed by the Chief Cataloguer. Improvements to its design were suggested as experience of its use increased. Basic principles for a database management policy which included standardization of input and quality control to produce a good end-product were being established as a natural process of evolution.

The next area to be automated was cataloguing. A throughput of 25,000 titles per annum and the traditional problems of maintaining a manual card catalogue, with slow production by typewriter and filing times, were exacerbated by a need for a union catalogue in a multi-site organization. In 1975, choices for a library wishing to automate cataloguing were limited but it was decided that the Library would join the Birmingham Libraries Cooperative Mechanization Project which later became known as BLCMP (Library Services) Ltd. One of the reasons for the choice of BLCMP was the Cooperative's intention to develop other computer-based housekeeping routines such as circulation control and an acquisitions and ordering system both of which were areas that the Polytechnic Library wished to automate.

As with the subject index system the role of the Chief Cataloguer was crucial in the selection, implementation and successful management of the BLCMP cataloguing service. Of course at this stage the role was mainly concerned with database management, as the service was still a paper-intensive off-line batch system, but again the subsequent migration of a chief cataloguer to a systems librarian can already be seen in the making. Management of this 'system' included, as a basic requirement, proven skills in easily manipulating 'very large quantities of very large pieces of paper' and then being able to find them again later! Being a batch system the cycle of activities included delays of at least a couple of weeks, often longer, between initiation and completion of the cataloguing process.

In order to maintain some semblance of order in the flow of books, proformas, and computer printout through the department a type of 'production line' was created. Rather than cataloguers dealing with one particular subject area or site, all the material was handled on a strict rotation basis so that within the constraints of the aforementioned delays in a batch system, material received first was catalogued and processed first.

Another hope when the Library joined BLCMP and began to use MARC data was that a high quantity of the material purchased would have both a catalogue record and a classification number generated by somebody else, thus speeding up traffic through Technical Services. This hope is still fostered at Manchester Metropolitan University today, although whether it is achievable is a moot point, owing to variations in the quality of data available from an increasing number of sources. With a 'hit rate' of over 90%, data quality assumes a very high profile in the mind of any database manager.

With the staffing pattern referred to earlier of assistant librarians spending only half of their time in Technical Services and the practice of adhering to cataloguing and classification standards laid down by the national agency, the 'production line' was effective in achieving an efficient service to the Library.

Having established a system for dealing with current acquisitions the next development was towards the creation of a union catalogue. This involved large amounts of retrospective conversion. It was felt that the importance of quickly achieving one unified machine-readable database outweighed most other factors such as quality of records and the use of experienced staff. Thus all means to hand were employed towards this end such as recruiting temporary staff on Manpower Services Commission projects and Job Creation schemes, and using the substandard retrospective data available from the British Library via BLCMP. This may sound at odds with what has been stated already on the subject of quality end-products but in the light of subsequent developments it is still felt to have been the right decision.

The changeover from an off-line to an online cataloguing system, known as BOSS, had taken place by April 1981. The Library had installed five terminals which were connected to a BLCMP satellite minicomputer, itself connected to a 'main centre' computer at BLCMP through which the BLCMP database was accessed. Multiplexors and modems were also required to effect the transmission of data. Suddenly, 'hardware management' had joined database management as a responsibility of the Chief Cataloguer. Admittedly, in comparison with the hardware management of the systems librarians of today it may not have been much, but it was very different from what had gone before!

As well as having to adapt to the vicissitudes that this new hardware brought about, the software was still very much in its infancy and was already in the process of being redesigned. Trying to maintain a steady flow of work through all the changes was no easy task. New skills were being learnt all the time, particularly those relating to patience in the face of great adversity!

Procedures were in place not only for ensuring that standards of data quality remained high but which also allowed work to be easily tracked and if necessary re-created. Many of the principles enshrined in these basic routines and precautions are still practised at the Manchester Metropolitan University Library today – they appear to have stood the test of time. In spite of many frustrations with this early system there was never any question of abandoning it as unworkable. The Library offered BLCMP support and constructive criticism and a belief in the knowledge that they were moving in the right direction. One advantage of early involvement with these systems was that the many problems that arose enabled the staff in the library, particularly the Chief Cataloguer, to gain a very thorough knowledge of both hardware and software and, of course, the data itself. This knowledge was to prove invaluable in the future with the implementation of other systems, especially the standalone circulation control system.

Prior to the arrival and installation of this circulation control system the stock in the library needed preparing by way of being bar-coded. At this point the advantage of already having a complete machine-readable file (even if it also included warts!) was revealed, in so far as it was easy for BLCMP to produce labels from this file in class number order. Specially recruited temporary staff went systematically round the shelves matching up the books with their bar-codes. This project was again managed by the Chief Cataloguer and as expected, many queries and problems within the database brought about by the 'fast and dirty' conversion projects were resolved at this time.

A file of borrower data was keypunched by a bureau from registration proformas filled out by all library users within the year previous to the installation date. The state of this file was unknown until the standalone minicomputer had been installed a few weeks before the start of the autumn term in 1982. Inevitably there were some problems with it but, again, resolving them went towards the learning process involved in operating this totally new system.

It is difficult to imagine, looking back from today's perspective, what might have been expected when this system was planned and installed by the Library. Apart from the obvious problems of learning how to operate this 'machinery' the situation was exacerbated by the fact that the minicomputer had been installed in a totally unsuitable location outside the Library. The 'room' was little more than a cupboard outside the Polytechnic telephone switch room and was almost equidistant from both the Technical Services Division and the main circulation counter. This resulted in a rapid improvement in the fitness of both the Chief Cataloguer and the Circulation Librarian by virtue of regularly having to sprint the 100 metres distance down to the minicomputer to resolve problems and restart the system when it crashed.

At this point the responsibility for the operation of the circulation system was jointly maintained by Technical Services, in the guise of the Chief Cataloguer and Deputy, and Reader Services in the guise of the Circulation Librarian and Deputy. This involved a whole range of activities new to all the staff concerned and included operating the minicomputer, data backup and restore, system parameters, file utilities, learning about operating system software and application system software and, of course, problem solving. Naturally, all of this went alongside 'the day job'!

Although the renaming of Chief Cataloguer to some form of system manager was still a couple of years away, a reappraisal took place of how the Library would continue to implement its computer-based systems in the future. The catalogue file was no longer regarded simply as 'the catalogue' but rather it was seen as a master bibliographic database which could provide for a variety of applications in the future. The file of borrower information which had been created for the circulation system was seen more as a patron file which would do more than enable users to borrow material from the Library. The databases and their management were crucial to the orderly development of computer systems in the Library. Thus it was now acknowledged that it was necessary for the control and maintenance of these databases to be carried out centrally. So the section for which the Chief Cataloguer was responsible became renamed as the Database Management Section.

Technical Services, and more particularly the newly named Database Management Section, had by this time had considerable experience of managing databases and with the earliest versions of BLCMP's CIRCO system this was extremely useful. While the crucial upfront circulation functions for issuing and discharging material on CIRCO were fairly robust, the same could not be said of the software for accessing book and borrower information, and indeed the opportunity to corrupt data unknowingly was always there. This, in conjunction with the staffing policy of recruiting graduates on short-term contracts wishing to gain pre-library school experience as library assistants, made the policy of centrally maintained databases even more necessary. What this entailed as far as the circulation system went, was that no bibliographic or patron data was created or amended at service points. Proformas containing any new or amended data were forwarded to the Database Management Section to be entered into the system by staff who had experience of using the software and knowledge of its dangers. Thus data input was standardized, and quality control ensured that the master databases remained as uncorrupted, accurate, and reliable as possible.

Cataloguing continued using BLCMP's BOSS system although as yet there was still no direct link between this database, still maintained on BLCMP's IBM mainframe computer, and the author/title file used by the circulation system which was maintained on the Library's minicomputer. This latter file was updated on a weekly basis via a magnetic tape of stripped down records from the Library's continuous input to the IBM database. Close monitoring of this interface between the two systems was naturally the responsibility of the Database Management Section and as a result any problems were quickly identified and resolved.

This interface included not only the addition of new material but also the many amendments to the file brought about as a result of movements of stock around the various site libraries. This movement of stock around the system continues unabated in the University to this day as departments and courses seem to be regularly relocated. An adherence to a policy of only amending database records via the well-ordered route of the cataloguing system and its interface with the circulation system has certainly, with hindsight, been shown as most prudent. The temptation to amend circulation files on an *ad hoc* basis at service points has been resisted and as a result all the major stock moves that have taken place have been fairly easily managed as far as changes to the databases have been concerned. Stock has been identified and database records amended by means of machine change rather than thousands of records being individually amended.

The year 1986 brought about the change in job title from Chief Cataloguer to Systems Librarian/Database Manager. Chief Cataloguer no longer adequately represented the work involved in the post, and an acknowledgement of a new range of technical skills, expertise, and responsibilities had been made. One of these responsibilities, and indeed a very crucial one, was management of the Library's minicomputer now known as the System Centre. As referred to previously, operation of the minicomputer had been shared between Technical Services and Reader Services – it now became entirely the responsibility of the Database Management Section. This resulted in a further clarification of the function of the databases stored in the System Centre, and their relationship with one another.

The master files of bibliographic records and patron information were acknowledged to be the responsibility of the Systems Librarian/Database Manager. The subsystem files created from the master files such as issue file, reservation file, interlibrary files (still in the future at this stage), etc. were to be managed on a day-to-day basis by the relevant managers. The Systems Librarian/Database Manager liaised regularly with these managers to ensure that necessary file maintenance such as compressions, backups etc. were carried out as required. This situation still pertains today although there are now more subsystem files to be aware of such as files of orders, funds, serials check-in, etc. The management of the System Centre computer was made considerably easier by a major hardware upgrade and a relocation of the machine itself into an area adjacent to the Technical Services Division. This resulted in a corresponding downturn in the fitness of the Systems Librarian/Database Manager who no longer had to run the 100 metres to resolve a system problem!

The hardware upgrade enabled a quantum leap to be made in the area of systems development within the Library. The new hardware used the Advanced Operating System/Virtual Storage (AOS/VS) which provided a multitasking, multiprocessing environment which allowed modifications to the system parameters, amendments to macros, and so on to take place while the online systems were operational. Previously these activities had had to take place outside of library opening hours thus requiring a high degree of flexibility in the area of library staff hours and conditions. Real improvements to the development of the Library's system could now be made.

The first of these developments was the implementation of an online public access catalogue (OPAC). Here again the strategy referred to earlier of using all available methods to create a union catalogue proved itself to have been a good one. Once this OPAC had been generated, there was no necessity to guide users as to the whereabouts of various ancient card catalogues – everything could be located by using one source. Although the file was generated by BLCMP, its structure and record content was to be as advised by the library staff – in the case of Manchester Polytechnic this was the Systems Librarian/Database Manager. Detailed knowledge of the creation and content of the Library's catalogue file meant that the OPAC that was offered to the users in 1988 was good enough not to require re-creation at a later stage. Even later developments such as the addition of keyword access were thought through and catered for – early involvements with the management of the Library's subject index probably being in part responsible for this.

Following on from this early OPAC, BLCMP's integrated library system, BLS, was installed onto the Library's System Centre in December 1987. This was another highly significant development for the Library although in many ways it was a transparent change. An official recognition had taken place of a development from the use of 'shared' systems like cataloguing and acquisitions to that of a 'local' system like that of circulation control. Shared systems in this context refer to a situation where files are stored in a remote location outside the Library, in this instance on BLCMP's IBM mainframe computer in Birmingham. Editing and updating would be the responsibility of the individual library but storage and security would be the responsibility of BLCMP. Local systems put the files on the Library's own computer thus transferring all responsibility for editing, maintenance, security, and the like from BLCMP to the Library. At this stage the cataloguing and acquisitions functions were indeed still 'shared' but now software was in place for the migration of the local system.

This migration began with the transfer of the Library's order records and associated funds and currency conversion files. Acting in the role of test site for this software development was another useful opportunity for the Systems Librarian/Database Manager to gain knowledge and experience that would prove valuable in the future. This knowledge in the area of database management was transferred to the Acquisitions Department who were to be responsible on a day-to-day basis for their files of orders, funds, and currencies. Responsibility for the hardware and the efficient maintenance of these acquisitions databases lay with the Systems Librarian/Database Manager. In terms of systems development it was necessary for the Systems Librarian/Database Manager to provide the Acquisitions Department with accurate and up-to-date management information to enable, for example, expenditure to be monitored and chasing reports to be provided. These activities require close cooperation and understanding to take place between the Systems Librarian/Database Manager and the subsystem manager – in this instance the Acquisitions Librarian.

This model for the installation and continued operation of the different modules of BLS has been worked out and followed with the implementation of all the other modules. These have included the serials check-in system, inter-library loans, and, the latest addition, a local authority index of name headings.

During all these developments the Systems Librarian/Database Manager has acted in a coordinating capacity between BLCMP and the managers responsible for these subsystems. Presumably, this works to the advantage of both BLCMP and the Library in so far as the new developments are effectively integrated into the whole system. As remarked by Dwyer: 'A library is only as good as the information it provides. A system is only as good as the database it operates upon.'[1] Therefore, effective integration is merely the first step and efficient management of the databases that support these systems must follow.

In order to achieve both efficiency and effectiveness a sound knowledge and understanding of the creation and content of the databases is required. This in turn leads to a sensitivity to the needs of all the users of the system, both library staff and library patrons. An integrated system requires an 'integrated manager' and therefore if this is to be believed, separation of the responsibilities for system management and database management would not seem to be an advantage for the Manchester Metropolitan University Library.

The latest implementations, referred to earlier, of the addition of an authority index of name headings to support the cataloguing function has demonstrated the benefits of this 'dual role' at Manchester Metropolitan University Library. Having volunteered as the test site for this new software, problems with its installation were anticipated and allowed for in the day-to-day organization of the Database Management Section. Indeed, problems did arise but the smooth flow of material and data was maintained, as was an uninterrupted provision of the online services to the public. The nature of the authority control system required a knowledge of cataloguing and cataloguing rules, an understanding of the relationship between the BLCMP IBM database and the Library's own author/title file, OPAC, with its associated indexes, and knowledge of how the cataloguing module functioned in association with the rest of the BLS system. It is felt that the difficulties that were encountered with all of this would have been considerably more difficult to resolve without the 'integrated manager'. A clear view of the day-to-day operation of the system, and the requirements of the Database Management Section and of the Library as a whole, again hopefully allowed constructive criticism and encouragement to assist BLCMP in refining the software for the benefit of all the potential users.

TECHNICAL SERVICES – ORGANIZATION

Technical Services in general have been described as 'one of the more dynamic areas of the library'[2] and although this may not be the view of everyone it does seem to be the case at the Manchester Metropolitan University Library. The evolution of technology and the continually increasing demands placed on the library service make stagnation almost impossible. The organization of both staff and work-flow in the Database Management Section make the section well able to cope with change and extra pressure. The staffing policies in place at Manchester Metropolitan University Library also enable these methods to be successful by the employment of graduates on short-term contracts as library assistants and newly qualified librarians, usually in their first professional posts, as assistant librarians.

Both these groups of staff tend to be enthusiastic, well motivated, willing to learn, and, as might be expected, questioning. The corollary of this is a continual demand for staff training brought about by a high staff turnover. However, this brings with it a constant examination of work methods and practices so it is to be hoped that freshness of vision will always overwhelm stagnation.

The Database Management Section has only three full-time professional members of staff apart from the Systems Librarian/Database Manager. It is this group of four who manage the orderly flow of work through the section and the Library's System Centre computer. This latter responsibility includes all aspects of hardware and software management from routine security backups and the running of overdue notices to database restoration and rebuilding after hardware failure. The hardware and software now operational in the System Centre make many of these tasks fairly easy to manage by being capable of running automatically and without operator intervention. Management of the network which delivers the system to all areas of the University is carried out by the Computing Services Division who work closely with library staff to provide an uninterrupted service.

The other 16 (8 Full-Time Equivalent) assistant librarians spend only half of their time in Technical Services, the other half being in Reader Services areas. It is also worth noting that they work not only in the Database Management Section but also support the Acquisitions and Serials sections of Technical Services. All of this makes for a very flexible staff, sensitive to the needs of the Library as a whole.

Work in Technical Services is organized on a team basis, each team being responsible for creating, updating and maintaining an area connected with one of the Library's databases, for example orders, catalogue, subject index, or circulation. Staff work on all of the teams rather than specializing in a single area, again encouraging flexibility. A sound training programme and well-documented procedures for all teams aim to ensure continuity and consistency. A clear understanding of team objectives is also vital. Day-to-day planning and organization of the work of each team is the sole responsibility of the team leaders. Graduate trainee library assistants are assigned to each team on a daily need basis as indicated by the team leaders themselves. This system gives newly qualified staff a good opportunity to learn much about planning and organizing not only their own work but also the work of staff assigned to their area, and most importantly how to work successfully with others to achieve a set of objectives.

Alongside all of this a concern for quality control and the end-product is emphasized. This is relatively easy to achieve when staff are not only responsible for creating and maintaining the databases but are also users in their capacity as Reader Services librarians assisting 'the public'. As far as the catalogue database is concerned standards of data input are maintained by following cataloguing rules as interpreted by the national agency and used in the production of the British National Bibliography. This is also a requirement of BLCMP for any library contributing to the BLCMP database. The use of the authority index of name headings held on the Library's System Centre computer also assists in maintaining consistency for the entry of names.

Subject classification is similarly the responsibility of the Database Management Section. The twentieth edition of the Dewey Decimal Classification (DDC20) is applied, again using the scheme as interpreted by the national agency. This practice of following cataloguing rules and classification schemes as seen in the British National Bibliography should achieve consistency of input and speed. The theory behind this being that if the majority of the material that is purchased has data produced by the national agency then adding it to the local catalogue should be a quick and easy operation with little input required from the team leaders. In practice, although the theory may be sound the reality is not always as could be hoped for. However, database standards and quality within the British National Bibliography are not the subject of this chapter.

The adoption of DDC20 at Manchester Metropolitan University Library took place in January 1991. Up until that time, the Library had continued to use the eighteenth edition of Dewey (DDC18). This had been perfectly acceptable at the beginning of the use of MARC data when the Library joined BLCMP but became increasingly difficult to apply with the passage of time. The speed element of utilizing classification numbers prescribed by the British National Bibliography was simply becoming lost because they were no longer using DDC18. Consequently, the Systems Librarian/Database Manager recommended to the Librarian and Reader Services colleagues the benefits of switching to DDC20 and undertook to arrange for an extensive programme of reclassification to take place during the summer vacation of 1991. This was successfully achieved to the tune of something in the region of 25,000 titles reclassified over a period of eight weeks. This project continues today. If additional copies are purchased for items which would require reclassification then the existing copies are recalled and converted as required.

SYSTEMS LIBRARIAN/DATABASE MANAGER – ROLE INSIDE AND OUTSIDE THE INSTITUTION

The Systems Librarian/Database Manager, then, has overall responsibility for the operation of the Database Management Section including everything from participation in staff selection and appointments, progress monitoring and appraisal to problem-solving on both the hardware and the databases when necessary. This may well add weight to the view expounded by both Chan[3] and Muirhead[4] of an individual possessed of mysterious powers which enable them to operate in many different guises, but as a foundation and background for the 'in-touch system manager' these varying tasks and responsibilities are invaluable. It is to be hoped that the image of the tail (in this instance 'the system') wagging the dog (the Library) would not materialize at the Manchester Metropolitan University Library. The involvement of the Systems Librarian/Database Manager as a member of the senior management team is another factor that militates against this (see Figure 7.2). Similarly, attendance at Reader Services team meetings and any relevant working parties also enhances all-round understanding between Technical Services and Reader Services. Effective management of the system and its databases needs close involvement with all aspects of the operation of the library service.

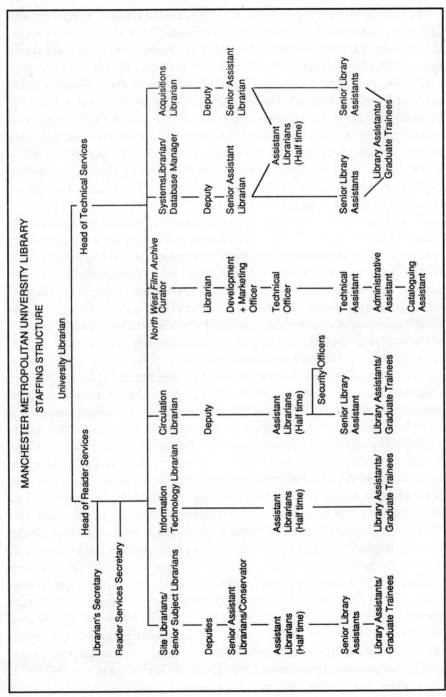

MANCHESTER METROPOLITAN UNIVERSITY LIBRARY STAFFING STRUCTURE

University Librarian

Librarian's Secretary

Reader Services Secretary

Head of Reader Services

Head of Technical Services

Site Librarians/Senior Subject Librarians

Deputies

Senior Assistant Librarians/Conservator

Assistant Librarians (Half time)

Senior Library Assistants

Library Assistants/Graduate Trainees

Information Technology Librarian

Assistant Librarians (Half time)

Library Assistants/Graduate Trainees

Circulation Librarian

Deputy

Assistant Librarians (Half time)

Security Officers

Senior Library Assistant

Library Assistants/Graduate Trainees

North West Film Archive Curator

Librarian

Development + Marketing Officer

Technical Officer

Technical Assistant

Administrative Assistant

Cataloguing Assistant

Systems Librarian/Database Manager

Deputy

Senior Assistant Librarian

Assistant Librarians (Half time)

Senior Library Assistants

Library Assistants/Graduate Trainees

Acquisitions Librarian

Deputy

Senior Assistant Librarian

Senior Library Assistants

Library Assistants/Graduate Trainees

Fig. 7.2

The most recent example of the diversity of tasks charged to the Systems Librarian/Database Manager has been a successful installation of a self-service issue system for the use of library patrons. Beginning with early discussions between BLCMP and library staff to map out the basic requirements, this project again demonstrated the essential liaison role of the Systems Librarian/Database Manager in bringing together the library system suppliers, the hardware suppliers, library circulation staff, and, of course, library users. The diversity comes with ensuring the hardware functions correctly, liaising with both Computing Services to make the telecommunications operate, and circulation staff to ensure understanding of how the system operates on a day-to-day basis and, of course, in communicating with library users to monitor operation of this new system.

While this example may be quite different from tasks such as restoring software and database files after a serious hardware crash or organizing a project to convert from one classification scheme to another, they all illustrate the benefits of 'the integrated manager' to the Manchester Metropolitan University Library. One of the images portrayed is of a plate-spinning juggler. If successful, at the end of a week, the Systems Librarian/Database Manager goes home tired but contented, having managed by judicious running about to keep all plates spinning. Lack of success, on the other hand, brings exhaustion, lack of contentment, and much broken crockery!

Among the tasks listed in the job description (see Appendix) for the Systems Librarian/Database Manager at Manchester Metropolitan University is to 'liaise with and participate fully in the work of the various agencies associated with the Library in the provision of computer-based systems . . . .' This role is probably the one that is fundamental to the success of all other tasks charged to the post. Within the institution, this liaison is principally with the Computing Services Division who are not only responsible for the provision of networking facilities to deliver the system around all of the service points, but also hold the funds for capital expenditure on all computing equipment. The Systems Librarian/Database Manager must also liaise regularly with both the Student Registry and the Personnel Division who provide the Library with data for the patron files.

Externally, the most important relationship is with the Library's system supplier, BLCMP. This relationship was, and still very much is, one of mutual support. As one of the earliest libraries to join the cooperative and indeed as a 'shareholder and owner', BLCMP's survival and continued growth are important to the future of the Manchester Metropolitan University Library. To this end library personnel have always tried to take an active role in all of BLCMP's committees, working parties, and, of course, user groups.

In the early days of the Library's association with BLCMP, user groups consisted of, presumably, interested parties getting together at very small quite informal meetings to exchange views on particular topics. The early history of BLCMP and the development of its user groups up until 1987 has been documented by Stubley.[5] It is interesting to note that at the time Stubley was writing it had been deemed appropriate that 'major groups were chaired by a Board Member or an executive director of the company'. Nowadays things have moved on to such an extent that the user groups are more appropriately chaired and managed by the users themselves. Thus, rather than a member of BLCMP's staff or a board member, who by their nature will be chief librarians or heads of service, the user groups are chaired by cataloguers, circulation librarians, system managers, etc. The Systems Librarian/Database Manager at the Manchester Metropolitan University Library currently chairs both the System Managers User Group and also the Systems Development Group. This new arrangement was set in place during 1989 when it seemed that the previous arrangements were no longer achieving what was required. Determining just what *is* required is easier said than done in so far as the relationship between BLCMP as a non-profit making limited liability company, a cooperative, and its customer/owners, has been and always will be an intriguing one.

The user groups as they exist today cover all of the main business areas – acquisitions and serials, cataloguing, OPAC, circulation, and system management. There is also a separate group for public libraries. Each separate group is convened by an individual from a BLCMP member library and each of these individuals also attends the Systems Development Group. This latter group acts as a coordinating advisory committee for all the user groups and, subsequently, communicates directly with the BLCMP board. This direct communication is effected by virtue of the meetings being attended by both the Chairman of the Board and at least one of the executive directors of BLCMP.

The meetings of all these groups provide a vital forum for the exchange of both information and experience between BLCMP and its customers and also between customers – individual cataloguers, system managers, etc. – themselves. They normally include a review of current software and identification of problems associated with running the system. Future developments of the software as a whole, together with new products, are also discussed alongside any general issues that may be raised by members. Minutes of all the separate user groups are then considered by the Systems Development Group in order to discuss priorities and to seek to influence planning by making recommendations directly to the BLCMP board.

It is interesting to note here that representatives from the individual user groups played an important role in the design of BLCMP's new system, TALIS. User group convenors together with a small number of representatives covering the different types of libraries in BLCMP membership spent several days reviewing the designs proposed for TALIS. Stepping right back and starting afresh without simply putting a new look on top of BLS should enable this new system to develop in the right way. Drawing on the collective experience of members of the user groups for this early validation of TALIS is an example of BLCMP's continuing commitment to both the user groups and its customers as a whole.

It is, nevertheless, also worth remarking that apart from a commitment from BLCMP to the value of user groups it is vital that the same commitment is forthcoming from the users themselves. BLCMP's strength as a cooperative lies with its members and the user groups will only be successful as forums for change and development if the users themselves are prepared to offer both support and/or constructive criticism where required.

Turning back again to that element from the job description referred to earlier, the task of liaising and participating fully 'in the work of the various agencies associated with the Library in the provision of computer-based systems . . .', there are now new relationships developing not known of at the time that the job description was devised. Within the Manchester area the Consortium of Academic Libraries in Manchester (CALIM) has been formed with the aim of cooperation on a variety of fronts between the major higher education institution libraries. As four of the five member libraries of CALIM are now BLCMP members this is bound to impact in some way on the development of systems at Manchester Metropolitan University and indeed on the Systems Librarian/Database Manager. Similarly the increasing role of research and the quest for funding will also impact on the Library, not just on the increasing demands made on the service by researchers but on a potential requirement for library staff to become more involved in research themselves. As a university with a Department of Library and Information Studies a strong relationship already exists between the Library and staff and students of that department. The Systems Librarian/Database Manager has previously taken part in the teaching process and this may be expected to continue with perhaps more emphasis on pure research. The plate-spinning juggler may find that even more plates need to be kept aloft.

THE FUTURE – A 'VIRTUAL' SYSTEM MANAGER?

Looking to the future, the Systems Librarian/Database Manager as an integrated manager with an all round view of the library service will continue to have a crucial role to play in selecting and managing one of the new generation of library housekeeping systems on the market. Doubtless these new systems will bring with them new requirements for their successful management (they may well manage themselves) but the history of technical services operations and the implementation of computer-based systems at the Manchester

Metropolitan University Library clearly demonstrate adaptability, so these latest developments may simply be seen as 'more of the same'! Whether this will also be the case for the post of Systems Librarian/Database Manager remains to be seen.

REFERENCES

1   Dwyer, J. R., 'The evolutionary role of technical services', in Cargill, J. (ed.), *Library management and technical services*, New York, The Haworth Press, 1988, 13–26.

2   Riggs, D. E., 'Leadership versus management in technical services', in Cargill, J. (ed.), *Library management and technical services*, New York, The Haworth Press, 1988, 27–39

3   Chan, G. K. L., 'The systems librarian', in Revill, D.H. (ed.), *Personnel management in polytechnic libraries*, Aldershot, Gower in association with COPOL, 1987, 175–99.

4   Muirhead, G. A., 'System management in UK libraries : some preliminary findings of a survey', *Information services & use*, **12** (1992), 177–93.

5   Stubley, P., *BLCMP: a guide for librarians and systems managers*, Aldershot, Gower, 1988.

**Appendix: Job description for Systems Librarian/Database Manager,
Manchester Metropolitan University Library**

JOB TITLE:
Systems Librarian and Database Manager

LOCATION:
In the Technical Services Division at the All Saints Library. Will also visit site libraries.
All appointments are made on the understanding that staff may be required to work in
any capacity at the appropriate grade anywhere in the University Library as directed
by the University Librarian.

RESPONSIBLE TO:
The Head of Technical Services, and the University Librarian.

OTHER ESSENTIAL CONTACTS:
Deputy Systems Librarian, Acquisitions Librarian, Serials Librarian, Circulation
Librarian, Site and Floor Librarians, Head of Reader Services, Head of Computing,
Computing Services Division.

MAIN PURPOSE OF THE JOB:
Responsible to the Head of Technical Services for the organization, operation and
maintenance of the Library's computer system centre and for the efficient creation
and maintenance of the bibliographic and other databases used in the Library's
computer-based systems.

MAIN TASKS:
1.   In charge of and responsible for the efficient organization and operation
of the Library's computer system centre and for the care and maintenance
of equipment, including telecommunications, where these are a Library
responsibility.

2.   Ensures the equal and effective provision of the central system to the
managers of services, including the circulation, floor, and site librarians
and other responsible staff charged with the operation of the specific services for the management of the Library and the provision of services to
end-users.

3.   Liaises closely with all staff using the central system in support of their
job function in order to ensure that all their requirements are adequately
provided for and that services can be operated satisfactorily.

4.   Advises the heads of Technical and Reader Services of equipment requirements in the computer field.

5.   Assists in the setting up and start of new services supplied by the system centre, in conjunction with the librarians ultimately responsible for the service, and helps in the briefing and training of staff involved in their operation.

6.   Organizes the training and instruction of staff in the control and operation of the computer system centre, to ensure that at all times staff with adequate training and experience are available to maintain the Library's service.

7.   Produces or provides up-to-date guides, manuals, and instruction packages designed to describe and explain system centre operations to support the training and instruction of library staff, and staff and students of the Department of Library and Information Studies.

8.   In charge of the Database Management Section with overall responsibility to the Head of Technical Services for the efficient creation and maintenance of the bibliographic and other databases used in the Library's computer-based systems.

9.   Responsible for the establishment and implementation of procedures for carrying out effectively the work of database management.

10.   Liaises with and participates fully in the work of the various agencies associated with the Library in the provision of computer-based systems, e.g. BLCMP, Computing Services Division.

11.   Keeps abreast of new developments in computer systems and computer applications in libraries and advises the heads of Technical and Reader Services on possible improvements to increase efficiency in working practices or to improve services to the user.

8   Systems management in the University of Limerick Library

❖   Lindsay Mitchell

1   INTRODUCTION

The University of Limerick Library offers an example of a library which has chosen not to create a post of systems librarian.

From the beginning, the University's Information Systems and Services Division has adopted an approach which emphasized the need to take advantage of emerging technologies. A strong ethos of customer orientation has driven the uptake of systems which facilitate service for users. Library services are continually being monitored for improvement by both managers and staff who operate them on a day-to-day basis. These services include background technical and administration areas as well as public services. Given this desire to encourage services to be improved in a 'bottom-up' fashion, underpinned by as much delegation of responsibility as possible, staff need to be able to avail themselves of systems which are flexible in supporting their policy decisions. We have always been clear that we have bought standard products to run our housekeeping systems and that local bespoke tailoring would be minimal. We have preferred to influence enhancements to the standard product and, while this has sometimes meant that changes are less speedy than we would like, it has also avoided costly software development and the additional work caused by applying the supplier's standard software upgrades to a non-standard product.

Another influencing factor on systems has been the growth rate of the University in a very short time: from an initial intake of 113 undergraduate students in 1972, when the then National Institute for Higher Education, Limerick was first set up, to a complement of over 6,000 undergraduate, post-graduate, and research students in academic year 1993/4. All systems on campus, including library housekeeping systems, need to support this rapid growth.

The University of Limerick network provides a range of tools and services which include information resources provided by the Library. This network is under the management of the Library's 'sister' department, the Information Technology Department. While this overview will focus on structures and responsibilities within the Library, it will be obvious that there are close common interests between the two departments.

2 AUTOMATION BACKGROUND

2.1 Library housekeeping systems

Prior to the implementation of an integrated library system, URICA, in November 1985, a number of in-house systems had facilitated acquisitions, cataloguing, and circulation since 1975. They were minimally connected. For example, accession numbers formed the only link between a very basic circulation system and the technical services systems, and batch processing was used. However, having been customers of the British Library's LOCAS service, we were able to obtain a tape of our holdings for loading on to our URICA system. Prior to this, a microfiche catalogue had been offered for the majority of stock and very early acquisitions had been indexed by a card catalogue. All material, either on order or in stock, is now visible to users through our database: items received, but not yet classified and fully catalogued, will be made available on request within 24 hours.

In May 1985, the decision was made to purchase McDonnell Douglas's URICA software, following an evaluation exercise which included the usual functionality factors as well as the need to interface to the campus network.[1] The functional needs were defined by groups of staff from different areas. Between May and November 1985, a number of training courses took place for library staff to prepare them for the implementation. These included keyboard skills and 'training the trainers' courses since Librarians and Senior Library Assistants would be expected to play a major role in training staff in their functional areas in the use of the software. When the system was delivered in November 1985, training in three modules commenced: acquisitions, cataloguing, and circulation. This was conducted in-house using a small database of our records which had been loaded as a test prior to loading our full tape. This small database is still used for training and testing. The system initially went live with these three modules (acquisitions, cataloguing, circulation), commencing in January 1986, followed by the OPAC and serials modules. The Lancaster University Interlibrary Loans package (which uses the PICK operating system, as does URICA) is currently in use but we intend to take the interlibrary loans module from URICA. The British Library Document Supply Centre's Arttel service is used to transmit the majority of our interlibrary loan requests.

The implementation of URICA, surprisingly headache-free for Library staff and without disruption for users, was welcomed by Library staff who had been operating increasingly inadequate systems. The computer which runs the system is located in the Library and is the responsibility of the Library staff. This has had some advantages which may be summed up by the fact that there is no 'middle party' to liaise with when handling faults, upgrades, and any urgent activities which need to be carried out on the machine. Since the same vendor supplied both the machine and the software, Library staff have a single contact point for engineering and software support. We currently have 40 lines, 15 of which are dedicated OPAC lines and of these, 6 are for external access to OPAC. The number of external ports will increase in the coming year.

2.2   Information retrieval systems

As a new institution, we were never in a position to satisfy all user information needs from library stock and have never seen it as our role to amass large collections. Instead, we have always emphasized the need to access remote sources, again taking advantage of communication technologies. Online searching of remote databases was offered as soon as possible, both for end-users to do their own searching as well as being provided as a service to users. CD-ROM products have been available on the campus network since February 1990 as a result of a joint project between the Library and the Information Technology Department.[2] Responsibility for loading CD-ROM products and for ensuring that the server is available lies with the Information Technology Department. There are a number of CD-ROM products which are not networked. In some cases these will be networked in future as extra drives are purchased and, more importantly, as funding becomes available for network licence charges. The University of Limerick campus is wholly networked and with over 1,200 nodes already on the network, the delivery of information resources to desktops throughout campus will increase. Figure 8.1 gives an overview of networked services.

The campus-wide office management system, Digital's 'All-in-1', incorporates a gateway to the Library's OPAC which is also available to campus users via a server on the network. The OPAC module has become very open to tailoring and this is done by a task force of Library staff representing the Information, Cataloguing and User Services departments. This task force has been in operation for almost one year. The Cataloguing department employs a new Cooperative Education student (via the University's work experience programme) every six months and this student is included on the task force, providing a valuable user viewpoint. Recently this student designed and administered a pilot survey of users' experience of OPAC. It is intended that the results will assist with specific tailoring decisions and that a further, more in-depth survey will build on the information gained.

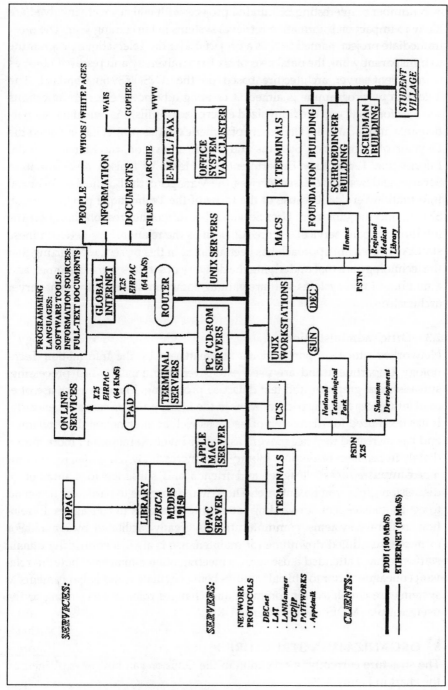

Fig. 8.1 University of Limerick: ISSD network services

A number of interesting EC-funded projects with which we are involved are likely to impact on information retrieval systems in the coming year. The most immediate project, named IRIS, is a project under the Telematique programme to transparently link the databases of six Irish university and research libraries using client-server architecture based on the ANSI Z39.50 standard. The Telematique programme is aimed at creating advanced telecommunications services for small and medium-sized enterprises (SMEs). As one of the six participants, input from the University of Limerick to this project has included the Director of Information Systems and Services Division, the Manager of the Information Technology Department, the Heads of Liaison & Information Services and Systems & User Services, the Manager of the Business & Technical Information Service (because of the focus of the Telematique programme on SMEs), and the Librarian, User Services (because of her responsibility for the interlibrary loans service). Figure 8.2 clarifies the relationships between these staff. Again, a team approach has been utilized in this project, recognizing that the technology is a tool underlying the delivery of services to the customer, and a number of non-systems staff are gaining some familiarity with client-server architecture.

2.3   Office administration

Networked office support systems are managed by the Information Technology Department and are used extensively for e-mail, word processing, spreadsheets, graphics, and text database processing. The pervasive use of e-mail influences many aspects of work in the Library and on campus generally. It has been used for discussion of issues as well as information dissemination and has increased the pace of work as well as involved more staff more immediately in problem resolution. Library staff increasingly use e-mail to communicate with remote colleagues and friends and subscribe to a number of discussion groups on the Internet. Those who subscribe to particular lists tend to act as gatekeepers, forwarding interesting messages to colleagues. In relation to library systems, communication is greatly facilitated by e-mail. For example, scheduled downtime for maintenance is always notified by e-mail; staff who have attended a user group meeting often e-mail brief notes to relevant colleagues prior to official minutes being circulated; and enhancements to systems are circulated for comment and changes prior to forwarding to the user group or MDIS, the supplier of URICA.

3   ORGANIZATION STRUCTURE

The structure currently in operation in the Division can best be explained by the chart in Figure 8.2.

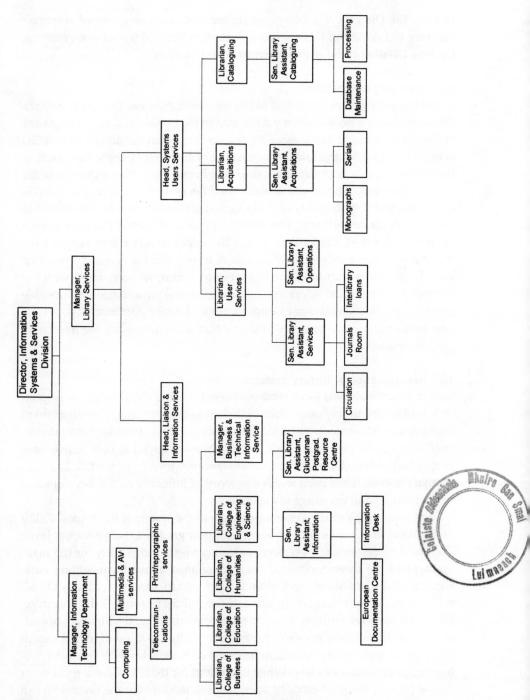

Fig. 8.2 Information Systems and Services Division, University of Limerick

In 1986, the Director of Library and Information Services assumed responsibility for the totality of Library and Information Technology services, forming the new Division of Information Systems and Services.

3.1 Staff responsibilities

It was the policy from the outset of library automation not to have a systems librarian, that is a person wholly dedicated to the operation and development of the library system. The reasons for this were to avoid the danger of systems being developed for the sake of the systems without reference to the needs of the customers, that is library users and other library staff. Also, expertise could be shared between those who actually used the system, avoiding the creation of an elite, and responsibility for training in a particular module is devolved to the appropriate department. This does not mean that nobody has developed a deep knowledge of the system, in fact the opposite: some few people have become very knowledgeable while others have gained a necessary working knowledge. More staff have the opportunity to become acquainted with the technology, not just the select few, and decision-making at the lowest possible action level is facilitated. For example, a Senior Library Assistant will set up a new borrower or item category in the system, after discussing the need with her Librarian.

3.2 Maintenance of library systems

Staff in functional areas (acquisitions, cataloguing and circulation) are responsible for the day-to-day operations of their systems, including identification of faults and enhancements required. Librarians in these areas also attend relevant user group meetings. URICA has always enjoyed a very active user group, and although travelling to such meetings, usually in the UK, is a substantial expense, it has been worth it in terms of influence on the development of the product and exchange of experience.

Fault reporting and the general overview of the system is the responsibility of the Head of Systems & User Services, a post graded at Sub-librarian level. The Head of Systems & User Services also carries responsibility for the management of the three functional areas mentioned above (acquisitions, cataloguing and circulation) and attends user group meetings of the OPAC sub-group, the technical sub-group and the full user group. If discussion on particular software faults is required following reporting, the librarian operating the module usually provides further information to the staff in McDonnell Douglas. In general, this structure has worked reasonably well from our system supplier's point of view. While it is useful for them to have a focal point in one person, the staff actually operating the module are the ones who can describe most vividly the way the system is working. Proposed solutions to faults or required enhancements may meet the criteria of a systems librarian but not those of the people who need to use the software.

Ad hoc reports are produced using the system's retrieval language, ENGLISH. Both Librarians and Senior Library Assistants have received training in this. College Librarians have used tailored reports for deselection and collection development, and special listings, usually by subject area or by a language or format, are produced for faculty. These are sent in hard copy or on a floppy disk or are e-mailed to the requester. Lists may also be loaded into word processing packages (available on the network) for tailoring and high-quality printing. The Acquisitions Librarian frequently produces bespoke reports for College Librarians and faculty, and extensive use of these report generation facilities was made earlier this year to analyse some aspects of our journals collection. With eight years of operation of an integrated system behind us, a substantial amount of statistical information is now available from the system and this is increasingly being used to assist decision-making. While we would like enhancements to this area within URICA, and the long-term collection and analysis of this information needs to be more coordinated, individual staff members can now satisfy many of their own statistical information needs in a fairly immediate fashion.

Daily routines, including printing notices, statistics, and orders, are carried out by the library assistants in the relevant areas. A daily complete backup of the system is done by a library assistant. This is not the responsibility of particular people: one of the library assistants timetabled for duty in the evening does it as a routine closing-up procedure. The responsibility for monitoring and logging security backups and transaction logging rests with the Senior Library Assistant, User Services (Operations).

As this type of post appears to be unusual, it may be useful to explain it more fully. Senior Library Assistants are not required to have library or information science qualifications but substantial experience of library work is a prerequisite. The Senior Library Assistant post shown in Figure 8.3 was created in late 1985 to cover a number of key responsibilities.

Having one person at this grade responsible for the maintenance and good order of physical plant and equipment has released other staff from this onerous work. These and other responsibilities ensure that the person is central to the provision of services and again is very directly involved with user demands.

This Senior Library Assistant reports to the User Services Librarian, a post graded at Assistant Librarian level. This latter post carries additional responsibilities in relation to the general operation of the system, compared to other posts at Assistant Librarian grade. These include loading software upgrades and patch tapes and arranging, with the Senior Library Assistant, for cabling

Senior Library Assistant, User Services (Operations)
Reporting to: Librarian, User Services

Staff:
. training, timetabling and supervision of Library Attendants
. prioritization of duties of Library Attendants, depending upon seasonality and changing demands
. participation in Library Attendant panel recruitment

Systems:
. daily security procedures for URICA system
. basic problem-solving and referral as necessary in relation to terminal, printer, and node faults

Administration:
. statistics of photocopier usage and card sales
. stationery, supplies and equipment – ordering, receipt, monitoring and distribution
. replacement bar-codes
. petty cash administration

Safety:
. regular familiarization of Library staff with current safety procedures
. checking of safety equipment and exits and reporting of problems to the Buildings Office
. representation on University Safety Committee
. keys

Physical plant:
. ongoing supervision of maintenance in all Library areas
. monitoring regular/special cleaning requirements
. equipment – checking and arranging repair and service and non-mechanical maintenance, e.g. cleaning
. stock – monitoring orderliness and condition and relocation as necessary
. furniture and shelving rearrangement as necessary
. provision of guiding signs and notices

Liaison:
. Buildings Office
. Suppliers
. all Library staff regarding hardware and equipment, safety, physical plant and general supplies

User behaviour:
. implementation of library rules and regulations

Fig. 8.3   Job responsibilities of Senior Library Assistant, User Services (Operations)

and new equipment to be installed.

This structure has helped to disperse responsibility to the most appropriate grades of staff – librarians are not involved in daily system maintenance routines. For anything more than routine, non-technical problem-solving, and maintenance, outside expertise is called upon. For example, staff from the Information Technology Department install PCs on the network, MDIS are contacted for engineering support, and maintenance contracts operate with suppliers of peripherals such as PCs, scanners and printers. It is also true to say that there is very little in the way of downtime: both equipment and engineering support from MDIS in Dublin are very reliable.

In addition, the User Services Librarian has been responsible for loading the Lancaster Interlibrary Loans software and upgrades, with only occasional assistance from staff in the Information Technology Department and Lancaster University during set up and ongoing troubleshooting. Backup and security routines are carried out by library assistants in the Interlibrary Loans department.

In short, library housekeeping systems are stable although, of course, as with any library system, we continually identify enhancements which are reviewed and prioritized by the URICA User Group before forwarding to MDIS.

4 BENEFITS AND PROBLEMS
So far, mainly the benefits of our current *modus operandi* and structures have been described:

- customer focus supported
- delegation of responsibility
- distribution of expertise among library staff
- speedy uptake of enabling technology, particularly via the campus network

In a rapidly changing information and technical environment, however, no structure ever reaches perfection and we are continually in the process of evolving the most appropriate structures for demands on services.

Liaison between the Library and the Information Technology Department needs to be developed. Some problems are caused by scarcity of staff to support the complex and extensive campus network infrastructure. For example, if the CD-ROM server hangs during the evening, there is only one staff member on duty in the computer room where the server is located. If that person is called away to deal with another problem, a frequent occurrence in a distributed computing environment, users have to wait for the operator to return and reboot the server. Additional cover has been provided by the Information

Technology Department at weekends and the possible relocation of the server and CD-ROM drives to the Library has been discussed.

At a deeper level, the development of an integrated user interface to networked information resources has been hampered by insufficient understanding of each other's primary focus and strategy. Effort needs to be directed to these areas: both the development of closer liaison and the development of the user interface to the network. Cultural differences complicate our relationships: library staff tend to feel that colleagues in the Information Technology Department should be more focused on service issues, but it would have been impossible for the Library to make such rapid progress in delivery of networked services without the focus by the Information Technology Department on implementing innovative technology. We rely on their expertise and vision in technical areas, especially networking.

It may also be said that library staff with a penchant for working with systems have missed a learning opportunity. It would seem that in libraries whose structure includes a systems librarian, that person may have the opportunity to enhance their knowledge of networking through more hands-on involvement. However, from observation, this level of involvement usually appears to imply development of a local network within the library, often for the specific purpose of networking CD-ROMs, rather than hands-on involvement in a campus wide network and global networking. One member of library staff has remarked that not having a systems librarian can lead individuals to feel insecure when dealing with computer department personnel but feels that this will pass as the emphasis in computing changes from technical brilliance to customer service. Of course, such insecurities ought to be addressed through appropriate training also, so that library staff have confidence in their own perceptions and do not feel inadequate when talking to technical experts.

In a library which sees technology and the network very much as tools, the Library's strategy regarding the network will concentrate more on the realms of user interface development, information retrieval, user education, collection development, and so forth.

5 THE FUTURE

The benefits and problems described serve to illustrate that our structures and procedures are still evolving. It can also be seen that a number of systems-related developments came to fruition together in 1985/6: the implementation of an integrated system, the creation of the Senior Library Assistant post in Operations and, of course, the bridging of Library and Information Technology services.

It is likely that further structural changes will now be needed to facilitate a number of areas of future systems developments, particularly in the support of networked information resources and document delivery. The shape of these changes is not yet apparent but many organizations are facing similar challenges. Evidence for this can be found, for example, in many job advertisements on the Internet for posts with titles such as 'Networked Information Resources Librarian'.[3] However, no dedicated systems librarian is needed to support the housekeeping systems within the Library and this is unlikely ever to be the case.

Systems choice in the University of Limerick Library has been informed by a desire to remove barriers between users and information. Indeed, users are becoming more sophisticated in their expectations of systems and, while staffed services and hard copy collections are available for between 8 and 16 hours per day (depending on time of year), an increasing variety of networked resources, both on campus and globally, is available for 24 hours per day, all year round. With a speed of penetration that leads librarians to use science fiction scenarios as a lever to the imagination, networks provide us with real challenges to exploit new electronic information resources and document delivery to the benefit of our user community while continuing to meet existing, very real, and very immediate, demands from our users for traditional book-based services. Considerable expertise and wisdom are needed in these areas and much of this will be found and developed within existing staff at all levels, as has happened with previous systems developments.

REFERENCES

1   Reddan, M., 'Systems evaluation at NIHE, Limerick', in Brunt, R. (ed.), *Systems evaluation*, Dublin, Library Association of Ireland Cataloguing and Indexing Group, 1986, 18–23.
2   Mitchell, L., 'OPTI-NET on a campus wide network', in Moore, C. and Whitsed, N. (eds.), *CD-ROM networking in practice*, London, UK Online User Group and Library Information Technology Centre, 1992, 55–60.
3   For an analysis of such issues, see Woodsworth, A. and Maylone, T., *Reinvesting in the information job family: context, changes, new jobs, and models for evaluation and compensation*, Boulder, Colorado, CAUSE, 1993.

9   Systems as teamwork: the experience of University College London Library

❖   *David Bovey and F J Friend*

1   INTRODUCTION

Tradition has it, passed by word of mouth from librarian to librarian, that University College London (UCL) Library was the first academic library in the UK to adopt subject specialization. Whatever the truth of the tradition, its existence indicates the importance attached to a staff structure based upon subject specialization in UCL Library. It is a tradition which is reinforced by the sense of identification UCL academic staff feel with 'their librarian'.

In a large institution (UCL has 12,025 students in October 1993) a sense of identification is important for the Library in retaining the loyalty and support of members of the College. Subject specialization therefore reinforces the Library's mission 'to provide, sustain and develop a library and information service to support UCL in maintaining and extending the excellence of its research and teaching', as described in the Library's Strategic Plan. Another factor in the emphasis upon subject specialization has been the physical separation of the Library. All libraries at UCL are under one management structure, but as UCL has grown, libraries which were previously independent have been added to the system. The individuals in charge of such libraries naturally retain a local management role and act as subject specialists for the collections they manage. Even some collections in the two major libraries have at various times in their history been physically separate, with a librarian in charge. Conversely academic departments some distance away from the main site whose collections have been in the Main and Science libraries have appreciated the appointment of a member of library staff who could act as a contact, drink coffee with them in their departmental common room, take suggestions for new books for purchase, and resolve any problems they might have in using the library. Generally, therefore, subject specialization has suited UCL, its staff and students, and its library. The individuals holding subject specialist appointments have been held in respect by their academic colleagues and have often held good degrees in one of the subjects for which they were responsible.

The first major break with the subject specialist tradition occurred with the establishment of the Central Cataloguing Unit in 1981. It was realized that modern automated cataloguing techniques could be handled more efficiently through a central unit, which would be conversant with the databases from which cataloguing records could be drawn. Moreover, the cataloguing system available at the time did not allow online working by 20 subject specialists scattered throughout the Library. Subject specialists did, however, retain responsibility for classification, for which they could use their subject expertise and their knowledge of the needs of staff and students in the departments they served. It must be understood that the Central Cataloguing Unit was established before integrated library systems were available, so when UCL Library began using the Geac circulation system in 1984 no bridge was built between the circulation and cataloguing systems. Perhaps the appointment of a systems librarian at that point would have encouraged a library-wide approach to automation, but it is difficult to see, given the systems available at the time, what such an appointee could have done to achieve more integration. Politically also at that time the emphasis was upon sharing in automated developments within the University of London as a whole, so the appointment of a systems librarian for UCL would have been difficult to justify. What did happen, in a natural way for very practical reasons, was the emergence of an Assistant Librarian as the member of staff who took the lead in implementing the Geac circulation system, and became the troubleshooter to whom other members of staff turned when they had a problem not only with the Geac system but also with any other piece of equipment, such as the PCs gradually coming into use. The Assistant Librarian took this lead because of his responsibility for readers' services together with a natural ability to bring people together to sort out problems quietly and efficiently.

The helpfulness and efficiency of the individual member of staff was greatly appreciated but the situation did contain dangers for the long-term efficiency of UCL Library. Firstly, there was the 'falling-under-a-bus' risk: if anything happened to that individual, even a temporary illness or a holiday, systems might grind to a halt, because too great a dependence had been placed upon one person. Secondly, there was a risk of loss of efficiency because of pressure upon the individual concerned. As more and more equipment became available, including equipment at scattered library sites, the telephone never stopped ringing: 'Can he come and sort out this problem?' As well as being too great a workload for one person to handle, it was not good for the career development of the person concerned to become a troubleshooter for automation problems faced by everybody else, including the Librarian himself. Thirdly, the impression developed that somehow automation was something different, something which required a specialist to look after rather than being a tool which all members of library staff should know enough about to use in their daily work.

2   IMPLEMENTATION OF LIBERTAS

It was with such feelings in the background that UCL Library began the investigation into the choice of an integrated system, an investigation which led to the choice of the SLS Libertas system. Because of the importance of the decision the investigation was led by the then Deputy Librarian, Jacqueline Whiteside, who for this particular exercise took on the role of systems librarian in the sense of evaluating the automation needs of different sections of the library and also evaluating the ability of various systems to meet those needs. The investigation formed part of a general University of London initiative to adopt an overall strategy for automation whereby all parts of the University could join and machines at individual sites would be able to talk to one another. UCL is the largest single institution within the University, but there are 45 libraries in total. The final choice of system was for Libertas. With UCL Library's previous background in mind, when the time came to implement the Libertas system in 1988, a conscious decision was taken to share the implementation amongst a team of six members of library staff. This had the effect of dividing up the very substantial workload and also involving a wider range of people in automation activities. The team was set up by identifying the various roles and tasks to be performed, and then finding volunteers to take on those roles and tasks.

Six main areas of activity were listed:

- **SLS liaison and communications**
  To act as the official contact in all matters relating to implementation of the Libertas system between UCL and SLS. In addition, to liaise with the UCL Computer Services over the communications network and coordinate its installation and links to the Libertas equipment.
- **Staff training**
  To prepare a programme of staff training for each Libertas module and section of the Library who would need to know about it, together with publishing a regular news-sheet to keep library staff informed of progress in implementation.
- **Bibliographic record creation and maintenance**
  To plan the transfer of catalogue records from the previous off-line files to Libertas, together with the enhancement of records of the previous online circulation system. To reorganize the Cataloguing Department owing to new work-flows created by the cataloguing and acquisitions modules.

- **Acquisitions and serials control**
  To plan for the implementation of these modules as a second stage.
- **Circulation and OPAC**
  To create parameters for the circulation module. To tailor OPAC screens to local requirements.
- **Financial control**
  To investigate the financial control and information available within the acquisitions and serials modules and to advise on their suitability and potential to interface with the College's central financial procedures.

Senior staff who had shown an interest in aspects of automation were approached, and they were matched up to the above jobs according to preference. Regular progress meetings were held under the Deputy Librarian and a news-sheet produced to keep staff aware of implementation. The success of the installation also depended very heavily upon the support of SLS staff, and our confidence in the support provided by SLS was an important factor in the decision on how to handle this development in the Library services. The SLS staff not only gave good advice in the initial recommendations on the hardware to be purchased, but they also provided advice at the right moments when upgrades were desirable in order to prevent system performance from deteriorating. Extensive practical help was given during the implementation period, as you would only expect but sometimes do not receive from a system supplier. Even more important has been the availability of a help desk for the immediate analysis of problems, covering the Libertas interface with VMS (the VAX system operating software), as well as the applications themselves. The knowledge that the system was receiving continuous online monitoring in Bristol also provided a comforting background for a Library which staff-wise was not equipped to run a system as comprehensive as Libertas. Obtaining the money for Libertas had not been an easy political task and the Library's future reputation had in a sense been invested in the success of Libertas. Much therefore depended upon the support structure both from within and from outside the Library, and fortunately all went as well as could be expected, thanks to our own staff and to the staff of SLS.

The team approach was particularly favoured as the Libertas system ran on a Digital computer which was not supported by the College's Computer Centre. Staff at the Computer Centre were very helpful in advising on and implementing the correct communications set-up, but the Library had to turn to other departments in College for advice on the VAX 6210 machine. Without the patient support of both the Mechanical Engineering Department and the Management Information Services Division (MISD) it would have been very difficult for the installation to have been accomplished so smoothly. The VAX was placed in the same machine room as the MISD machine, some hundred yards from the Science Library. The possibility of a shared support service was investigated but did not prove cost-effective. A very worthwhile investment, however, was the maintenance contract with Digital, which covered hardware problems, the installation of upgrades, and (until July 1993) software upgrades. Despite this outside help library staff were still faced with learning rapidly the rudiments of VMS software and bravely tackled the relevant Digital training courses while picking up expertise from others in College; but there remained a psychological barrier to be overcome for librarians to feel confident in running their own set-up. This feeling was enhanced by the fact that UCL was the sole installation among the College libraries in the University of London where the minicomputer was not run on behalf of the Library by a computer centre. One positive feature of being within the University of London group was that UCL was the fourth site to be implemented and so could build on the experience of the three installations within the previous nine months. However, UCL was the first to have a 6210 machine, and so had some pioneering to do.

The bulk of the implementation work initially fell upon the SLS Liaison offi-cer, with overall responsibility, and on the Chief Cataloguer, as the basis of the new system lay in its bibliographic database. These two undertook special training at SLS headquarters in Bristol, and then passed on this knowledge to the rest of the team. The fact there was a team greatly helped, rather than hin-dered, effective communication. The members of the Libertas team retained many of their regular duties in different sections of the multi-site Library and were able to disseminate current information very widely and quickly, which did wonders for morale and the feeling that staff were being consulted as well as informed. This was doubly important as the introduction of Libertas coin-cided with the formal amalgamation of the Middlesex Hospital Medical School and research institutes into the UCL Medical School, and also the Institute of Archaeology into UCL. The libraries of these institutions also merged with the rest of UCL Library and Libertas was an important tool in linking them to the Library and making the staff feel part of a larger whole.

Once up and running the implementation team was supplemented by sev-eral clerical staff undertaking the routine tasks of tape handling and report and notice printing. Again it was regular library staff who adapted to these tasks, and no special technical staff were co-opted.

3   DEVELOPMENT

When, after a few months, running the system became more of a routine oper-ation, the systems work devolved onto two assistant librarians, with the work spread 70/30. After a year, the Assistant Librarian who had shouldered the bulk of the work since the beginning requested a lessening of his systems work and a return to subject librarianship, so the two staff reversed ratios. The 30% ratio staff member retained a brief for systems communications but dropped being official SLS liaison. However, it proved very useful to have in reserve somebody who had undertaken the full range of work, and has led the Library to ensure that two staff have a working knowledge in the use of VMS operating software.

As the systems work matured it did not lessen. More sites needed to be brought into the system, new modules were added to Libertas, and the system reached its limit on number of terminals attached and required enhancing. Some in-depth investigations had to be undertaken. The two staff carrying out this work carried a heavy burden, which eventually led to further restructuring outlined in section 4.

The expansion of the system required a hard sell to the College so relatively soon after what had been a large initial capital expenditure. The Libertas installation was a victim of its own success as customers wanted to use facilities previously unavailable. Initial OPAC installation had been limited by space available for equipment and by cost. More terminals for library staff use were also required as additional Libertas modules became available. The Library wanted to raise its terminal limit from 70 to 90 and at the same time ensure response time was improved rather than just maintained. Detailed investigations were required to size potential new equipment, and quick answers sought to questions from committees who were being approached for funds. The systems people were drawn into a negotiating position for the first time and learnt to prepare briefs. The VAX 6210 was upgraded to a 6310 in July 1989.

A second enhancement was required within two years to provide for an increase in the number of sites to be hosted on the VAX machine and to provide even more OPACs to meet the demand from a large increase in student numbers enrolled at the College. The ability to make use of an external access module to outside databases and outside ports so that with the investment by the College in extending its network more users could access the UCL Library catalogue from their own offices was also required. In going to the College again for substantial sums of money, it was decided to opt for a bid allowing enough expansion for several years' growth, which was put in terms of increasing terminal capacity from 90 to 150, and resulted in the installation of a VAX 4000-500 range machine in summer 1992. This again involved the close cooperation of the Computer Services, whose procurement officer negotiated on the Library's behalf, and from the Mechanical Engineering Department as well as SLS itself. The bid had a rocky progress through College even though it formed part of the official information systems strategy, as there were many competing bids for limited finance. There was, however, a widespread ground-level support for improving access to Library resources which eventually won the day.

As UCL Library was the first Libertas site to install this new range of VAX equipment, it was asked to be a beta test site for Libertas software release 5.5-1 in October 1992. This was particularly in order to explore the possibilities of the new TF85 tape drive, which was expected to be recommended as the standard SLS drive after the test. The Library staff were to test the new software for COM fiche production. This was of benefit to the Library as it had not produced a backup fiche for two years, and had planned to produce one once a year. The tests also included the transfer of bibliographic records via Inter-Libertas Access and the SLS database, a test of the External Network Access, and improvements to the man–machine interface. The systems team were willing to carry out this extra work where they felt the Library would gain on having immediate access to desirable new features, and as long as the background running of the regular system was unlikely to be affected.

Much time was spent investigating the potential of the serials module received with the original software. One of the Assistant Librarians undertaking systems work also had responsibility for policy-making in the Periodicals Department. It was finally decided not to automate periodicals as some operational aspects of the module caused us concern, particularly on the management/accounting side, and would not show enough return on the enormous manpower required to input 8,000 serial titles onto the system. Work on the interlibrary loans module fell to one of the systems people in conjunction with the ILL staff. This involved not only setting parameters, but also a thorough overhaul of all ILL procedures, to ensure the most efficient and cost-effective service. It was, however, decided not to implement ILL requests on the OPACs owing to the copyright requirement for a requester's signature, rather than simply a machine acknowledgement of copyright conditions. The Inter-Libertas Access module had always been a pivot of the University of London's Library Resources Committee's plans for improving resource sharing. This became available in July 1990 and has accounted for a large increase in the number of both staff and students using libraries other than their home library within the University, as well as being of great value for cataloguing and collection development. It provides access from a Libertas menu to all OPACs of the other Libertas sites in London University, together with the option of downloading records from one site to another for cataloguing purposes.

4   A COMPUTER APPLICATIONS TEAM

The resignation of one of the two specialist systems staff led the Library to look again at the organization of this area. Since the dispersal of the Libertas implementation team there had been an increasing concentration of the systems work onto two members of staff. This was the very situation we had always sought to avoid. While heads of departments such as Cataloguing or Interlibrary Loans obviously contributed to developments in their particular fields, an overview as well as detailed knowledge of the system was being concentrated in too few hands. Certainly rapid decision-making was possible in these circumstances, but it was at the expense of overburdening the two individuals involved. Holiday cover and sickness were obvious problems. At the same time the Library employed a number of staff who had a particular interest in systems work even though they were not directly connected with it in their daily job. This included staff who had undertaken a Masters degree in related areas and who were anxious to keep up-to-date in the field. There was a log-jam of staff queuing up to be involved.

A parallel log-jam was building up in relation to the range of automated services to be made available to the user. No longer could 'automation' equal 'Libertas' in our thinking. The whole concept of automated information retrieval was continuing to develop at a fast pace, and the range of products and formats was widening so quickly that the Library needed to devote more resources to the area to keep at the forefront of providing the best possible service to its wide range of customers. CD-ROMs were now commonplace and in particular the launching of the BIDS initiative opened up a whole new way of providing information services. The mix of all these factors coming together resulted in the Library redrawing its staffing structure and reinstating its firm commitment to a team sharing of systems work. Different aspects of computing had so infiltrated every area of librarianship it could no longer be looked on as a separate part of library work. All staff needed a basic knowledge, but some would be given a little more than others.

In January 1993 the Computer Applications Team (CAT) was formed, drawing on existing expertise, and allowing a wider group of staff to participate in the detailed work. A senior medical librarian who had a higher degree in the field was designated as Coordinator and liaises with SLS, the UCL Central Computing Services and any other relevant body, together with directing the work of the more junior members and collaborating with the two Assistant Librarians involved. One Assistant Librarian works on communications, Libertas troubleshooting, and user education, and another on Libertas parameters and developments, and Libertas staff training; one senior library assistant looks after CD-ROMs and databases and another looks after personal computing. These staff retain other responsibilities and spend about 50% of their time on CAT activities. The Library sees this development as a great strengthening of its commitment in this area, which has the full backing of its governing bodies, and indeed there is now a budget line specifically for electronic information. It also means the remit of systems work has become much wider, with the opportunity to make an input directly into general Library policy.

The College's overarching Information Systems Strategy more clearly defines the role of the Library. As a result the Library and the Computer Centre are working much more closely together. There has been an opportunity for the Deputy Librarian and CAT Coordinator to develop a training programme in conjunction with the Computer Centre, so staff are systematically taught beyond the mere basics of Libertas, and are being encouraged to surf the Internet. The systems team is also given a more public role in training students. The College set up a Graduate School in April 1993, and from October 1993 all new research students for MPhil and PhD degrees (about 450 in all) will attend a first year Foundation Course, which includes two hours of information skills. This teaching will be split between the CAT and subject specialists.

The additional staff, together with some funding, are permitting the CAT to take part in research projects. Two are underway as this chapter is being written. The Librarian is coordinating the pilot application of SuperJANET for document delivery, using Ariel software designed by the Research Libraries Group. UCL Library is also one of the test sites chosen for the electronic delivery of a journal published by the Institute of Physics. This is being undertaken jointly with UCL Department of Computer Science.

It was the provision of the BIDS initiative that marked the opening up of databases to a much wider library clientele. The CAT has the exciting if demanding task of keeping library staff up-to-date as to what is available, and the easiest method of obtaining it. Work is progressing both on the local and wide area networking of CD-ROMs, together with the full exploitation of sources nationally and internationally via JANET and the Internet.

In this development, again there has been close collaboration with the College's Central Computing Service. Even more directly, in summer 1993, a cluster of 20 workstations has been installed in the Science Library. A major reorganization of open shelf stock and weeding to store has released prime space on the ground floor of the Science Library to house the facility. The CAT will have general overseeing of the rooms, for security and upkeep of printers etc., but there will be a 'hotline' to the Computing User Services for help with software.

5   THE FUTURE?

It is very doubtful whether any librarian 30 years ago could have predicted the automation situation in libraries today, so it would be foolish for anybody to attempt to predict what libraries will look like at the time people entering the profession now reach the peak of their careers. And yet those individuals and the libraries they are entering are taking decisions now which will affect their futures. One very clear sign is that future librarians and information professionals will have to be considerably more flexible in their attitude towards their careers than previous generations. No longer will it be possible to enter librarianship with a fixed plan for a career as a subject specialist. Some may have a long-term career in that role, but institutions will wish to recruit members of staff who can change their role as the needs of the institution change. As the management of libraries is merged with the management of computer centres, for example, the individuals who have a successful career will be those who can perform well in either service. That is not to say that subject knowledge will not be required in the future. Indeed, it could be very important if librarians are to continue their traditional role of intermediaries between information procedures and users, but the subject expertise will be exercised in an environment which will change more rapidly than libraries have changed over the past century.

The flexibility such a future will demand of individuals will have to be matched by a greater emphasis upon training opportunities for existing staff. The days are past when we could recruit members of staff fully trained and regard their training as being complete. As the library environment changes we shall have to arrange for staff who went through library school even as recently as five years ago, let alone 20 or 30 years ago, to attend courses which will equip them to meet needs as they change. Rather like collection development, these courses will have to be provided on a 'just in time' basis rather than 'just in case'. Their cost will have to be evaluated against the cost to the institution of not having staff trained to meet the institution's needs. Similarly individuals will have to decide what priority they are prepared to give to retraining in order to ensure a good future for themselves. Against this background UCL Library has embarked upon a rolling training programme for its senior staff, using the expertise of the Computer Centre and the School of Library, Archive and Information Studies at UCL. Even those members of staff who come closest to the concept of 'systems librarians' will need such retraining opportunities if they are to fulfil a flexible role in the future.

It will be realized, therefore, that all that has been written in this chapter about UCL Library's past and present staff structure should not be taken as inevitable for the future. The right decisions in today's circumstances are not necessarily the right decisions for the circumstances of the future. UCL Library has a Strategic Plan with a rolling five-year programme, and five years is about as far ahead as any institution can predict, given the face of change in higher education and in scholarly communication. There can be a good future for libraries and for librarians if managers and their staff members cooperate to find the role which provides the best services to users in the new environment.

❖ Part 3
Education and training

10　The training of systems librarians

❖　*Hazel Woodward and Jack Meadows*

The obvious first question to be asked regarding systems librarians is whether they require particular skills or knowledge that other librarians do not. Such a question is best answered in terms of what systems librarians are expected to do: this can be examined via job descriptions, surveys of activities, etc. After this, the next question is whether the training which is currently available satisfies the on-the-job requirements of a systems librarian. Finally, since the systems themselves are changing rapidly, it makes sense to consider briefly what additional training may be needed in the future.

WHAT KNOWLEDGE IS NEEDED?

It is easy to define a systems librarian as someone who manages a library's automated system, but the real question is what expectations does such a definition create in the minds of would-be employers? Something like a generalized (and probably idealized) job description is necessary in order to consider what education a systems librarian is likely to need. So it seems sensible to begin with an employer's comments:

> We have come to believe that it is easier to make a person familiar with library operations into a computer operator than it is to make a computer operator sensitive to library operations. . . . We look for people with a well-rounded knowledge of library operations. The more components of the system they have used, the better. . . . The second aspect we look for is micro experience. . . . The third aspect we look for is . . . the ability of the applicant to analyse situations with which he or she may never have dealt before.[1]

It is worth comparing this with some comments by the President of the Faxon Company in the United States. At the end of the 1980s, he was looking for an information systems director for the country. He sought candidates who were:

– looking for a place where information systems are central to the institution rather than peripheral;
– familiar with large-scale bibliographic and textual information systems;

– interested in being at the forefront of new technologies;
– seeking direct involvement in creating services and programmes for their institutions, rather than simply managing a 'service bureau';
– entrepreneurial risk takers, seeking an institution that supports innovation and risk taking;
– experienced at working very hard and delivering on time;
– effective negotiators and marketers of their services;
– visible and respected within their institutions and within their professional associations;
– inclined to stay with one institution for a long time;
– continuously learning, creating, and discovering;
– not primarily motivated by money, but by challenges and opportunities to contribute to society.

Eight candidates were identified as fitting in with these criteria. Some had relevant experience in library automation, but none had had formal library training.[2]

These comments can be expanded into three categories of knowledge required of a systems librarian: (1) library operations, (2) information technology, and (3) management. Knowledge of the first of these – library operations – is naturally most important in highly automated areas such as acquisitions, cataloguing and circulation. Some automated activities have hitherto been the domain of other specialists, as is the case with information retrieval. However, automation is increasingly seeping into all library operations, while the various aspects of automation are becoming increasingly integrated. Online public access catalogues (OPACs), CD-ROMs, campus wide information systems (CWIS) and the developments springing from them, are making the distinction between systems operation and information retrieval less and less important. Consequently, the purview of a systems librarian from a training viewpoint must be drawn broadly.

General information technology skills and systems knowledge must cover a broad spread of components (apart from the big number-crunching computers), extending over all sorts of hardware and software. Knowledge of networking has in recent years become as important as knowledge of computer configurations. One remaining question is whether systems librarians require programming skills. Though perhaps not absolutely essential, some low-level ability in programming is so useful that it is generally worth acquiring. It is true that most library software is now bought off-the-shelf, but it can often be made much more applicable to local circumstances by a small amount of tweaking. As new forms of technology come on stream, so systems knowledge must expand. A current example is the trend towards the networking of CD-

ROMs. Moreover, systems librarians are usually expected to have at least a working knowledge of general software packages used within the library – for example, word processors, databases and spreadsheets. In addition, they are frequently the person to whom enquiries about the burgeoning number of networked software products, such as personal bibliographic software (PBS), are directed.

An outline of the duties of an 'automation librarian' in 1990, listed the main ones as being: developing PC applications; software evaluation; hardware/software monitoring, maintenance, and upgrading; general troubleshooting; data protection; staff training; system documentation; communications and negotiations.[3]

Management knowledge, to the extent that it deals with organizational or personnel matters, is basically similar to the training required for other library posts. It has certain requirements of its own in terms of personnel management (for example handling technicians), organizational management (for example computer security), and budgeting (for example negotiating with diverse types of supplier). But the major managerial difference lies in the expected speed of response. Automated systems now dominate many libraries. Consequently, the phrase 'the computer is down' means that many key library functions have stopped. Hence, one special skill of a systems librarian is the management of crises.

EMPLOYERS' EXPECTATIONS

Another way of viewing employers' expectations of systems librarians is to look at job advertisements.[4] The specifications in such advertisements are often quite vague. Overall, three activities are likely to be mentioned: (1) planning, (2) installation, and (3) running and maintenance. The main housekeeping activities (basically acquisitions, cataloguing, and circulation) may be mentioned, but usually in the context of advising and assisting the library experts in these areas. In addition, the training of personnel appears in a number of advertisements. An examination of very recent job advertisements in the UK shows that they cover the same points, but emphasize additionally the use of networking and the management (or development) of integrated systems. 'The [person appointed] will be responsible for PC and Mac-based systems in the Library, including CD-ROM networking, and for the integration of Library IT developments with the University's overall IT strategy.' There is an increased stress on user support and training, together with an ability to plan for future developments. 'Can you advise, liaise with and train staff at all levels?. . . We need someone with the appropriate managerial and technical skills to take our system through the next phases of development, and progress our use of microcomputer applications, CD-ROM products and networking.'

The contents of the advertisements indicate that rather different types of activity may be expected of people working in the general systems area. This elastic scope is reflected in the range of titles attached to the advertised positions. The commonest is 'systems' librarian, but 'systems support', 'information systems', 'computer/library systems', and 'network management' all appear more than once as qualifiers. This vagueness suggests there can be a major problem in fitting educational requirements to employers' expectations. There are still many senior library staff who do not feel entirely at home in a highly automated library. They are rather uncertain how automated systems fit into the management of the library, and are not entirely sure what factors should be taken into account in planning for the future. Hence, they have problems in deciding just what duties a systems librarian post should encompass. The other side of this coin is that the range of expectations reflected in job advertisements certainly exceeds what can reasonably be expected of a single individual. They range from an ability to plan the future of a library to an ability to attack recalcitrant microcomputers with a screwdriver. The following excerpt from a job description for a systems librarian indicates just how many skills can, with some justification, be counted necessary:

> Exceptional communication and listening skills; positive and network-promoting relationship with library staff and administrators; good problem-solving skills; strong teaching skills; understanding of library processes and needs; strong organizational and reporting skills; quick learner; aptitude for learning the vendor software, including application software, report generator, and system utilities; not intimidated by computer, peripheral, or telecommunication equipment; tact; courtesy; good judgement; ability to communicate pleasantly and effectively with general public and co-workers; does not panic under pressure.[5]

The question of training, both for and by systems librarians, will be looked at in more detail later; but one point worth noting here is the necessity for systems librarians to act as a translator between computer specialists and librarians. Indeed, with the move towards much closer liaison between libraries and computing centres, in some places even merger, the need for highly developed interpersonal communication skills becomes even more crucial. There is an obvious need to explain otherwise incomprehensible jargon from each side to the other. In addition, and sometimes more of a problem, is the need to grasp when apparent mutual understanding covers an underlying incomprehension. To give a very simple example, both computer specialists and librarians frequently speak of documentation. They do not always realize that they are talking of different things. To a computer specialist, documentation relates specifically to software, whereas librarians use the word in a much wider context.

A study of job advertisements raises a further question. To what extent does an educational background appropriate for a systems librarian, provide an entry to other sorts of jobs? A study of the emerging market for information workers in the UK gives grounds for supposing that systems librarians possess transferable skills.[6] The job advertisements in a range of newspapers and journals were scanned for certain keywords (information, data, database, etc.). The skills being asked for were grouped into four categories: (1) established library skills, (2) applied information skills, (3) other basic skills, but related to library/information skills, and (4) no direct reliance on library/information skills. Over the course of a year 575 posts fell into the first three categories, and 531 into the fourth. Trained systems librarians could certainly hope to compete for many of the posts in the first three categories, and might well succeed for the considerable number of jobs related to systems analysis, etc. in the fourth category. In other words, systems librarians could hope to compete for over half of the 1,000+ jobs analysed in this survey – some indication both of their range of skills and of the direction in which the market-place is developing. A more specific study of systems librarians in the UK confirms that there is scope for a further expansion of numbers.[7]

Experience in the USA seems similar to that in the UK. Advertisements for systems librarian posts, specifically, require experience with library bibliographic systems, but regard a library qualification as useful, rather than essential.[8] Job responsibilities emphasize ability to select and install a system and/or to run an existing system. The concern is with existing systems and short-term planning, rather than preparing for the future.

Information gained from employers and job advertisements can be supplemented by an examination of what people involved with systems actually do when they are in post.[9] Nearly all are, or have been, involved in the main areas which have been described above – planning, installation and implementation, and running and maintenance. Most are involved in staff training and, to a slightly lesser extent, user training. Only about a third have been concerned with physical aspects of operating the system, such as programming and hardware maintenance.

THE EDUCATION OF SYSTEMS LIBRARIANS

The survey reported in the preceding paragraph found that formal education and library qualifications were not seen as highly relevant to a systems librarian's job. This raises the immediate question, to what extent do library schools provide in their curricula material that is relevant to the work of a systems librarian?

By the end of the 1980s, the content of library and information courses, especially at postgraduate level, had moved strongly towards emphasizing the automated handling of information. This can be seen readily by comparing the main features of a postgraduate course in the UK and the USA.

UK syllabuses: information management, information technology, information sources, use and searching, human factors in information systems design, database structure and design, information handling.

USA syllabuses: information systems analysis, management principles, information structures and strategies, computer technologies, information processing, concepts of information resources, managerial statistics, economics for information, national and international information policies.

Both these courses cover the librarianship requirements of a systems librarian, and some of the systems requirements. (The USA syllabus does rather better in this latter respect.) However, the computing-oriented components are underplayed. For example, both cover software selection and evaluation, but are less good on the corresponding activities for hardware. Neither pays much attention to programming (though a few postgraduate courses – mainly those concerned with information, more than library studies – do incorporate a significant amount). Neither does much to help future trainers of staff and users.

With the exception of this last deficiency, most of the gaps can be filled with courses typically offered by computing departments: this is the route down which some courses in the UK and USA are now going.[10] Such an 'add-on' approach is not necessarily ideal because computer professionals are not usually acquainted with the sorts of problems faced by librarians. Consequently, the material in computer courses may be only partly relevant to students of librarianship. For such a student, a computer course may also represent overkill. This can be true in programming, for example, where a systems librarian may need only a nodding acquaintance with BASIC and is, instead, inundated with C.

The recent development of degrees planned and taught jointly between library and information departments and those in other subjects avoids some of the problems of purely modular degrees and helps bridge the gap between the different approaches to information technology. For example, one British university now has an MSc in Information Systems and Technology taught jointly by the Departments of Information Science, Computer Science and Business Computing. The course covers, 'in approximately equal depth, the hardware and software associated with information technology, the analysis and design of information systems, and aspects of information itself'.

Are postgraduate courses necessarily the best way of educating systems librarians? After all, an undergraduate course allows for more time for exploring all parts of the syllabus. Studies carried out in the UK during the 1980s suggested that the career prospects for librarians were much the same seven years after graduation whether they had taken undergraduate degrees or postgraduate diplomas (though postgraduate degrees had a slight edge in terms of career development).[11,12] Some undergraduate degrees now can provide a reasonable basis for a career in systems librarianship. Consider, for example, the following BSc course available in the UK:

First year Applications of information technology; information sources and searching; introduction to information studies; organization and retrieval of information; understanding organizations; introduction to computer systems; systems analysis; computer programming; problem-solving methods; ergonomics and design.

Second year Business planning and marketing; human resource management; online information retrieval; research methods; subject analysis and indexing; introduction to computer systems; information processing; programming projects; trends in information technology; skills analysis.

Third year Compulsory subjects: advanced information retrieval; practical financial management; legal and professional issues; software project management – plus options (including networking and software implementation).

Along with course content, there is the question of student background. Many students taking library courses are female, and arts-oriented (as compared with the more male, and science-oriented information courses). Does this represent an obstacle to the training of systems librarians? As we have seen, though existing library and information courses may not provide all the background required by a systems librarian, they do include considerable material relevant to library automation. It is typically found on such courses that females can perform as well as males, and arts-oriented students – given proper motivation – do not perform significantly less well than science-oriented students. A study of postgraduate students from one British university compared the careers of those with science and technology qualifications on the one hand, with those possessing social science qualifications on the other. Some differences could be found in the initial jobs taken by the two groups. However, their subsequent jobs fitted more closely to a common pattern: in both cases this involved a more intensive use of information technology.[13,14]

According to McLain *et al.*, 'the optimal solution to producing qualified library system analysts is to locate individuals with the necessary technical background (and inclination) and teach them to be librarians. Unfortunately, this may also be the least feasible method on a large scale.'[15] The difficulty is how to attract technically trained individuals onto a library and information studies postgraduate course. Students with a first degree in computer studies will almost certainly be able to command salaries in excess of those paid to new entrants into the library profession.

A final problem in the education of systems librarians relates to resourcing within library and information studies departments particularly in the UK. Training for automation requires instruction in the use of sophisticated and up-to-date hardware and software. Investment is therefore required in setting up laboratories containing workstations linked to both internal (CWIS) and external (JANET, the Internet) networks, as well as obtaining expensive new software products. Even when this is possible, such provision clearly has an impact on staffing, both in terms of technical laboratory staff as well as teaching staff. Attracting suitably qualified teaching staff is as problematical as recruiting suitable postgraduate students: once again salary levels are a key factor.

ON-THE-JOB TRAINING

The type of on-the-job training opportunities required by and offered to systems librarians inevitably depends upon a number of highly variable factors, including: academic background (library or computer studies) and previous work experience of the individual; the position of the post within the library hierarchy; and the current state of information technology developments within both the library and the parent organization. A recent survey of UK systems librarians by Muirhead (see Chapter 1) indicated that, on the whole, systems librarians are computer-trained librarians rather than library-trained computer people. They were found to have experience in a broad range of library work with no particular specialization predominating. A number of respondents taking part in the survey felt that their lack of computing skills was a source of stress and placed them at a disadvantage. Other interesting facts to emerge were that few respondents had become systems librarians immediately after leaving library school, and a massive 66% were internal appointments, suggesting that employers prefer candidates who have both considerable library experience and an inside knowledge of local practices and systems. In the light of such information, the issues of on-the-job training and continuing professional development (CPD) are clearly important ones for library management. These points have been emphasized by an American university librarian:

> Those currently in library management positions - not just senior people, but 'middle managers' and younger people who are being groomed for moving up in larger libraries as well – are in urgent need of new automa-

tion training. I would argue that every employee needs to understand computing better and that we should spend every training dollar we have on automation education at all staff levels. Librarians need to reorient themselves in their approach to computing – away from the long-articulated position that librarians will not 'do' automation but 'use' automation, toward a much more involved stance in which participation in the 'doing' of automation becomes a matter of course. The necessary training can be started through investment in short courses or other formal educational experiences, but must be pursued further than that; librarians must be provided the resources to 'get their hands dirty' with local automation experiments so that they may grasp the full potential that computing holds for improving access to information and managing library processes.[16]

As stated earlier in this chapter, although job advertisements vary enormously, the three main categories of knowledge required of a systems librarian are (1) library operations, (2) information technology, and (3) management. Perhaps the easiest of the three for library management to address is that relating to library operations. A newly appointed systems librarian should be expected to undertake the same general library induction programme as colleagues in more traditional areas of work. A thorough knowledge of library organization, management structure, and basic operational procedures is a prerequisite. A well-designed induction programme should allow the new appointee to spend time in all the various departments or sections of the library and to learn from colleagues information about both the specific tasks, and aims and objectives of individuals and sections. Shadowing of key individuals can also be a useful exercise. It can help in developing an understanding of library culture and jargon; building essential contacts with the staff; and introducing the new systems librarian to the needs of individuals and departments both within and outside the library.

Crucial during this induction period is the imparting of an understanding of the structure of the library and of a clear and unambiguous reporting structure. Due to the permeation of information technology into all aspects of library services, systems librarians 'wield considerable power (potentially) and also at times enjoy the mystique of possessing what appears from the outside to be arcane and esoteric knowledge'.[17] A 1986 survey by the Association of Research Libraries (ARL) in the USA found that reporting lines varied tremendously in different institutions and were often based on historical precedence rather than current reality. The survey found that in most libraries the systems librarian reported either to the Director (39%) or the Head of Technical Services (14%).[18] However, the 1991 Muirhead survey[19] found that 66% of respondents reported directly to their Director (Chief Librarian or his/her deputy). Perhaps more significantly, 52% of systems librarians were members of their senior management team. It is interesting to note that as far back as 1980, Sherwood wrote: 'If a systems librarian is being properly utilised by a library, the incumbent will bear considerable responsibility for the present and future operations of that library. On his judgement and advice will ultimately rest a great deal of effort and expenditure. The position should therefore be a senior one.'[20]

Discussions with systems librarians reinforce this assertion. Furthermore, it is generally acknowledged that an early introduction, by senior management, to the longer term strategic planning of the library service is highly desirable. Moreover, up-to-date knowledge of management policies and strategic plans is an essential, ongoing requirement if the systems department is to support the library's IT developments. Participation in the senior management team and senior staff meetings is therefore crucial.

Such an assessment of seniority certainly reflects the increasing importance attached to the post. In terms of training, the level of reporting and status within the hierarchy, clearly has a direct impact on the person's responsibilities in budgeting, planning, staffing, and decision-making abilities, and thus on their overall training requirements.

The second category of knowledge required of systems librarians is information technology. Training to an appropriate level in this area should ideally form part of a formal continuous professional development programme. The potential benefits of such a programme would appear to be indisputable but it is unlikely that, in the majority of organizations, such training could be offered in-house by the library. (However, the experience available from other organizational resources such as Computing Services and Computing Departments should not be overlooked.) Consequently, at some stage, most libraries turn to external bodies for off-site training courses, conferences, and workshops, including:

- professional bodies and their groups, for example The Library Association (LA), Institute of Information Scientists (IIS), and Aslib;
- commercial suppliers of library hardware and software, for example DIALOG, Silver Platter, BLCMP, Geac;
- commercial organizations specializing in information technology training, for example TFPL and computer schools;
- cooperative library automation groups, for example BLCMP, Libertas, OCLC;
- user groups associated with a particular system or product, for example BIDS, ProCite, BLCMP;
- schools of information and library studies and other educational organizations.

Owing to the rapid pace of change within the whole area of information technology, the systems librarian will need to participate in various forms of CPD activities offered by a wide range of different organizations. Given the plethora of advertised off-site training courses in information technology and the fact that they are generally at the more expensive end of the market, it is important to ensure, as far as possible, that the course matches the needs of the individual. It must also conform to predetermined criteria, for example facilities for hands-on experience, experienced trainers, and backup documentation. Discussions with systems librarians emphasize, in particular, the importance of supplier training – especially that of major library systems suppliers such as Geac, BLCMP, and Libertas. Such user groups play a central role in the work of systems librarians, enabling them to influence the development of software, articulate and discuss complaints and problems, and develop a network of contacts. As in any specialized field (people) networks are of paramount importance. Telephone, fax, and e-mail form essential personal links to colleagues in similar library environments.

More generally, electronic discussion lists and bulletin boards provide a forum for discussion of common interests. Other information sources include: library IT exhibitions; IT-related journals, magazines, and newspapers (for up-to-date information and benchmark testing); and junk-mail flyers! Several systems librarians expressed concern that day-to-day pressures made it increasingly difficult to find the time to look forward and investigate new developments and new technologies. This is an important issue for library managers. In the field of IT, it is imperative that someone in the organization has both the motivation and the time to concentrate on forward thinking. Lack of such initiative could cost an organization both efficiency and academic/commercial advantage.

One aspect of training which should not be overlooked is that of self-learning, where staff initiate their own learning process and have control over what, when, and where they learn. In a well-managed library environment where motivation is high, self-learning is frequently used by library staff to teach themselves – often with the help of manuals – how to use particular systems. Many software packages include training materials (of various quality) and both system-based or print-based guides can mean quick and effective learning. Most systems librarians would agree, however, that manuals are not an adequate substitute for systems-specific training as they do not give a true overview of the system. Detailed training courses from suppliers are an essential starting-point; well-written, structured manuals should be available to refer to after the course.

Self-learning also includes flexible, open, and distance learning and offers individuals the opportunity to improve their knowledge-base and skills in a variety of IT-related areas. Many such courses exist and are well-documented in the various open learning directories. Flexible self-learning is probably the best option for the systems librarian who wishes to add to and improve his or her technological expertise. The typical librarian with a limited technical background and a full-time professional position to maintain, would almost certainly find it very difficult to pursue either an undergraduate or postgraduate degree in computer science. Such a course of action would be difficult, long-term and costly.

By implication and exclusion this conclusion is supported by Durrance[21] who identified five levels of continuing education programmes relating to information technology:

1   Those that give librarians the desire to embrace a particular technological innovation.
2   Those that provide the knowledge or information necessary to become involved or to purchase the technology.
3   Those that transmit the skills necessary to manipulate the technology.
4   Those that provide specialized or advanced skills.
5   Those that focus on the management skills necessary to oversee the technology.

To produce individuals capable of operating at level four she suggests that the person should obtain a second Bachelor's or Master's degree in computer science. Given that it will take three years full-time to accomplish the former and one year full-time to achieve the latter, Durrance has inadvertently identified the major problem with continuing education for systems librarians. Systems staff already working in a library will seldom have the time, or even the inclination, to obtain these types of degree – even part-time.

Many on-the-job training requirements are inevitably associated with the technical aspects of the systems librarian's job: IT-related tasks such as choosing systems, implementation, development, systems maintenance, and programming. These are clearly essential elements of the post. However, if we cast our minds back to the various job descriptions discussed earlier in the chapter it becomes apparent that there is also another very important requirement of a systems librarian's job – management skills.

Obvious management skills include planning abilities – both at an operational and strategic level – and budgeting. After all, '. . . the automated system may be, and most likely is, the most expensive and visible thing you will ever put into the library. The cost of both procuring and maintaining the automated system are significant'.[22] The systems librarian will usually have to endure frequent complaints from other senior library staff about the high proportion of library funds being consumed by the automated system and IT developments in general. An ability to formulate budgets, justify expenditure, and present well-planned and argued cases for systems expenditure is an important aspect of the post.

This leads on to perhaps the most important of management skills – dealing with people. Systems librarians must of necessity deal with people just as much as machines. This is particularly well-illustrated by the following extract from a job description: 'Personality traits: exceptional communication and listening skills; positive and network-promoting relationships with library staff and administrators; strong teaching skills; tact; courtesy; ability to communicate pleasantly and effectively with the general public and co-workers.'[23] Training in this area can frequently be provided in-house. Many forward-looking organizations offer management training courses, interpersonal communication skills training, etc. as part of an organizational staff development programme. Indeed, forward-looking library managers are increasingly investing staff time and money in tailored, targeted courses specially for library staff.

In addition to general staff management responsibilities a systems librarian's job impinges on virtually every other section within the library system. An essential task is to keep staff informed about work in progress and involve all relevant staff in the planning process. As well as frequent informal discussions, systems librarians will usually be required to chair, or at least contribute to committees and working parties, make presentations at staff meetings, and write articles in library and parent organization newsletters, magazines, etc. Although interpersonal relationships with library staff are extremely important, there are two other groups of people with whom systems staff are required to interact on a daily basis – computer centre staff and system suppliers. Relationships with staff in the computer centre require a great deal of tact and diplomacy but also quiet persistence. As pointed out by Chan: 'Systems librarians will be uneasily aware of the pressure on the computing department, which like the library will always be overstretched, but nevertheless, when their help is needed, the systems librarian will often have to prod them repeatedly as they may not appreciate the urgency of the situation or they may simply be overwhelmed by the other demands being made on them.'[24] Dealings with system suppliers need not be so restrained. Market forces apply and there is no reason to be polite and friendly with a supplier who is not fulfilling his or her part of the contract.

TRAINING LIBRARY STAFF

A final aspect of a systems librarian's job is that of training other library staff. In the majority of large libraries, all staff – from library assistants to senior managers – will have some form of daily contact with IT. A survey of the impact of IT on senior managers in academic libraries showed that nearly 60% of senior staff have a computer of some description in their office. Computerized work activities included writing reports, preparing budgets, sending and receiving e-mail, online information gathering and maintenance of personal diaries and databases.[25]

Staff training has to be seen as an ongoing requirement as new staff are appointed and new developments in IT are integrated into library services. While written documentation, for both library staff and users, is essential, this can never be a substitute for hands-on experience. In-house seminars and workshops incorporating demonstrations and practical exercises provide the best learning environment; here, once again, the communication skills of the systems librarian come to the fore. Clearly, staff do not learn effectively in a training session that is pitched at too high a level and permeated with computer jargon and unexplained acronyms. Frustration and annoyance will be the only outcome.

The depth of training given by systems staff to their colleagues will necessarily vary from institution to institution. What is important to remember is that ultimately, the better the initial training, the fewer subsequent calls there will be on systems staff time to fix minor hardware and software problems. In an ideal situation, the systems librarian should eventually be able to delegate most of the routine training functions and systems maintenance to other staff. Moreover, from a management perspective, spreading knowledge and responsibility throughout the library avoids the danger of concentrating them on one person or one small group of people. Such delegation also overcomes a potential problem for systems librarians – that of feeling isolated from colleagues by one's specialist interests. (One reason why training courses outside the institution are currently worth supporting is to allow systems librarians to mix with their peers, who have similar job concerns.)

Although this discussion of training has been illustrated mainly by examples from the UK and USA the points made are applicable to most developed countries. However, systems librarians are also becoming needed more and more by major centres in developing countries. Their importance there may be even greater than in developed countries, since the infrastructure (for example as regards equipment maintenance) is often less well-organized than in developing countries, and so more is required of them. At the same time, they are likely to feel more isolated, and to have less adequate access to training than their counterparts in developed countries. Initial training may be provided abroad, but frequent trips overseas for updating are rarely possible. Hence, there appears to be an urgent need for an effective system of distance education aimed at systems librarians in developing countries.

CONCLUSION

It is clear from job advertisements, surveys and anecdotal evidence that systems librarians are in increasing demand. In terms of their initial education, library and information schools in a number of developed countries (though by no means all) provide a reasonable basis of knowledge for systems librarian work. In many cases, some additional computing knowledge is desirable: the modular course system, now increasingly common in universities, allows this to be obtained by an appropriate selection of courses from other departments. Such selection presumes that students are aware that they wish to pursue a career as a systems librarian. This is not true at present, since many systems librarians are converts from other posts. However, the trend towards recognizing systems librarianship as a distinct specialism suggests that an increasing number of students will come to see it as a possible career. Because computer-based systems and their applications will continue to change and diversify into the foreseeable future, access to further training is likely to be more important for systems librarians than for any other single group.

REFERENCES

1 Schuyler, M. and Swanson, E., *The systems librarian guide to computers*, Westport and London, Meckler, 1991, 18–19.

2 Rowe, R. R., 'Managerial competence for library automation', *Library hi tech*, **7** (2), 1989, 104–6.

3 White, F., 'The role of the automation librarian in the medium-sized library', *Canadian library journal*, **47** (4), 1990, 257–62.

4 Chu, F. T., 'Evaluating the skills of the systems librarian', *Journal of library administration*, **12** (1), 1990, 91–102.

5 Epstein, S. B., 'Administrators of automated systems: a job description', *Library journal*, 15 March, 1991, 66–7.

6 Moore, N., *The emerging market for librarians and information workers*, London, British Library, 1987 (LIR Report 56).

7 Muirhead, G., 'A survey of systems librarians posts in libraries in the United Kingdom: a summary of the main findings', *ITs news*, **27**, 1993, 31–4.

8 Martin, S. K., 'The role of the systems librarian', *Journal of library administration*, **9** (4), 1988, 57–68.

9 Meadows, A. J., 'Educating the information professional', *Perspectives in information management*, **1**, 1989, 169–86.

10 McLain, J. P., Wallace, D. P. and Heim, K. M., 'Educating for automation: can the library schools do the job?', *Journal of library administration*, **13** (1/2), 1990, 7–20.

11 Large, J. A. and Armstrong, C. J., *An investigation into the criteria applied by employers in the library and information sector when appointing staff*, London, British Library, 1986.

12 White, B., *Impact of LIS education on subsequent career progression*, London, British Library, 1986.

13 Wood, F., Richardson, D. and Schur, H., 'Scientists and information work: the careers of the 1979–1985 M.Sc. graduates from the Department of Information Studies, University of Sheffield', *Journal of information science*, **13**, 1987, 197.

14 Hulme, A. J. and Wilson, T. D., 'Professional education and subsequent careers in library/information work: a follow-up study of former students on the M.A./M.Sc. Information Studies (Social Sciences) course at the University of Sheffield', *Journal of information science*, **14**, 1988, 109–17.

15 McLain et al., op. cit.

16 Nielsen, B., 'Comments on developing managerial competence for library automation', *Library hi tech*, **7** (2), 1989, 109–11.

17 Muirhead, G. A., 'System management in UK libraries: some preliminary findings of a survey', *Information services & use*, **12**, (1992), 177–93.

18 Manchovec, G. S., 'The broadening role of the systems librarian', *Online libraries & microcomputers*, **7** (10), October 1989.

19 Muirhead, see ref. 7.

20 Sherwood, M., 'The systems librarian, or library systems analyst', *Australian library journal*, **29** (4), 176–9.

21 Durrance, J. C., 'Library schools and continuing professional education: the de facto role and factors that influence it', *Library trends*, **34** (Spring 1986), 683.

22 Epstein, op. cit..

23 Ibid.

24 Chan, G. K. L., 'The systems librarian', in Revill, D.H. (ed.), *Personnel management in polytechnic libraries*, Aldershot, Gower in association with COPOL, 175–99.

25 Hayter, M. and Heery, M., 'Use of IT by senior managers in UK academic libraries', *Aslib proceedings*, **41** (4), 1989, 203–11.

11 What's the use of systems?: the role of library systems in the education of young professionals

❖ Shelagh Fisher

1 INTRODUCTION

A knowledge of library systems is important to those who aspire to be systems librarians; but is it of value to anyone else? This chapter argues that it is and that all library and information students can benefit from the approach used at Manchester Metropolitan University, where students on first-professional courses in the Department of Library and Information Studies benefit from hands-on experience of 'real' library systems. The integration of library systems into the curriculum fosters a number of educational and course objectives. The management of this experience is recounted in this chapter and is supported by examples of students' own reflections of their educational experiences. Profiles of recent graduates in their first professional posts are included to illustrate the wide variety of learning outcomes derived from using library systems in the educational context.

The Department in Manchester offers an extensive programme of courses, both full-time and part-time at undergraduate, postgraduate, Masters, and research degree level, in order to meet the fast developing needs of the library and information profession. A major area of the Department's activities is focused on teaching state-of-the-art information technology. This is supported by a comprehensive range of hardware and software. Such facilities are continuously under development.

Important steps forward have been made possible in the past three years with the implementation of 'real' library systems software in the Department for use in teaching. The BookshelF and Heritage systems are available with the full complement of working modules, while TinLib and Librarian are available as demonstration systems. The latter, although limited in record capacity, do simulate the actual systems. Demonstration disks of TALIS and Genesis are also available.

It is argued here that learning experiences provided through the use of library systems have implications for education and professional work far beyond the immediate objectives of any one syllabus. Indeed, student experience with library systems can be seen to provide a significant platform for many areas of development in library and information work.

2   COURSES

The Department offers first-professional education in the form of the BA (Hons) Information and Library Management and the PG/Diploma/MA Information and Library Studies. Both these courses may be taken full-time or part-time. Post-experience courses are offered in part-time mode for the MA Strategic Library Management and the MSc Information Management. Full and part-time research degrees are offered at MA, MPhil and PhD level.

The particular application of library systems discussed in this chapter are based on the BA (Hons) Information and Library Management, which is the main undergraduate programme in the Department.

Components in the BA course comprise Management, Information Technology, Information Systems, Information Sources, Information Retrieval, Information and Society, Research Methods, Communication Skills, and one of a number of electives. Electives focus either on one particular group of users, such as adult public library users, students and teachers in further and higher education, business and commercial users, children and young people, or on the design of computer-based information systems.

The course is designed so that students are actively involved in the teaching and learning process. Methods range from lectures through to seminars, practical computer workshops and visits, with an emphasis on group work.

Students undertake periods of work placement in organizations which are relevant to their study and specific interests. Placements vary significantly in their nature, from those in large public and academic library systems to others concerned with information management in organizations. Some students may be involved in the establishment of information collections and databases for local community groups and significant information users (such as medical consultants) or in the production of training videos. Students on the BA course, with no previous library experience, have the opportunity of spending half a day per week in a working environment throughout their first year.

3   DEPARTMENTAL IT FACILITIES

The library systems available to students in the Department are installed on standalone PCs, on the local area network (LAN) or on the central University's Prime 6350 super-minicomputer.

In the Department, a dedicated information access laboratory contains 20 Mitac PCs which can be used as standalones, as part of an Ethernet Isolan LAN, or as intelligent terminals to access the University's Prime system, and through the latter, access to PSS and JANET. A second information technology laboratory provides 20 Tulip 1Mb AT COMPACT 2 286 EGA workstations, each with 40 Mb hard disk. These machines are now four years old and are rostered to be replaced by 20 MITAC 486 PCs. A 3Mb Tulip AT 386 SX 160 Mb hard disk machine acts as a file server on the Isolan Ethernet LAN, supporting Novell Advanced Netware linked to the workstations. Networked versions of several applications software packages are installed. These include Paradox, WordPerfect, Quattro Pro, Framework III, and Papyrus. Students also have access via JANET to NISS and BUBL, of which extensive use is made in the teaching of OPACs worldwide and searching online information services such as DIALOG. Information servers around the world can also be accessed using the Gopher software installed on the local fileserver.

The BookshelF library system is installed on the central University Prime 6350 computer, TinLib and Librarian on standalone PCs, and Heritage is available across the local area network. The tutorial versions of TALIS and Genesis are also available on the LAN.

4 LIBRARY SYSTEMS IN THE CURRICULUM

Three core components of the BA course are Information Access, Information Technology, and Management.

The objectives of the Information Access component are to enable the student to create bibliographic and data records for appropriate materials, evaluate specific information resources and to match user needs to information resources. Topics include printed, online and CD-ROM-based information sources, networked information sources, bibliographic control, cataloguing codes and standards, OPACs, classification, information retrieval (IR) theory and techniques, subject indexing, thesaurus construction, and evaluation of IR systems.

A library system provides the framework for students to create a working catalogue with appropriate subject access which can utilize natural and controlled indexing languages. Since the systems in the Department are networked on different platforms, students are able to evaluate hardware and software capabilities. Students also test and evaluate the databases which they have created, utilizing a range of interfaces, OPACs, command languages, and search devices. IR theory is related to the practical issues involved in creating an information system to match user needs.

The Information Systems component of the course has the general objectives of enabling the student to develop foundation skills in systems analysis and design, and enabling the student to select software for a particular library or information environment. The focus for the course is systems analysis, design, and implementation. Topics which are explored include systems theory, systems methodologies, data gathering techniques, data analysis and modelling techniques, software and hardware evaluation, implementation, security, and user training.

Library systems allow students the opportunity to develop their understanding of the process of systems analysis and the need for system specifications. Students examine at first hand the ways in which a commercial software package matches or does not match the requirements of a specification. An integrated library system also provides a working model of relational database design.

The objectives of the Management component of the course are to enable students to acquire a body of knowledge and skills relevant to the management of resources in library and information units with specific regard to decision support systems, finance, stock, personnel, planning and public relations.

From the library system, students learn about fundamental library operations, which is a good starting-point in their training and education as future library managers. A working library system contains core information about a library's stock and clientele. Library systems provide management information on which decisions may be made about budgets, staff deployment, and stock control.

Each of these objectives and the ways in which library systems facilitate the learning experience, are explored in the following sections.

5   HOW STUDENTS USE THE SYSTEMS

Students are introduced to library systems in year two of the Information Access component. As a starting-point, they examine the menus of the main modules – Catalogue, Acquisitions, Circulation, and Serials. Secondly, students are given practical exercises designed to lead them through the processes of ordering, receipting, cataloguing, and issuing a book, in effect, tracking the item through the system. Thirdly, students undertake a number of projects which provide a means for furthering their learning and for assessing their understanding of specific applications. Fourthly, the systems are subjected to close scrutiny, when students are required to match the functions of a system to a system specification, in the form of a supplier's proposal. Finally, by using a range of systems students are able to make comparisons about system configurations, software functionality, interfaces, etc.

The specific teaching and learning methods are explained in more detail below.

5.1   Exploring the menus

Figure 11.1 gives an overview of menus and functions for the version of the BookshelF library system, available in the Department. The menus are very revealing, providing a neat summary of all the routines and operations which any automated or non-automated library is likely to perform.

5.1.1 *Exploring the menus – learning outcomes*

The menus in the Catalogue module, in addition to outlining the main cataloguing processes, raise a number of key issues about cataloguing codes and standards, record creation, retrospective conversion, record content, indexing languages, retrieval, and output.

The menu options available in the Acquisitions module represent the key processes involved in the process of managing the ordering, financial control, and receipt of new material in the library. From an examination of the menus, students can see that the Acquisitions module links directly to the catalogue. Menus in the Circulation Control module, in addition to highlighting the key operations, raise a number of further issues for consideration including uses of management information, the need for rapid response times, staffing issues, and library-defined parameters.

The menus in the Serials module, in addition to pinpointing the key operations of serials control, raise further issues in relation to patterns of serials publishing, sources of supply, efficiency of supply, and the uses and management of serials in different types of library.

1.	System Reference Data
1.1	Locations
1.2	Media
1.3	Default Values
1.4	Last Numbers
1.5	Accession Status
1.6	Accession Streams
1.7	Order Streams
1.8	Subject Definition
1.9	Areas
1.10	Sites
1.11	Users
2.	Catalogue Menu
2.1	Catalogue Maintenance
2.2	Accession File Maintenance
2.3	Catalogue Prints Menu
2.3.1	Sorted by Author
2.3.2	Sorted by Title
2.3.3	Sorted by Subject
2.3.4	Sorted by Specified Field
2.4	Catalogue Enquiry/OPAC
2.5	Execute Catalogue Indexing
2.6	Labelling continued/

Fig. 11.1 BookshelF menus

2.7	Acquire from Labelling
2.8	Journal Article Definition
2.9	Reference Data
2.9.1	Define Indexed Fields
2.9.2	Stop-List Maintenance
2.9.3	Users Enquiry File
3	Thesaurus Menu
3.1	Descriptor Definition
3.2	Synonym Definition
3.3	Thesaurus Enquiry
4	Acquisitions Menu
4.1	Order requests and catalogue update
4.2	Process Order Requests
4.3	Orders: write, review, cancel
4.4	Prepare orders for printing
4.5	Print Order Slips
4.6	Print Order Forms
4.7	Receipts/Claims menu
4.7.1	Receipts
4.7.2	Receipt of bar-coded stock
4.7.3	Claims
4.7.4	Print Claims
4.8	Assign Accession Numbers
4.9	New Accessions Listing
4.10	Reference Data
4.10.1	Suppliers
4.10.2	Budget
4.10.3	Currencies
4.10.4	Countries
5	Circulation Control Menu
5.1	Issues
5.2	Returns
5.3	Reservations
5.4	Reservation Priorities
5.5	Readers
5.6	Catalogue Recommendations
5.7	Calculate Overdues & Fines
5.8	Print Overdue Items
5.9	Reservation Notifications
5.10	Circulation Rules

continued/

Fig. 11.1 (cont.)

continued/

Fig. 11.1 (cont.)

6.11	Serials Reference Data
6.11.1	Issuing Body
6.11.2	Publishers
6.11.3	Countries
6.11.4	Issuing Frequency
6.11.5	Issue Copy Holding Details
6.11.6	Change Serial Standard Number
6.11.7	Budget Codes
6.11.8	Reader Categories
6.11.9	Locations

Fig. 11.1 (cont.)

5.2 Practical exercises

Staff in the Department have designed a number of practical exercises to familiarize students with the integrative nature of systems, with the functionality of software, and with the ways in which various systems handle the same set of data. The exercises are not assessed and therefore their use in teaching is not dependent on student access to their own workspace and ownership of data.

5.2.1 *Exploring and comparing systems*

A number of systems, including BookshelF, Heritage, TinLib and Librarian, can be examined and comparisons be made. Worksheets are provided, which instruct the student to perform two main tasks. The first is to create local parameters of their own choice. The second is to create a record for a document and perform operations using this record in the Cataloguing, Circulation, and Ordering modules. The record is then tracked through the system to examine its status, to understand the impact which various routines have upon it, and to determine the levels of integration of data for different routines.

Thus, in a workshop session, students will 'use' a type of library of their choice – this may be the University, their own public library, or a library or information unit in which they have worked, or have done their fieldwork placement. They then create:

- location codes for library sites in their chosen library organization;
- media codes for specific types of material - these may be related to the general material designations in AACR2 or may be related to a special library collection, for example a film library in which the range of physical formats may be given separate General Material Designations;
- reader categories for different types of library user, for example undergraduate, postgraduate, academic staff, etc.;

- a reader record with their own personal details, including their 'category';
- circulation rules for their own reader category – these will determine loan periods and fines according to the type of material and location of the borrowed items;
- supplier details and codes for use in ordering material;
- budget codes for use in ordering material, for example by subject, by location, or by type of material.

Once students have set up these parameters, by following the worksheets, they are required to:

- create a new record for a document;
- assign accession numbers to two copies;
- issue, return, reserve a copy for themselves;
- search for the title in the OPAC;
- examine its loan status;
- order additional copies;
- generate order forms;
- examine the status of the order;
- receipt orders;
- examine the holdings data for the title.

Students perform these operations using the range of systems available.

5.2.2 Practical exercises – learning outcomes

Use of library systems by students raises issues about hardware and software, providing students with foci for discussion. For example, should the computer be library-dedicated or shared? What are the benefits and problems of using proprietary and industry standard hardware? Who, in the organization, maintains and repairs it? How does one 'size' and configure a system? Should printers be available for public use? What are the effects of using DOS and non-DOS-based operating systems? Who supports the software? How is system security ensured? Is it password controlled? Are there different levels of system access?

By using and comparing different systems, students also experience the variables which affect system response times, such as the number of records in the system, 'size' of a record, other users on the system, system configuration, record locking, indexing routines, and phantom routines. Students compare OPAC interfaces, not only of the in-house library systems, but also with those available over JANET. They experience the complex variations which occur in the use of function keys. Some systems utilize only standard F1 to F12, while others use these combined with CTRL, ALT, SHIFT, END, HOME, and up/down arrows. The RETURN key also performs various functions in different systems. Comparisons are also made between database structures, record formats, and input screens. Facilities for the provision of management information within systems are also examined, from menu-generated reports to report generators and query languages – it is usually the inadequacies of these which come to the fore!

5.3   Assessment of students' learning

Using BookshelF, students gain practical insight into methods of organizing and accessing information, and into the functions of a computerized library housekeeping system. In addition, students develop skills appropriate for creating systems specifications. This approach also provides a mechanism for the assessment of individual student's efforts and depth of understanding.

A common approach to the use of library systems in LIS education has been to demonstrate the features or, at best, hands-on experience of a shared data-file (that is, all data held in the system can be accessed by all users). Such an approach does not allow for assessment of an individual student's input. Students at Manchester, however, can access their own individual BookshelF systems which are located via personal Prime directories. Programmers in the University's Computing Services Unit have created a 'Virtual BookshelF Environment'. This means that pointers have been created in the student Prime directories to the BookshelF programs so that each student appears to have access to their own versions. Students working simultaneously, therefore, can create catalogue entries, index them, construct thesauri, set up local parameters, search their own databases, etc. without accessing any other student files nor using other students' data.

5.3.1   *Projects*

Two system-related assessed projects which the students undertake would be impossible without the facility outlined above.

5.3.1.1   *Database creation and retrieval*

The first project focuses on bibliographic record creation, access points, and headings and the second on subject indexing and thesaurus construction. (It should be noted that both these projects and the system specification-based project described in section 5.3.1.3 below, function both as a means of assessing learning and as vehicles whereby learning is facilitated.) Students, for the first project, are required to provide bibliographic descriptions for a set of book and non-book items in accordance with AACR2 and then enter this information into the BookshelF Catalogue Maintenance program. The students' submission for assessment includes a printout of their set of catalogue entries arranged by author (a hard-copy catalogue) and a written discussion of the role of the main heading in computerized cataloguing systems, based on their practical experience of data entry, searching, and output from the BookshelF system.

The second project which necessitates student 'ownership' of their own BookshelF workspace focuses on subject indexing and thesaurus construction. For this project, students create bibliographic records for a set of journal articles, including abstracts, using the Journal Article Definition program. Each student is assigned the same set of records which relate to the subjects 'alcohol', 'drugs', and 'crime'. (These records have been downloaded, with abstracts from the National Criminal Justice Reference Service database, available on DIALOG.)

In addition to standard fields (author, title, source), two further fields allow for subject enhancement of the record – abstract and keywords fields. The inclusion of an abstract in a designated field allowing for up to 999 lines of text and a free-text search facility, gives students the experience of retrieval using natural language. The 'keywords' field links directly to the thesaurus program, and therefore a controlled indexing language. Students create their own thesaurus, in the specified subject area and assign relevant controlled terms to records in the keywords field. This automatically checks whether a term is in the thesaurus. In addition to printouts of assigned index terms and thesaurus relationships, students are required to submit an analysis which compares the effects of searching the database globally, that is using natural language, and restricting the search to the assigned keywords, thereby invoking the thesaurus, that is using a controlled vocabulary.

5.3.1.2 *Database creation and retrieval – learning outcomes*
Learning outcomes from such project-related uses of the system are manifold. The direct evidence for learning is in the students' written analyses and in the required printed output from the system. For example, in the first project, the process of creating a multimedia catalogue, gives students the opportunity to evaluate the role of AACR2 in a non-MARC-based environment. The problems of accommodating non-standard data in a standardized database record format (which is primarily book-oriented) are examined. Although BookshelF provides a field for a coded General Material Designation, there is no designated field or subfield for a number of key elements of description, for example scale and projection (maps), running time (video cassettes), material specific designation, provenance, manufacturer (3D artefacts), distributer (software, motion pictures), and so on. Conversely, a free-text IR system such as BookshelF demonstrates that in retrieval terms, the record format is of sec-

ondary importance when all data elements are indexable and are entered somewhere in the record , for example the notes field.

Students also examine the issues concerning the value and use of main headings and added entries. There is no uniform heading or authority control in the version of BookshelF used in the Department. The personal author and corporate author fields are multi-value. Multiple authors, therefore, have equal status in BookshelF when creating a record, or searching for a known item. When listing records on screen or in hard copy, in author order, multi-value personal and corporate author fields are 'exploded' to provide a listing which includes all author-based access points. Author headings are, in fact, modified statements of responsibility. Where there is no identifiable statement of responsibility for a document, the field is left blank, so there is no filing element for that particular record in the listing. This emphasizes the value of headings in computerized cataloguing as well as in manual systems.

In the second project outlined above, in which students index a set of articles and create a thesaurus, the principles of vocabulary control are reinforced on an experiential basis. The complexities of recall and precision ratios (always difficult for students when taught in the abstract) become meaningful in a practical application working with a limited set of documents. The effect of using primary and secondary concepts as index terms on recall and precision is demonstrated at close quarters. The assessment of students' written submissions clearly reveals an understanding of the effects of exhaustive indexing on the relevance of the recalled records. Automated retrieval systems – in this case BookshelF – allow for more exhaustive indexing than manual or printed systems. This factor may precipitate a degradation in the specificity of the indexing language, thereby reducing the precision ratio. Furthermore, students not only find that terms entered in the thesaurus should be confined to the relevant subject area, but also that the thesaurus should only contain terms which are collection-specific, otherwise searchers are led up blind alleys in pursuit of a specific subject for which there are neither records in the database, nor documents in the collection.

In general terms, students find that the use of the thesaurus in searching increases recall and lowers precision. The evidence for these relationships, however, is in no way determinate. Students also realise that the relationship between exhaustivity, specificity and precision is a highly complex one. While such findings underline the fact that the success of any retrieval system (that is high recall and high precision) is very dependent on the accurate analysis of document content and assignment of terms at the indexing stage, the project demonstrates to students that 'relevance' is a subjective interpretation and therefore very difficult to ensure at the search stage.

5.3.1.3 *System specifications*

A third project on which the students are assessed involves matching one or more systems to the requirements of a system specification. Firstly, students examine a range of system specifications which have been kindly donated by a variety of public, academic, and special libraries.

Secondly, students are supplied with selected extracts from the system specification for Sandwell Public Libraries and with corresponding extracts from the suppliers' proposal – permission was obtained from the originators of both documents. The system eventually acquired by Sandwell Public Libraries was, in fact, BookshelF.

Thirdly, a system specification for the fictitious 'Watermouth College of Higher Education' is distributed to students. This document has been created from a number of 'real' academic library system specifications. Students are required to respond to the mandatory and desirable requirements in the time-honoured fashion of library system suppliers. This entails examining a system to investigate whether and how the system can perform the required functions. The activity is project-based and students are assessed on the basis of their submitted proposal. However, as with other project work outlined above, the activity is designed to be supportive of the learning process, in addition to providing measurable output. The real worth of such projects is in the process of 'doing' them, rather than in the final grade achieved.

5.3.1.4 *System specifications – learning outcomes*

The examination of systems specifications generates lively discussion on the level of detail required in the specification, the problems which may arise from trying to match a system to a library's current manual operations, the importance of the systems analysis process before specifying requirements, the use of ambiguous terminology and jargon, and different requirements of public, academic and special libraries. The opportunity for scrutinizing real system specifications also provides students with some insight into demands made on suppliers for supplying 'total' solutions, that is supplying hardware, software, communications, ongoing support, and staff training. Indeed, many aspects of the library/supplier relationship are examined in the context of the tendering and supply processes.

Students are able to examine the specification, the supplier's proposal and the BookshelF system, giving them a total view of the whole decision process and the rationale for choice and outcome.

The project based on the model specification not only provides the student with the practical insight into the design of specifications and the expectations of proposals, but also necessitates the student subjecting the library system to close scrutiny.

The teaching methods and learning approaches outlined above are intended to enable students to acquire a range of skills relating to library and information systems and to understand some of the more theoretical aspects of information retrieval. In the following section, the students' own perceptions of their learning outcomes and experiences are explored further.

6   THE STUDENT EXPERIENCE

In their penultimate term the undergraduate students are required to submit a 4,000 word Learning Development Report (LDR) based on their reflections of their learning experiences over the previous 12 months. An analysis of 120 LDRs over a two-year period, reveals a number of educational and professional learning outcomes by students who have made extensive use of library systems in their project work and in class workshops. The extracts given below were selected as representative of the range of comments reflected in the reports of other students and to illustrate the style and content of the LDRs. These extracts focus on several students' experiences of using library systems as undergraduates in the Department.

> This month, using BookshelF, I have been made aware of just how much my past experience of library work ties in with topics on the syllabus. Information Access, as the most 'library' oriented area of the course is probably the most obvious example of this. Again and again I find that procedures which I performed with little understanding at Lancaster Library are becoming clear for the first time. For instance, the concepts of precision and recall, which we have been covering recently, was a little like discovering the theory of grammar for the first time.

> It was extremely helpful to learn about computerized integrated library systems, but I found it hard. In a real working situation, a person would be trained to do such a task. I learned the ins and outs of the system. I feel I would be able to write a specification.

> In Information Access this month, the BookshelF catalogue and thesaurus evaluation project was submitted . . . I now appreciate the difference between using a thesaurus and a global search strategy . . . something which was causing me considerable difficulty until I came to examine them for the project. I was reminded of one of the endless supply of Chinese proverbs: 'Tell me, I forget. Show me, I remember. Involve me, I understand'.

> In the systems specification project, I could not find how BookshelF dealt with standing orders but other students found several solutions. One of the

best things about a project like this is that I got to work with other students, who have different outlooks and approaches to the problem which can help make sense of it. On my placement, I got to sit in on some training sessions of BookshelF which they were installing. I had used BookshelF in the second year so I found it easy to understand the trainer. This gave me a chance to observe training techniques and methods which I can reflect on for the future and maybe use these to train my own staff if I have the chance to become a manager.

The experience I had with BookshelF on the course immediately seemed more meaningful on my placement. It gave me confidence using the DS system. The knowledge gained in computerized cataloguing and retrieval gave me great satisfaction in being able to use this knowledge to provide a service.

The evaluation of library systems enabled me to identify flaws in the software and also their good points and as a result, taught me to be critical and not just to accept things the way they are. Using the BookshelF library housekeeping system gave me experience and a new insight that have helped build my confidence in this subject and extend my IT experience.

On the visit to [a library book supplier], I saw how Information Technology for information access is used and that it was something I was actually capable of using myself, especially with my experience of using a similar integrated library system. It was interesting to see the end products such as order slips which were produced. Seeing the IT and information retrieval skills I had acquired at college effectively used by others, made me feel more confident that I could assume responsibility in this kind of environment.

On field work – at [a special library in London] – they asked me to evaluate their user guide to their OPAC. The evaluation skills that I had learned in information access from the BookshelF projects were very useful and they appreciated my comments and thought they were worthwhile.

Using library systems in Information Technology and Information Access was, for me, of major importance and because it was practical in nature, was one of the most beneficial areas in relation to future library work. I learned 1) an understanding and appreciation of the workings of a library housekeeping system and the advantages of them 2) an appreciation of library housekeeping routines 3) understanding of the benefits and limitations of IT 4) insight into the process of changing from manual to computerized systems.

In doing my Information Access projects, I felt I could finally see how cataloguing, indexing and retrieval slotted together. Suddenly all these subjects that I knew were connected, but found difficult to put together from my notes came together in the form of the projects.

The IT project made it essential to look at all the technical documentation that went with the library system. I felt that in a work situation, I would come across similar manuals and I know I would feel more confident to tackle them.

6.1   Summary of learning outcomes – the student perspective

These extracts from a small, but fairly typical, sample of Learning Development Reports, highlight a number of benefits and learning outcomes which are perceived by the students to be directly related to their experience of library systems.

The evidence here is that the library system is a focus for enhancing the learning accrued in previous work experience, and provides students with insights and skills on which they can draw on fieldwork placement and on visits to 'real' libraries. Understanding difficult concepts is facilitated by the marrying of theory with practice. Students are provided with marketable skills, enhancing their employability. They learn about systems training techniques, the complexities of technical documentation and issues in retrospective conversion. They also gain some life skills – working in groups – and develop powers of critical thought. Their library systems experience also gives them confidence in using information technology and in pursuing careers as information professionals.

7   GRADUATE PROFILES

A number of graduates, now in their first professional posts, were contacted and asked to supply details of their work responsibilities. In particular they were asked in which ways, if any, their use of library systems as undergraduates had impacted on their current jobs. They were selected for inclusion here on the basis of their contrasting work roles and responsibilities. In employment, or further study, they have all been able to draw on their undergraduate experience of using library systems. Their profiles are given below. (Names have been changed to protect their innocence!)

Name:	Karen Baker
Job title:	School Librarian
Organization:	School of Music

Responsibilities

Since my post is the first of its kind at [the music school], I am compiling my own job description as I go along. In the past there have been two teachers managing the music and academic libraries with the assistance of two part-time librarians. The new Head felt it was time for the library to develop and that a full-time librarian was the best way for this to be achieved . . . My duties include everything from issuing material to holding junior story times, writing overdues to choosing a library software package.

On my first day, I was asked to think about choosing a system for the library. That was my one and only instruction – I was given a set of keys, directed to the library and from then on I was on my own. Choosing a library system is not something that can be carried out quickly. Apart from assessing our requirements, cost was also a consideration. I did pay [another college of music] a visit to look at their system as it was specifically designed to cater for music, but at £40,000, it was a touch out of our price range.

My main starting point was the Computers in Libraries exhibition. A quick look at what was on the market led me to arrange demos with Alice, Heritage and Documedia. Assessing the packages and how they fitted in with our requirements was my first priority. The system specification project using BookshelF came in very useful here. In fact it was commented on by one salesperson that I was very thorough compared to most schools, which was a reflection of my project experience. All the packages were very good for schools and they could all cater for our needs with the general material, but with music it was less straightforward. I felt that Heritage came out on top and could cope best with music. Having examined BookshelF in some detail, I could quickly grasp the basics of all the systems, and concentrate on my major concern of how it would handle music. I also think that my use of BookshelF had some impact on my selection of Heritage because I felt knowledgable and comfortable with the system.

The salespeople representing the various packages all said their system could handle music in the way I wanted. This in fact was not true. Again, my hands-on experience as a student was of great value. For example, students would search for the contents of the Brahms book of piano music and not the title, 'Klavier Werke'. The Notes field in Heritage enabled us to create our own field, i.e. Contents, and enter the various titles. Not all the systems provide such a facility e.g. the Alice Notes field is not free text. I first entered the titles as they would be written, but searching for them was very difficult e.g. 'Op 1' is treated as 2 search terms, as is 'C major'. Numbers and letters are on the stop list, so searching for them results in no hits. Ultimately, I decided that the best way of recording such titles, was to leave no spaces i.e. 'op1' and 'CMajor'. Students are instructed to search the database in this way and help screens are edited to indicate this. Another example was 'F#major' – the system does not recognize punctuation marks in searching, so the suppliers of Heritage wrote a small programme to allow the system to recognize the #key in searching and retrieval.

The retrieval facilities were an important issue in my choice of package for the library, and again the cataloguing and indexing project, in which I created a multi-media database proved highly useful. In fact all the exercises I did using library systems, especially BookshelF, have proved to be worthwhile. In my case it was a dummy run for the real thing. I have been able to put them to good use.

Name: Paul Blackwell
Job title: Assistant Librarian
Organization: Government Department, London

Responsibilities
Management and production of the current awareness service; routine system administration for DOBIS/LIBIS and STAIRS; development of the photograph database on Picture Cardbox; generating enquiry statistics using Supercalc.

There are three main areas of competence in my current post in which I think I have been influenced by using library systems on my library school course. Firstly, I am familiar with the complexities and detailed functions of an automated library system. For example, one of the jobs I run on the IBM system is to extract and print the overdues from DOBIS. Normally 49 out of 50 are OK but there are usually one or two which don't get printed due to an error in the system. For these, I have to manually enter the system to get the details. I think that the use of library systems at library school has enabled me to appreciate the size and scope of document searching, fields in circulation control and the reader records. Secondly, I understand the processes involved in choosing a library system. The [Department] is currently looking at library systems to replace the existing one. The librarian to whom I report, is directly involved in the decision-making process. The whole project is being run using the Prince methodology to maximize efficiency and meet deadlines. The system specification project using BookshelF, which I undertook as a student has helped me to (i) understand how an organization chooses a library system (ii) how and why a library specifies its operational requirements (iii) understand what a supplier has to do in order to sell a system (iv) understand how, in spite of steps one and two, the wrong system can be chosen. Thirdly, after using BookshelF at college for cataloguing and indexing, I understand the principles of thesaurus construction and how a thesaurus is used in indexing and searching. There is no thesaurus module on DOBIS and I have to update it manually on a word processor where it was originally created. The BookshelF thesaurus is a better way of creating and maintaining one, because it displays existing relationships when a new term is entered. When it comes to usage, however, there is no doubt that it is better to have a printed copy next to you. I have to assign subjects to the periodical articles for the current awareness service. I understand that BookshelF are updating their system and will run it in a Windows environment. This might help the user who will not need to leave the indexing function in order to consult the thesaurus.

Name: Laura Taggart
Job title: Postgraduate student – MSc Computing
Organization: UMIST

Course content
Systems analysis and design; Mathematical foundations of computing; Programming; Principles of Computation; Data structures; Database design; Artificial Intelligence; Information in Management; Knowledge-based decision support.

No previous knowledge of computing was required for the course. I found, however, that the experience and knowledge gained during my first degree aided my progress because I was already familiar with computer systems. This familiarity was more than many on the courses had – some were not sure what floppy disks were, or how to switch on a computer! At the other end of the spectrum, however, some members of the course were professionals in the computing world such as systems analysts and programmers. The options I chose were influenced by the work I had done on the library degree course. I was more inclined towards the database and systems analysis type modules, due to the use of BookshelF and other library systems, and to my final year undergraduate option in Information Systems.

My final dissertation for the MSc involved setting up a database for student records. I used Omnis 7, a relational database system. Much of the

BookshelF and library systems work I did as an undergraduate was relevant to the work I did on my MSc project. Although I didn't realize it at the time, the relational aspects of BookshelF helped me to understand the basic concepts of relational databases. The systems specification project was very useful because I had to write one for my MSc project, from the interviews which I conducted with the potential users of my student records system. I also came to realize that systems usually cannot always exactly meet the users' requirements. Having experienced the problem of poor response times when I used the BookshelF system, I then knew not to expect instant responses from systems which had many users or were mainframe or networked. Many on the MSc course complained about the poor response from the UMIST network. I however found it much faster and easier to use than BookshelF on the Prime computer.

For my project database, I also had to design the user interface. I think that all the systems I had used in the past probably had a bearing on the design I used for my system.

Name: Anne Barber
Job title: Development Analyst
Organization: An established library systems supplier

Responsibilities
To develop the OPAC for the next generation library system.

The classroom experience of BookshelF gave me some relevant experience for the job I have gone into after graduating. The projects which we did focused on front-end use and gave useful insight into the housekeeping aspects of library systems such as acquisitions. This was better than just looking at OPACs on JANET and in the University library. The main criticism I have of using BookshelF for project work was that I had little experience of using MARC-based library systems – which is what [this library system] revolves around – but this is just one supplier's perspective.

A familiarity with BookshelF, gained in my second year undergraduate course, however, enabled me to undertake my fieldwork placement with the suppliers. It was on my placement that I actually got to edit help screens, overdue letters and have more time to investigate the operating system. This helped when I started at [this library system supplier] as the use of SQL was familiar. The placement also gave me an insight into the library suppliers' working environment, the help desks, account management, programming, sales and most useful, the analysis and design process. It also provided me with an interesting final year project on the way BookshelF was used to generate management information. The use of library systems software at library school and my third year fieldwork placement were significant experiences for my CV, and I consequently achieved my ambition of working for a systems supplier.

Name: Lydia Davies
Job title: Information Officer, Datalinks project
Organization: A City Council

Responsibilities
To collate information on childcare and children's services within the city; evaluating software and designing a computerized information system.

I have been involved in the creation of a printed directory of services, in part, output from the database. This data, however, links into a plethora of systems which are crying out for computerization. Each 'childcare' facility has to undergo a lengthy registration and inspection process, demanding progress charts and standard letters. It has been impossible to create a grid reference of what is available without considering the underlying sources and their systems. So the Datalinks project is attempting to address these problems with a view to improving data flow, reduce duplication of effort, produce statistical information and at the same time, make the information more accessible to those who need it. Thus, I am involved in assessing systems and collaborating with staff to design more appropriate ones. Currently I am working with the development officer to computerize the District Offices. This involves staff training and preparation of guidance notes.

That library systems offer different modules to cater for different functions is, in itself, instructional, raising awareness of background information needs for management purposes, statistical recording, etc. as well as for its primary functions. Using such systems has highlighted the fact that a single record or data set can have many functions (the complete data, a subset of that data or that data combined with other data) required by different people for different reasons.

These simple concepts have been reflected in assessing systems in my current job, where there are competing demands over a single set of data. Computerization has many knock-on effects beyond the immediate need. In the case of library systems, the decision to computerize may involve questions about retrospective conversion, thesaurus construction, public access, one database for everything, or different files for different media. All these considerations were highlighted by the exercises using library systems and that knowledge is relevant in my current job. I can identify correlations between the creation of library records with records for childcare facilities, background requirements for management and planning, as well as security and levels of access.

A direct consequence of my use of library systems, was that I was able to take decisions on the choice of a text-retrieval package, and to include a keyword field in the design of a disability information database. I get the impression from non-library IT professionals that they tend to be ignorant of text-retrieval systems, indexing principles and conventions, stop/go lists – all of which are critical to the effectiveness of databases.

Using library systems as an undergraduate, I think I learnt about compromise. Such systems usually involve some kind of trade-off and the system may only be as good as the searcher or the indexer. For students doing the BookshelF exercises and projects, I think there was a great deal to take in. With hindsight, I can definitely see the value.

Name:	John Savage
Job title:	Assistant Librarian
Organization:	Medical research institute and teaching hospital

Responsibilities
Running the interlibrary loans service; literature searching – online and CD-ROM; training users in the use of computer software – CD-ROMs, Wordperfect, Papyrus and software on the VAX network; production of user guides to computer systems including the library system, Sydney; evaluating new software packages for library use.

My first special project at the library was to tailor the Circulation system on Sydney to the library's needs and implement it alongside the existing catalogue module. Previously, circulation control had been a manual paper-based system. Previous knowledge of library systems, especially BookshelF, gained during my degree course helped in that I already understood the functions of an automated library system. I only really needed to familiarize myself with the individuality of Sydney. This involved a single afternoon session at Soutron. The circulation module of any automated library system appears to centre on the same basic principles – tagging a user to an item and tracking that item's progress. The relationship between different types of data – i.e. bibliographic information and user information (name, department, status, number of loans, etc.) – is an important issue. Experience of systems such as BookshelF on the course helped to visualize the idea of relational data and their importance in automating well structured functions such as library operations. My success in implementing the circulation control made me look at my own area of ILL. I looked at what was available among the commercial interlibrary loans packages and tested a number of versions. I found them lacking in that they had too general a perspective of the ILL process – not all requests are supplied by the British Library DSC, for example. Therefore, we decided to write our own ILL module.

I place immense value on the knowledge gained on the course on systems analysis and design. The ability to look at a problem and put it into a database structure scenario removes an awful lot of work with regard to planning. Although as a student I had used dBase IV, the switch to Paradox 4.0 in my work was relatively simple. Programming skills acquired using dBase IV were transferable to Paradox's PAL language i.e. variables, loops, procedures, etc. Once the system was running, I knew that testing it was crucial, so I ran the manual and automated systems in parallel for 3 months, until I was sure that the system was working and that no further problems existed.

An important role of anyone introducing new computer-based routines into a service is training novice users. The problems I had with using BookshelF as a student helped in understanding that there are common problems which exist across the library system – fear of loss of data, duplication of records, the importance of using standards to ensure consistency, etc.

7.1 Graduates at work – developing the learning

The evidence here suggests that students have developed an understanding of and abilities in designing, creating, and implementing systems to provide an effective service to users. They have acquired competencies which they have built upon and developed as information professionals in their first posts. They are now managing and designing systems, dealing with commercial suppliers, planning for change and making informed decisions in the implementation of new technologies.

8 SUMMARY AND CONCLUSIONS

The ways in which students use library systems as undergraduates have been described in the previous sections, and specific learning outcomes have been identified. Some examples of students own reflections on their learning experiences (in their Learning Development Reports) suggest a number of more general benefits. In addition, recent graduates in their first professional posts have commented on the relevance of this undergraduate learning to their current posts. This evidence suggests a range of benefits and learning outcomes from using library systems in an educational context. These may be summarized as follows:

1   Library systems provide support in the teaching and learning of specific topics and concepts embedded in the core curriculum.
2   Library systems in the LIS curriculum have unifying functions. Their use relates theory to practice, integrates seemingly fragmented aspects of the course, and relates the academic experience to the workplace.
3   The student experience of using library systems provides them with professional and personal transferable skills.
4   The use of library systems as a vehicle for teaching and learning provide a basis for continuing professional development in first professional posts.

At the beginning of this chapter, it was posited that the use of library systems in teaching supported the objectives of three core components of the BA (Hons) course at Manchester Metropolitan University. On reviewing the outcomes presented in the previous sections, it becomes apparent that the use of library systems in the professional curriculum does more than that. Indeed, this approach to teaching and learning results in a much broader range of outcomes for students.

The outcomes noted may be compared with the aims and educational objectives for the *whole* undergraduate course. The aims may be summarized as enabling students to:

- develop the ability to understand the needs of information users;
- organize information for retrieval;
- create and use information systems;
- use manual and computerized systems in the achievement of work tasks;
- understand the role of management;
- understand the role of information professionals in organizations and society.

In the pursuit of these aims, students are required to develop a range of personal transferable skills, in particular, the ability to:

- identify problems and devise solutions;
- research, analyse, and synthesize information;
- use numerical, IT and expressive skills in the research and presentation of information;
- apply what has been learned in practice and practical situations.

Considering the learning outcomes achieved by the approach discussed in this chapter, against the general aims and objectives for the BA course, it can be strongly argued that the use of library systems in the curriculum has implications beyond the immediate course components and makes major contributions to the total educational experience.

12 Supplying the systems training

❖ *Christine Dobbs and Frances Richardson*

1 THE NEED FOR TRAINING

Why is more education and training required for the systems librarian? If systems today are really as intuitive and easy to use as the suppliers claim, then surely the intelligent user can pick up the essentials quickly, with the aid of a manual or two. Some people do indeed follow this principle, but with varying degrees of success, for although manufacturers may say that their products are idiot-proof, not all of us are idiots! However, the trend is toward even greater demand for training, and this is because there is much more to continuing education than learning how to operate a system.

While library software applications may have become more user-friendly in terms of the screen design and use of windowing techniques, the environment in which they run has become increasingly complex. The growing complexity is due to the development of better systems technology, notably:

- Open systems which allow software to run on a variety of hardware platforms.
- Client-server architecture to improve performance by distributing the processing time between more than one computer.
- High availability systems which minimize system downtime.
- Networked systems which improve communications and connect to databases.

Open systems in particular offer benefits to the library in terms of flexibility. 'Open' means that the operating system conforms to international standards (usually UNIX), which makes it possible to run on different hardware. This leads, however, to a choice which can be bewildering to the uninitiated and, moreover, if a mix of equipment and applications from a variety of suppliers is used, it will raise attendant issues of integration, management and problem resolution. The systems librarian who is able to understand at least some of these issues will be in a much better position to make informed choices and to keep everything running smoothly. This kind of knowledge can usually only be acquired on the job, as technology changes so fast.

The flexibility of the system is not confined to greater hardware choice; it is generally also possible to change the screen layouts, the types of standard reports produced, and other aspects of the system to suit the library. The setting of these system parameters is one of the tasks of the systems manager. As parameters need to be changed at intervals it is not sufficient merely to rely on the system vendor to set them up at the installation stage. Full training in this area can be extensive, particularly as few systems librarians have prior knowledge of UNIX.

Nowadays, the computer system is increasingly at the heart of the library services – it has become the central nervous system that links and controls all the departments and functions of the library. It affects everyone, either directly or indirectly, and a new system installation becomes a major project to manage. The systems librarian is often expected to be the project manager and must therefore acquire the necessary planning and implementation skills to see the project through from start to finish, including the liaison with suppliers and colleagues.

The role of the systems librarian may vary from one library to another but there is one core responsibility common to all, that of ensuring the efficient and effective use of computer systems throughout the library. This means more than setting up the systems and keeping them running during service hours, and more than staying ahead of new technology for planning purposes. It also means ensuring that the library staff use the system efficiently. Systems librarians can therefore play a crucial role in training their colleagues in the use of the system, and indeed the effectiveness of this training may determine the systems librarian's own role and status in the library.

All of this makes the job of systems librarian both varied and interesting, demanding a multiplicity of skills. Thus good quality education and training is vital to the success of the systems librarian.

Training for the systems librarian can be obtained from a variety of sources:

- library schools
- the Library Association
- external specialists
- system vendors.

The first of these has been considered in the previous chapter, and the occasional courses offered by the next two are outside the scope of this book. Systems suppliers, however, can provide a wealth of training, not just as an adjunct to the system purchase, and it is this area which is explored more fully in this chapter. Specific reference will be made to TALIS courses run by BLCMP. (TALIS is the UNIX-based library system designed by BLCMP in consultation with its member libraries.) At BLCMP it is held that good training is very much in the interests of the company, for this will lead to the most efficient and creative use of the systems in the libraries and minimize future support requirements. To this end BLCMP has always included the planning of training as part of the installation process for a new system, for this is the best route to customer satisfaction.

2 ANALYSIS OF TRAINING REQUIREMENTS

The biggest single need for training arises when a new system is to be installed in the library, whether or not the library has previously been automated. Project management skills such as planning, resource management, and implementation are required for this, and these can be provided by BLCMP as part of the installation project.

One of the first stages is to analyse training requirements and it is important for this analysis to start early and be viewed as an integral part of the project. In this way training can be tailored to the specific library requirements and circumstances which will make it most relevant and effective. The key points to identify at the beginning are (as with almost any project): why, who, what, when, where, and how.

2.1 Why

It is essential to be clear about training objectives, so that the training is placed in context and the effectiveness can be measured.

2.2 Who and What

Consideration needs to be given both to the systems librarian's training and to all the library staff who will be affected by the new system. Different functions have different training requirements, and so do people. Some may have used a similar system before elsewhere, others may never have touched a computer keyboard. Some may need a really good grasp of all functions while others would only use it occasionally. Still others may hardly ever have to use the system but need to understand the main functions. All of these categories require clear definitions.

2.3 When

For training to be effective it must be timely. Train too early and people may forget and need to relearn it all when the system goes live. Train too late, and there may not be enough time for people to gain confidence in using the system.

2.4 Where

Unfortunately, most training still takes place at the point of use – at the issue desk, for example. Some libraries, however, are starting to set aside a training area equipped with half a dozen terminals. The latter is, of course, more conducive to learning, because the everyday interruptions are kept away from the training sessions. An alternative is to go to the offices of the system supplier, but this may prove impractical for large numbers of people.

2.5   How
There are many alternatives including:

- one-to-one training
- classroom style
- computer-based training
- video training
- self-training through workbooks
- trial and error, through using the system
- cascade training.

Early discussions will establish which best meets the needs of both the library and individuals.

3   BLCMP APPROACH TO TRAINING
With each new TALIS installation BLCMP provides a training consultant to work alongside the systems manager and implementation team at the library. A professional trainer, the consultant works with the team to evaluate the training requirements and advise on methods and motivational approaches.

At many large libraries the cascade approach has been chosen for training staff on the TALIS system. This means that 'key trainers' are identified, who receive training direct from BLCMP and then pass the knowledge on to their colleagues. The 'key trainers' are representative members of each department or functional area, and the choice of the right people can be quite difficult, although in the end this approach is very satisfactory for several reasons. Firstly, the trainees feel more involved; secondly, the 'key trainers' can identify potential problem areas and sort out solutions before they start; and last but not least, the method is very cost-effective. In many situations people learn how to do some aspects of their job from a colleague, so this is usually accepted quite naturally, and frequently preferred to other methods.

Using 'key trainers' does, however, demand a well-documented and repeatable package, and BLCMP provides this. Flexibility is nevertheless retained, and the package is tailored early on to suit the library. The details of the approach are worked out in the regular project management meetings which form part of all major installations, and these also provide a forum for monitoring the progress of system training and tailoring as necessary.

A training consultant normally delivers most of the initial training, and can also call upon various business specialists from within BLCMP for specific areas. This is particularly useful when, for example, the Acquisitions Librarians want to examine Fund Accounting or Electronic Data Interchange subjects in depth. The BLCMP business specialists are themselves librarians and are thus able to focus the training on the areas of greatest need in the library.

There is a great variety of courses to choose from when planning the training. The 'Understanding BLCMP' course provides a high-level overview for senior management, and product demonstrations can additionally be arranged to familiarize staff with the new system well in advance of installation.

Pre-implementation workshops allow librarians to study the implications of the new system and how to prepare for it. Then comes the applications level training, together with sessions on technical support and management reporting.

The primary objective is for the library to make the most effective use of the system as quickly as possible.

The following is a list of all the courses currently available, and examples of the Acquisitions and System Manager course contents are also described in subsequent sections:

- Understanding BLCMP
- Pre-implementation workshops
- UNIX
- System Manager
- MARC Cataloguing
- Functional training: – Acquisitions
                          – Circulation
                          – OPAC
                          – Cataloguing
                          – Management Information
                          – Serials
                          – ILL

Some of these will be included within the contract price for a new installation, depending on the nature of the contract.

As most of the training is usually delivered at the customer site during the installation process, tailoring it to the library's specific needs is not a problem, but ongoing training such as the System Manager course is aimed at new systems librarians at existing BLCMP sites. The System Manager courses are held at BLCMP and carry the problem of varied audience experience levels because delegates have different skill backgrounds.

In addition, delegates are from both academic and public libraries, which gives them different experiences of the system. While it is a strength of the BLCMP community that both types of library are well-represented (about half of BLCMP member libraries are universities, a third, local authorities, and the others colleges or special libraries), it can also mean that more detail is required to satisfy everyone's needs on the System Managers course. On the other hand, the exchange of experience between public and academic libraries is found to be very useful, and the problem of mixed backgrounds is solved by providing fully comprehensive training course contents covering all areas.

4   TRAINING FOR SYSTEM MANAGERS

4.1   Pre-implementation workshop

This has become a standard part of the after-sales process to prepare customers for implementation. Although the systems librarian plays a pivotal role at the workshop sessions, other colleagues become involved in various stages as appropriate.

Effective pre-implementation training means that no surprises are likely to arise for the library or for the systems supplier. During the tender process and the period leading up to the decision to purchase the new library system, the library and system supplier reach general agreement on all primary issues, but there are frequently some points of detail to be resolved, which can be done during the pre-implementation procedure. It also allows for the other training to be planned as part of the preparation for the arrival of the new system. There are three main elements.

4.1.1   *Preparation of the system centre*

This includes hardware configuration, cabling, and software elements other than TALIS. The first aspect to be considered is what routines should be generated on a regular basis, and who should be responsible for each of these. For example, the printing of reservation notices and regular reports for management can be scheduled to run automatically at specified times on any modern system. TALIS is designed to be run by librarians rather than by computer staff, and the routines are straightforward.

Formats need to be agreed and sometimes standardized, including the layout on computer stationery, and print formats must be specified. Reports need to be customized, and a slice of the pre-implementation training might be devoted to the setting up of management information reports, although detailed training in the use of Microsoft Access would be provided in a separate course (Access is the PC package recommended for downloading and manipulating TALIS data into graphical and presentation format for management reports).

In addition, the pre-implementation workshops cover setting up the network, or improving it as appropriate.

4.1.2 Setting up the database

Converting all the borrower, book, and other item records for use with the new system is no small matter, and depending on the size of the stock, can take months to complete. The first stage is to determine how much needs to be converted before the system can go live – less frequently used stock can perhaps be left for a second phase. Then it becomes relatively straightforward to determine which would be the most cost-effective method of conversion.

The BLCMP Database can simplify data entry, because casual labour (for example students) can be used to input item bar-codes, which are then matched against the Database and the full bibliographic records downloaded to the local system. This minimizes cataloguing effort, although some is always required, for example when a hit is not found on the Database (in about 10% of cases), to add site/shelf details, or to improve records to meet local library standards.

If the existing system is BLS (BLCMP's older proprietary system), then migration of the data must be planned to avoid disruptions to the data at the point of changeover.

4.1.3 *Parameterization*

This mainly involves thinking of the way in which the system is to be used and learning how to customize the screens. To simplify the process, grids are prepared (see Figure 12.1), samples of which are filled in at the pre-implementation workshops for each functional area. The process often results in clarified objectives for the whole library. For example, some multi-site libraries which have arisen as the result of college mergers may still have inconsistent loan rules. One site may have a policy of allowing all teaching staff to keep their books out for three months and renew them three times, whereas another site may restrict the same group of borrowers to six-week loans renewable just twice in a row. While the system will cope with such variations, the introduction of a new system is the ideal time to review practices of this nature, and the workshop provides a perfect forum for discussion and resolution of such issues.

The workshops are led by the BLCMP Training Consultant and the Project Manager. Libraries are also provided with a pre-implementation handbook which includes detailed check-lists and forms to be completed in a structured manner, to ensure all aspects are covered completely. The handbook provides

220 *Education and training*

5.4.1. Borrower Rules

For each site, each borrower type must have a "rule" set up.

Please list below the rule for each type of borrower. If you use different rules at different sites then use a separate sheet for each site.

Borrower Type	Site	Borrower Expiry (days)	Loan Limit	Res	Res last date or days
STAFF	NOR	12/12/95	10	10	30
EXTERN	WEST	12/12/94	1	0	0
STAFF	REF	12/12/95	0	30	30

5.5.6. The LOAN RULES Table

All the above rules come together in the loan rules table which contains one line for every type of borrower/item combination identified in each site. Below is an example built up from the illustrations above at a single site.

BORR	LOC	ITEM	LOAN	ROLL	Ordinary	Renew	RES	REN
AD	DUL	CDC	STAN	Y	STAN	STAN		
AD	DUL	CDP	STAN	Y	STAN	STAN		
AD	DUL	CDJ	STAN	Y	STAN	STAN		

Fig. 12.1   Examples of TALIS Parameter Tables

a useful record of all the decisions reached between the customer and supplier, as well as documenting all important parameters.

4.2 System centre installation
The procedures for setting up the system centre are covered in this course, aimed at system managers and their assistants at the time of installation. The course lasts for half a day and includes start up and shut down procedures plus basic UNIX commands. The content will vary according to the needs of the individual library, and it will normally be followed by the UNIX and/or System Manager course.

4.3 System Manager course
This course may or may not be taken as part of a new installation. Frequently delegates include system managers who have recently changed jobs, and although they may have picked up the rudiments of system operation they need to become better acquainted with the system. As the course is intended for systems librarians BLCMP has involved systems managers from member libraries in its design. A trial course was run recently to ensure that customers were satisfied. It is suitable for people who are responsible for the running of a TALIS system, to give them a deeper understanding of the UNIX and TALIS environments and how to manage them.

The System Manager course lasts two to three days and includes practical sessions. The specific objectives are:

- to connect and manage terminals;
- to set up and manage printers and print jobs;
- to understand the TALIS software structure and how it works;
- to use error and log files to help diagnose system problems;
- to backup and restore the TALIS system;
- to understand the basic concepts of the database;
- to backup and restore the database.

The course does not cover TALIS internals or specific functionality, database internals, the network, or troubleshooting.

4.4 UNIX course
This course is for systems librarians who are new to UNIX, with the specific objectives as follows:

- to understand the UNIX environment and use appropriate system commands to manage it;
- to set up and manage user accounts;

- use the vi editor (visual, text editing software) to create or modify files;
- to understand and use scripts;
- to understand and use CRON (this is a process for running time-scheduled routines).

5 TRAINING OTHER LIBRARY STAFF

An important part of introducing any change to a library is to ensure that the rest of the library staff are informed and involved so that they feel ownership and enthusiasm for the new system. Human beings are by nature resistant to change, and the systems librarian can play an important role in minimizing the upheaval.

Enthusiasm can be achieved through education about the need for change, and by including staff in the decision-making process, where possible. This is needed at a very early stage, and can be done through workshops and newsletters. An internal newsletter which explains and charts the progress of automation is a very effective means of communication, and raises the visibility of the new system, as well as initiating the process of training other library staff.

These activities will help to reduce the trauma some people experience when change occurs, especially if they feel it has been imposed on them. The systems librarian needs to understand these issues and be able to discuss them with library staff supportively. If staff can come to realize the value of the system in overcoming previous problems, and if they are also consulted about the kind of training to be done, they will feel positive about the forthcoming changes.

The attitude of the systems supplier can be of paramount importance in this respect, as the supplier can guide the initial pre-implementation workshops to include staff consultation sessions, and can communicate the benefits of the system, as opposed to confining the training to basic functionality. This will encourage teamwork, and avoid any potential frustration on the part of the librarians who will have to use the system in the future and who, if not properly trained, could vent their frustration on the system, the supplier, or even the systems librarian!

While some of these aspects are covered in the pre-implementation workshops, BLCMP also provide courses for specialist staff in all functional areas. Examples of the content of the Acquisitions and MARC Cataloguing courses are given here; the other courses are broadly similar in style and content.

5.1 Acquisitions

This course is designed for users who are new to TALIS and require a full working knowledge of Acquisitions functions, including the creation and modification of orders and funds, receipting and payment. It lasts a full day, and would also be suitable for systems librarians who desire an overview of acquisitions functionality in order to be able to cover for absence and help with any problems which may arise.

The objectives of the course are:

- to create a new order;
- to search for and use Work information;
- to receipt items;
- to enter payment for items;
- to change order details;
- to add new suppliers;
- to change supplier details;
- to create new funds;
- to change fund details;
- to understand Electronic Data Interchange and set up supplier accounts for electronic transmission of the data via the BLCMP Database;
- to know what to do if a problem arises.

Practical sessions are included, which would normally be on a tutor system set up with a practice database of suppliers, funds, orders, and items.

Similar sessions are available for each other area of functionality, including Circulation, Cataloguing and Management Information.

5.2 MARC Cataloguing

This is a course which BLCMP has been running for many years to help libraries maintain the quality of their catalogue records, both for their local purposes and for contribution to the BLCMP Database of bibliographic records. It is in the interests of all BLCMP libraries to maintain the high cataloguing standards on the Database, which all members use for the creation of their local records.

6   ONGOING EDUCATION

Continuing education does not have to consist of formal training courses. People learn in lots of different ways, including through the exchange of experience provided by conferences, seminars, and user groups, and from the use of system supplier documentation and help desks.

6.1   Documentation

A way of supplementing the formal training courses may be provided by comprehensive system documentation. Systems librarians who are already familiar with different types of computers and who are used to PC packages may be able to orientate themselves using manuals and online help if it is well written and easy to follow.

Context-sensitive online help enables librarians who are experiencing difficulty with a specific area to get immediate and relevant help by pressing the 'Help' function key, as if a customer service analyst were at their sides prompting with the right advice at the right time. This kind of facility can be particularly valuable when the functional specialists are away ill, should it fall to the systems librarian to cover. Individual areas can be quite complex and even if the systems librarian followed the initial training courses on the system, new features may have been introduced such as Electronic Data Interchange for acquisitions, which complicate a procedure already only partially remembered.

Good documentation will help to refresh the systems librarian's memory so that work can continue in the event of a colleague's unexpected absence, but there are limits even to the best documentation. There is no substitute for the team spirit created in the training sessions, for the personal touch which clarifies complex areas, or for the customer support provided by the supplier once the system is in place.

6.2   Help desk

A small but essential part of the training of any systems librarian by the vendor is initiation into the mysteries of the help desk. Most large system suppliers provide a help desk facility of sorts, although this can vary in terms of coverage and response times. The help desk is there to provide customer libraries with a contact point for all their queries and requests.

The points to look out for in a help desk service are:

1 Is there one point of contact for hardware and software problems and development issues? If there is just one phone number it can simplify contact, although sometimes direct access to regional hardware service centres could be an advantage. This will depend on the relationship between the software vendor and hardware supplier.

2 Are all calls to the help desk logged on a formal fault-logging system which ensures efficient handling and progress-chasing? A computerized system is probably more efficient than a manual one.

3 Are the staff manning the help desk, librarians, programmers, or neither? Librarians may well understand your problems better than others, and technical staff will be able to answer technical queries, but the most important factor is probably the level of staff turnover, because experienced systems support analysts will be the best people to solve your problems. Also, do they have other jobs and are just doing rota duty on the help desk, or does system support command their full attention? The latter will provide greater consistency if the query takes more than a day to sort out.

4 How busy is the help desk? Are there enough staff or will the phone be constantly engaged?

5 Is the response time immediate in the case of a system failure? Are there guaranteed response times for hardware problems? Is there a formal escalation procedure so that if you are not satisfied with the progress of the situation it will be dealt with by a manager?

6 Is the service available outside normal office hours if required?

The BLCMP Help Desk is staffed by qualified librarians and computer staff, who have many years of experience in customer support. Libraries with any kind of query ring a dedicated number and are assured of a personal response, rather than a recorded message. The Help Desk switchboard operators log the query on a computerized system which follows a standard procedure to ensure that all relevant information is recorded. The query is then assigned a number for progress-chasing and a priority based on the nature of the problem before it is passed to a support analyst. This analyst will ensure the query is resolved, escalating if necessary, to meet the agreed time-scale. The initial system contracts include guaranteed response times, and extended cover is available if required.

Librarians use help desks for a variety of reasons, some of the most common being lack of time, ability or confidence to deal with the problem themselves. Good training will minimize the number of calls they need to make. Many calls also arise from misunderstandings as to the capabilities of the system or the implications of interrupting jobs, which can also be reduced with efficient training, both at installation stage and ongoing.

The systems librarian is generally the first line of support if anyone in the library has any problems with the system. Training is also useful, therefore, to assist the systems librarian in this role. It is even more valuable if other members of library staff have training on problem analysis to enable them to state problems so they can be dealt with quickly. Experienced systems support analysts on the help desk will normally be able to unravel any problem, but it could take half the time if reported in a structured way using the industry terminology as opposed to a vaguely defined statement. If the problem is stated in the right way, the systems librarian has a fair chance of being able to intercept the query and solve it without ever resorting to the help desk. This will speed up the process even more – and help to gain the systems librarian an enviable reputation for efficiency!

It is generally in the interests of the vendor to ensure efficient training of customer library staff as this reduces the incidence of calls to the help desk. Some systems suppliers (not including BLCMP) even go to the lengths that they restrict all calls to the help desk to one or two nominated people in the library, in order to keep the number of calls to a minimum. It is probably wise for a systems librarian to encourage colleagues to share their problems with him/her before ringing the supplier help desk, but this would mainly be to keep a broad view of what is happening with regard to the system, and, of course, to try to solve the problem first, if possible, rather than to prevent direct contact with the supplier. A network of contacts across the organization can not only promote generally good relationships, but will help to keep everyone informed and involved, leading to better working practices.

The help desk does, of course, offer a backup to the systems librarian in case of insufficient training. This may occur through no fault of the supplier or library, for example when the systems librarian changes jobs, and before new training can be arranged. Support analysts can refer users to the correct place in the documentation and in many cases can dial in to the library's system using a modem to diagnose problems quickly. The most important aspect is that the librarian should never feel their call is unwelcome or unnecessary, the help desk should be there to help!

6.3   Technology seminars

For those librarians not implementing new systems or requiring initiation or revision in the intricacies of specific system management, there are a variety of seminars designed to help them improve working practices and plan for the future.

Technology days are arranged by BLCMP in conjunction with hardware manufacturers Data General and Sun Microsystems, and these provide explanations of how the hardware functions, demonstrations of emerging technology, and options for future systems planning.

Systems librarians sometimes bring their colleagues from computer departments, to assess how the technology can meet the objectives of the library and still comply with the information technology policy of the organization as a whole. Although it is not necessarily difficult to match the objectives, it is often easier to use the Technology Day to go into a subject in detail than for the systems librarian to act as go-between.

A typical Technology Day might include the following topics:

- Why client-server architecture is desirable.
- Developments in multimedia and image processing.
- Explanation and demonstration of high-availability disk storage systems.
- Networking standards and options.
- How open are open systems.
- Factors affecting the choice of terminals, PCs, and workstations.
- Protecting current investment in hardware when migrating to open systems.

6.4 New systems awareness seminars

With the demand for open systems a new generation of systems has arisen, and systems librarians should discover the make-up and potential benefits of each of these. Because they are new, independent training organizations are unlikely to offer formal assessments, and librarians must rely on the system vendors' own evaluation. This is not necessarily a disadvantage, however, for the vendors know their own system best, and can give more detailed information than other organizations. Contrary to some popular belief, most vendors prefer to sell systems which are well suited to the libraries in question, not least because it simplifies support issues later on.

BLCMP arranges regional seminars on TALIS, which look at the system from an objective viewpoint, to inform librarians and allow for questions and discussion. Where possible, opportunities for 'hands-on' trial of TALIS are also provided.

6.5 User groups/Exchange of experience seminars

A user group meeting provides a forum for sharing problems and their solutions as well as discussing development schedules. BLCMP's user group structure is fairly complex (see Figure 12.2) in that there are approximately 18 meetings a year, two each of the various special interest groups, but the programme certainly allows for a free flow of ideas. In addition, BLCMP has organized special exchange-of-experience seminars, structured to allow users to share their expertise, particularly in regard to setting up online public access screens.

6.6 Conference

BLCMP's customer conference, also known as 'BUG', is an opportunity for all BLCMP member librarians to meet, not only to exchange experiences but also to learn about new developments in library systems and to influence future

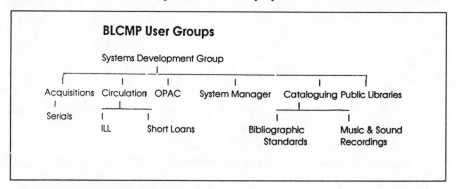

Fig. 12.2   BLCMP user group structure

strategy. Acquaintances made at the conference are frequently continued afterwards, with librarians ringing each other to exchange information.

7   SUMMARY

Training, or the lack of it, can help or hinder the life of a systems librarian. With the rapid changes in systems technology and increasing complexity of the skills required, the systems librarian needs to keep abreast of all the latest developments, and ensure colleagues are well-trained, in order to make the most of the job.

❖ **Part 4**
The future

13   Reasons to be cheerful?

❖   *Graeme Muirhead*

Several of the preceding chapters have discussed forces which will influence the future direction of systems management in libraries. The networked environment, competitive tendering, new managerial thinking, and the development of open systems are some of the trends which have been mentioned. This chapter aims to draw together the various strands of this theme, and at the same time provide some conclusions for the collection as a whole. To do this we shall be returning to the survey reported in Chapter 1. The questionnaire which was used in the survey included several questions designed to elicit information about what the future might hold. The findings are presented here, beginning with the prospects for individual systems librarians or aspirants to the position, and then speculating about the future for systems librarians collectively.

1   THE JOB MARKET
Anecdotal evidence suggests that systems librarians have often drifted into their posts by chance and with little forethought. Now that the position has become firmly established it is likely that the areas covered in the survey and reported in Chapter 1 will attract the attention of the increasing number of professionals who make a definite career choice to work in this field. Of particular interest to this group will be the job market and career prospects for systems specialists.

From the evidence of the survey, the number of systems librarians has expanded rapidly over the past five years; 77.8% of respondents being appointed in this period. Those posts which were newly designated accounted for 47.5% of the sample, 56% had been in existence for under five years, and 85% under ten years. However, there are good grounds for believing that the period of rapid growth is over: the specialist nature of systems work means that the total number of posts available is inevitably smaller than for more mainstream library posts, and the evidence of job advertisements seems to suggest that demand has levelled off: only 27 systems posts were advertised in the *Library Association record vacancies supplement* in the period April 1991–March 1992. Despite this, there is still some way to go before saturation point is reached. Of 135 libraries without a systems librarian which were planning to automate or to upgrade their existing system within the next two years, 8 (5.9%) said they would definitely appoint a systems librarian, while 49 (36.3%) said that they might. Of these 57 potential posts, the majority were in the public library sector (32), with the rest in special libraries (13), colleges (8), polytechnics (2), government libraries (1), and others (1). Meanwhile, those libraries which already have a systems librarian will continue to expand their systems to bring more service points online and improve the functionality of the growing number of ageing systems nearing the end of their lifespans. Whether these libraries upgrade their existing systems or migrate to a different system, demand for the skills identified at each of the three stages of the automation cycle will probably continue to grow. It is conceivable that some of the responsibilities involved could be farmed out, and systems knowledge diffused to a core of trained, computer-literate staff, as already happens in many institutions. But there is no evidence at present to indicate that libraries are reversing their decision to appoint a specialist to oversee system management and thus ensure a coordinated and consistent approach to IT systems: only eight institutions had disestablished a systems post, either because of restructuring or because it had been a temporary post to investigate and implement automation. Only one library commented that this was a deliberate policy decision to avoid overdependence on one individual. There is in fact a small but discernable trend in the opposite direction, with systems teams and deputies becoming more common in larger organizations. Ten of the libraries in the survey fell into this category, with systems units of generally between two and four full-time staff, and a variety of internal structures in which line responsibilities and a division of labour (for example library housekeeping system/micro applications) were sometimes evident. If others follow suit it would open up more opportunities for junior professionals and new entrants to the profession. Perhaps more likely in these recessionary times is that matrix structures will become more widespread without necessarily replacing the systems specialist. As many libraries have already realized, even where there is formally only one systems person, it is operationally desirable to familiarize other staff with routine aspects of system management to provide cover during absence and to spread the workload. In this respect, the survey showed that 58.3% of systems librarians said they had a designated deputy who was capable of running the system in their absence. These flexible staffing patterns and dual-function positions would provide an alternative route into systems work.

The survey also provides data about recruitment patterns for systems librarians; 66.5% intimated that they had been appointed internally, which confirms not only that when looking for a systems post it helps to be in a job, but also that employers prefer an inside knowledge of local systems and practices. Most of the remainder had learned about their posts through the *Library Association record vacancies supplement* (44.7% of 76 responses). The other sources of information were: other professional press (34.2%), national/local press (7.9%), word of mouth (7.9%), and internal civil service trawls (5.3%). No one had obtained their job through a recruitment agency.

Many of the sample were relatively new to their posts as systems librarians: 45.4% had been a systems librarian for two years or less, and only 22.2% had been in their present post for over five years. In view of the importance of a broad overview of library operations, though, it is not surprising perhaps that few if any seem to have been appointed fresh from library school.

Further evidence that the post requires some maturity and experience emerges from an analysis of the sample by age. Table 13.1 compares the ages of the systems librarians with those for Library Association members as a whole (expressed as a percentage of the 1991 membership whose age was known).

Table 13.1 Age of systems librarians compared with LA membership[a]

	n (100%)	<25	25–9	30–4	Age 35–9	40–4	45–9	>50
Systems librarians	203	2.5	9.9	23.6	27.1	22.7	8.4	5.9
LA members	21463	7.4	13.3	15.9	18.7	19.6	11.4	13.8

[a] Based on figures supplied by the LA Membership Department.

Only five systems librarians were under 25 years old, and the central bulge in the systems librarians ages contrasts with the more even spread for the LA members as a whole.

2 CAREER PROSPECTS

For prospective and existing systems librarians alike, the absence of a well-defined career structure with opportunities to progress to more senior positions or return to mainstream library work is a consideration of some importance. Obtaining first-hand information about the career moves of former systems librarians presented a problem, as their numbers are likely to be still fairly small and potentially widely dispersed. It was decided, therefore, to ask respondents to state the job or employment sector into which their immediate predecessor had moved. Of the 198 replies received, 47.5% said that they were the first appointee (that is they had no predecessor), and 7.6% said their predecessor was no longer in employment (that is through death, emigration, retirement, or pregnancy). The remaining 89 replies were sorted into categories which it was hoped would give a rough indication of the kind of job and whether the move had been sideways or was a promotion. The results showed that 14.6% had moved into senior library management, 7.9% had taken up a middle management position in support services, and a further 7.9% had gone to a similar post in mainstream library and information work. Those seeming to have moved horizontally to other support services posts accounted for 3.4%, 12.6% have moved to mainstream library posts, and 16.9% into posts as systems librarians elsewhere. As we saw in Chapter 1, one of the findings of the survey was that in the 'technician versus manager' debate, management skills in the widest sense are at least as important, if not more so, than technical know-how. The overview of library service operations which the systems librarian's post requires are part of the apparatus of the generalist rather than the specialist, and so is an excellent preparation for a move into senior management. It is encouraging to see that systems librarians are indeed able to use their abilities and experience and make this transition. A further pattern which the survey revealed – not unpredictable given the hybrid nature of systems posts – was for systems librarians to move into the related fields of library system supply (18%) and computing/data processing (10.1%), and also for small numbers of systems librarians to be recruited from these employment sectors.

3   THE FUTURE

Heseltine has written that:

> In the future, as networked information and electronic document delivery come to play an increasing role in the work of libraries, as access strategies finally start genuinely to overtake holdings strategies, then we might find that our perspective on IT changes. The automated systems with which we are so preoccupied today may become relatively low cost items, routinely managing a range of internal functions, and exciting very little attention. The development of real information services may occur outside of those systems, using different hardware and software, thus causing a relative shift of investment emphasis away from the traditional systems.[1]

We are here moving towards the concept of the 'virtual library' in which the library *is* its systems. What will be the role of the systems librarian in this future? Will today's systems librarians be the 'virtual librarians' of tomorrow? It is impossible to make firm predictions about a post which has been in a process of change since its beginnings, which is characterized above all by its diversity, and which operates in an organizational context of political and economic uncertainty; a post, moreover, which is concerned with the management of a rapidly and continually changing resource developed by an industry which is itself likely to see further structural change in the fuure. With these qualifications in mind, the questionnaire set out to try to answer the above questions by asking respondents how they felt the systems role was changing as a result of technological and other developments, and to speculate about how it might evolve in the future.

3.1 Technological developments

Most of the repondents chose to concentrate on technological developments. The most frequently mentioned of these were: cheaper, more powerful, more reliable hardware; cheaper, more sophisticated, more user-friendly software; the proliferation of PCs and CD-ROM; and the increasing use of networks. OSI (Open Systems Interconnection) would have important implications, and there would be a merging of technologies with transparent interfaces. Surprisingly, artificial intelligence, which could have a major impact in several areas which have till now been the concern of systems librarians (for example staff training, management decisions regarding the choice of system, troubleshooting, etc.), was mentioned only once (for some of the potential applications of expert systems, see Ercegovac,[2] Gunson,[3] and McDonald and Weckert[4]).

Respondents expressed virtual unanimity that these changes would lead to yet more responsibility and a wider role for the systems librarian. The main reasons for this would be the expansion of ongoing automation projects and the involvement of systems librarians in an ever more diverse range of IT applications. Accompanying these changes would be an intensification of the pressures on systems librarians, a need for more flexibility, and for continuous training and upgrading of skills. Many respondents also felt that the systems librarian's sphere of activity would increasingly extend beyond the library, and that this might lead to higher status.

Although there was general consensus that technology would not undermine the position of the systems librarian, there was less agreement about how the content of the job would change. One view expressed was that the burden of routine maintenance would increase, either because of the increasing flexibility and sophistication of library management systems, or because of the trend to smaller, distributed hardware units and the proliferation of software. For some this would lead to more specialization and a need for greater technical know-how, while for others, the pace of change and diversity of technology was making it more difficult to specialize and stay abreast of new developments.

An opposing view expressed by a significant number of respondents was that system development, strategic planning, and information management would become increasingly important for them. The advisory/support and promotional roles were other areas highlighted by many systems librarians, though here an interesting divergence of views came out. A few respondents felt that more user-friendly systems and more system-friendly users would lessen these functions, but the majority of those who commented on their role as trainers thought it would increase:

> There appears to be a trend towards end user searching and consequently training will become increasingly important.

> Increasingly processing will be distributed to intelligent workstations. Staff will become more responsible for how they decide to use IT, which will require considerable training effort.

> More non-library staff gaining access to the system – growing and varying training needs.

Finally, a handful of replies suggested that the technological changes mentioned would have less impact than might be supposed:

> The increasing sophistication of systems on sale has increased complexity, but that is a change of degree rather than nature.

> The *role*, as link between libraries and new technology, will remain the same, but the *job* will change as technology changes.

> The actual problem will remain the same i.e. identifying improvements and managing the changes.

3.2   Other changes

Some of the non-technological changes which were cited were: organizational change; possible local government reorganization; reductions in funding; the prospect of compulsory competitive tendering (CCT); greater demands from more computer-literate users and staff; increases in the use of management information; and changes in educational methods.

While technology was generally seen as reinforcing the position of the systems librarian (even if the increased pressures and workload it created were not always welcomed), there was much more disagreement about the possible effects of the non-technological changes and external factors. Some would secure the systems librarian's future role:

Change in teaching techniques has placed much greater importance on information retrieval within coursework, and consequently it's a high-pro-file, high-use, 'critical' area.

More and more computer-based learning, and this impacts on me for advice and support.

Others would undermine it:

Hopefully as more technically aware students enter the profession the need for a 'systems' librarian may diminish and better overall exploitation of the technology will become possible.

In the long term I suspect that systems librarians will not remain as posts. Right thinking authorities will buy in system management, and all librari-ans will be familiar with newish technology.

Political and organizational factors in particular were perceived as especially hostile. For some this is expressed as a vague impending uncertainty, but in other cases the threat was more precise:

Local government in any of the forms suggested ... would split the current library authority into three. The implications of this are numerous and var-ied. (Early retirement could be attractive!)

Biggest non-technical worry: effect of the 'unitary authority' move by gov-ernment. We could end up having to sell the computer service to a number of boroughs, just as Schools Library Service are having to sell their service to the schools. Horrendous!

Mergers of libraries and computer centres may make employers feel that systems librarians are redundant.

4   CONCLUSIONS

The post of systems librarian which emerged in Chapter 1 and the other chap-ters in the first part of this book is one which is more often determined by local conditions and constraints than by any universally agreed model of what a systems librarian should do. The diversity of the duties performed requires the systems librarian to traverse a number of milieux in what is in essence an inter-mediary function. The demands of the post are such that it has often, though by no means always, developed into a reactive role.

Doubtless this situation will continue in many organizations for the foreseeable future – this is borne out by the predictions of respondents summarized above. Existing automation projects will continue, more service points will be brought online, and system enhancements will be introduced. Lack of resources will in many cases prevent systems librarians from breaking free from routine maintenance work to consider the wider issues. The problem of stress will not be properly addressed. However, the views of the systems librarians also seemed to suggest two alternative and more hopeful visions of the future. In the first, the systems librarian will have increasing opportunities to assume a role in IT strategy, system development, and information management. The second vision, which does not exclude the first, pictures the systems librarian acting less as an intermediary and more as an enabler and facilitator, providing advice and support about reliable, easy to use machines and a range of IT products and services, to users, both within and outside the library, who are computer-literate but unable to devote time to maintaining current awareness of the increasing choices available to them as IT develops. While today's systems librarians are by no means purely reactive, this enabling role implies a more proactive approach.

'Today there are many observers who see fissures within the profession growing wider in the future. One writer worries that the great unifier, the computer, may actually lead to further divergence.'[5] One of the objectives of the survey reported in this chapter and in Chapter 1 was to investigate how far this concern is true of systems librarians' posts. Despite the apparent lack of homogeneity which has come out of the study, it has shown that there are, nonetheless, broad similarities between the functions performed by many systems librarians. Although the survey suggests that the range of tasks and duties will widen as new functions are added to the systems librarian's responsibilities, and although the execution of these functions will vary widely according to the resources of individual institutions and the needs of the community they serve, the functions themselves will be shared, and any diversity will be relatively superficial. In the short history of the system librarian's post chance and individual opportunity have been much in evidence; it is a story that has unfolded 'more by accident than by design'. In today's climate of change the only certainty regarding the future is that the functions performed by systems librarians will grow in importance. Systems librarians as *individuals* will therefore be well placed to capitalize on this and consolidate their position as key players in an IT-dominated service, and, as in the past, chance and opportunism may well be significant factors. For systems librarians collectively the future is less predictable. To the cluster of paradoxes and contradictions surrounding the post which were noted in the introduction to this volume (pp. xxiii–xxv) may be added another: the intermediary nature of the job, which is its very essence, not to mention the source of much of the variety and satisfaction it offers, also leaves it vulnerably exposed. In a trend which may well strengthen, several library system suppliers have already contracted to manage their customers' systems for them. An equally serious threat is posed by the generally improving levels of computer literacy among library staff. Here the danger is not so much that the systems librarian post will prove in retrospect to have been an evolutionary dead end but that in the future all librarians will evolve into systems librarians.

This discussion is an important one, not just for systems people but also for the wider library and information community. As the introduction to this volume contended, the issues which converge on the systems function have a much wider application and relevance than for systems librarians alone. Are librarians sufficiently computer-literate to deliver an effective service in an increasingly automated society? How can we equip new entrants with the IT skills they will need? Are we in danger of losing control of an important area of professional expertise to the suppliers who design our systems and on whom we depend for support? How is IT being implemented and managed in library and information centres? How does the library relate to the wider organization to which it belongs? Will there be 'virtual librarians' in the 'virtual library'?

As a focus for these questions and many others like them, the systems post can be seen as a microcosm of the profession at large, in the face of dramatic social, political, economic, and technological changes. It is an indicator of how we as a profession are facing up to and coping with these challenges, and as such should promote critical self-examination not just among those concerned with automation, but in all areas of library and information services. The fate of the systems librarian is in itself of little importance. But what is at stake, ultimately, is the future of library and information services.

REFERENCES

1   Heseltine, R., 'Choosing in the dark: strategic issues in the selection of library automation systems', *ITs news*, **27**, 1993, 13–18.

2   Ercegovac, Z., 'Knowledge-based expert systems: a profile and implications', in Williams, M. E. and Hogan, T., (eds.), *Proceedings of the 5th National Online Meeting, New York, April 10–12, 1984*, Medford, NJ, Learned Information, 1984, 39–45.

3   Gunson, N., 'Will sophisticated computer systems replace professional librarians or complement their skills?', *Aslib proceedings*, **42** (11/12), 1990, 303–11.

4   McDonald, C. and Weckert, J. (eds.), *Libraries and expert systems*, London, Taylor Graham, 1991.

5   M. S. Freeman, quoted in Webb, T. D., *The in-house option: professional issues of library automation*, New York, Haworth, 1987, vii.

❖ Index

Note: Topics have generally been entered directly rather than as sub-headings of the term 'systems librarians', except where this was considered to be unhelpful or unsatisfactory. Filing is letter by letter, with acronyms and abbreviations treated as words.